Emma Jane Holmes has spent most of her adult life working in death care, and her passion for writing led to the publication of her blog, Heels and Hearses, which amassed readers worldwide. The popularity of her adventures in the funeral home surprised her, landing a book deal. The blog has since been unpublished, the stories to be found exclusively in the book you hold now.

When not working with the dead, Emma Jane could be found on stage as an exotic dancer, trying to be sexy. She attempted to maintain a divide between the two worlds but the adult industry was as fascinating as the funeral home and is the backbone to her strength and character today. Dancing is still an important part of her life; she often attends pole fitness classes pretending she doesn't know all the tricks, and wears sequins during the day, just because.

Emma Jane has left the city and mortuary behind her, currently living on the Mid North Coast of Australia studying a Bachelor of Arts.

ONE LAST DANCE

EMMA JANE HOLMES

All events in this book are real, but some names, appearances, dates and locations have been changed.

First Published 2021
First Australian Paperback Edition 2021
This edition published in 2024
ISBN 9781867298557

Published by
HQ Non Fiction
An imprint of Harlequin Enterprises (Australia) Pty Limited (ABN 47 001 180 918),
a subsidiary of HarperCollins Publishers Australia Pty Limited (ABN 36 009 913 517)
Level 19, 201 Elizabeth St
SYDNEY NSW 2000
AUSTRALIA

A catalogue record for this book is available from the National Library of Australia
www.librariesaustralia.nla.gov.au

Printed and bound by CPI Group (UK) Ltd, Croydon, CR0 4YY

For the dead who saved me.
To the rest of us, may our last dance be sweet.

AUTHOR NOTE

I consider it a privilege to be entrusted with the care of the dead. My account of dealing with the dead is designed to throw light on the processes of death and break down some of the taboos surrounding it.

It is common for funeral directors to be asked why they chose the profession, and more often than not they reply, 'It's my calling. I just *knew* it was what I wanted to do.'

I truly believe funeral professionals are little messengers to the world. People rarely consider mortality when on the school run, stuck in traffic, while grocery shopping or climbing the career ladder. So, summoned by a greater power to tackle death head-on, in suit and tie or mortuary scrubs, death-care professionals keep hearts and biceps strong. Taking care of the dead and their survivors, they teach the grieving what they've learnt. Gazing down into dead faces daily, they are reminded that every moment in life is beautiful; even the mundane ones. No one appreciates a dentist visit like a funeral director. Hey, we're alive to have our cavities tended to. And the pain, well, another reminder our nerve endings are still awake. Funeral directors are a grateful bunch, and enjoy being the beacon of education to those who seem to forget their own headstone inscription is not too far away. If there is a Creator, I imagine He (or She) sat up in the clouds with all His (or Her) human-creating ingredients and when sculpting the funeral director, with a huge twinkling smile, blessed us with a magic wand: *You are going to be friends to the dead and teach the living because I have far too much on my plate to do it. Off you go, and stay strong!*

* * *

This is a true account of my experiences but dates, names and locations have been disguised to protect the dead and their families as well as the stage performers I worked with, some of whom prefer anonymity. Utmost regard for funeral home confidentiality has been applied by concealing all company details. While I have worked as a funeral director, there is no A Touch of Comfort funeral home. Events may be out of sequence, and some characters are composites of more than one person drawn from different workplaces. Conversations have been recreated to the best of my ability.

There is some dark humour in the book, drawn from some of my more complex experiences. There is no intention to offend anybody but with such a confronting subject, I know it is likely that I will, and for that I beg pardon. We all have our methods of coping with what we experience and, for me, finding humour and lightness in the midst of death is an affirmation that life continues.

Emma Jane Holmes

Motorists are rushing past the things worth seeing,
instead of stopping to enjoy them.
Travel slowly, stop often.

George Ade
1866–1944
RIP

PROLOGUE

'Rumour has it, Brad Pitt might be there!' Josie's voice chimed through the bluetooth as I switched lanes on the M5. 'This is huge for our agency, Emma Jane. Can I lock you in?'

Normally I'd never answer the phone while on body collection duties—my hand had bumped the 'answer' button while reaching for the radio in the company vehicle and technically, I didn't have a corpse on board. Just part of one.

'Emma Jane? The waitressing gig?'

'Sure, Jo, I'll be there.'

'You sound distracted, honey. Are you busy?'

I'm sure many girls would squeal at the prospect of seeing Brad Pitt's glorious hair in person, but no famous actor could spur excitement within me the way death did. My eyes darted to the box in the seat beside me, fastened with yellow tape, *Complete Organ* written across the side in marker.

Mr Stephen's brain was inside, finally released from the forensic pathologist. Tests finalised, the organ was now in the care of A Touch of Comfort funeral home.

'I'm just in traffic.' My voice reflected Josie's upbeat tone, omitting the fact that a brain in a box was sitting in the passenger seat, activating the 'turn on passenger seatbelt' light on the dashboard at every corner. Josie was my manager—well, one of my managers. The cheery entrepreneur owned one of the most popular lingerie/bikini waitressing agencies in the city, which made me ... a bikini waitress. Adjusting my tie in the rear-view mirror, I saw heels, bottles of hairspray and fake tan littered across the back seat. While Josie had no idea I drove across the city collecting body parts when not working for her (okay—I do much more than collect body parts), likewise, my colleagues at the funeral home had no clue I wore sequinned heels after dark, serving drinks in a bikini with a garter full of cash.

'Shit!' My foot slammed the brake to stop me from careening into the back of the vehicle that had switched lanes abruptly. The Brain in the Box fell to the floor with a light thud, my latte splattering it. Great. How would I explain a coffee-sodden box to the mortician when I handed her the brain? I scrambled for the organ and wiped the damp cardboard with some tissues from the glove compartment. With the traffic at a standstill, I buckled the brain in with the seatbelt and patted the box. Safe now.

I know this scene might appear rather odd to most people, but situations like this are my everyday reality. The previous day when delivering a decedent to a crematorium, I had flown to the rescue and removed a pacemaker from the dead lady's chest before she slid into the cremation retort (the pacemaker had been missed on her paperwork). In case you didn't know, pacemakers must be removed prior to cremation to prevent an almighty *bang* and considerable damage to the retort. With no pacemaker storage container available in that moment, I popped it into my pocket and for the rest of the day walked around with a mechanical object that once kept someone alive in my pants, covered in yellow, slimy chest fat.

'I have to go, Josie. I'll be there, Saturday.'

'Okay, love, take care. Talk soon.'

Mr Stephen's brain and I steered into the manicured lawns of the funeral home and a funeral director, suit pressed and shoes polished, bounced down the stairs to meet me.

'Great timing.' Kevin beamed, meeting me at the driver's side window. His moustache was set in twirls at the ends. 'New case just arrived in the mortuary for you.'

'Awesome.' Disguising exhaustion with a smile, I stepped out of the car. 'Anything interesting?'

'Decomp.' He winked, taking the brain from my hands. 'Lucky you! Wasn't found for days—brains everywhere!'

* * *

I'm not that unusual. There are double lives taking place all around us. The handsome father in conservative 'dad clothes' at the supermarket? He may wear leather underwear beneath those golf shorts and have a mistress.

That lovely co-worker with a lip-glossed smile? She may go home at the end of the day all alone and curl up in a ball of sadness and binge-eat.

The good-looking pool cleaner with the chiselled back muscles and a fantastic tan? Yeah, he's a stripper after dark.

Wearing suits by day and stilettos by night, I didn't dip my shellac toes into the adult industry to spice up my life. My day job was not only exciting, it was deeply fulfilling. I was an FDA (Funeral Director's Assistant) and Mortuary Assistant. By day I polished hearses, bathed bodies and dressed them, applied their lipstick and even helped the embalmer with the duty of reconstructing a skull following a vicious accident. The head mortician was quite the artist, and no request was too challenging for her. If the family wished to view their loved one who had just skidded into a tree on his motorbike, cracks would be filled. And I was the assistant by her side, passing implements and holding pieces of skull together as she glued and bandaged. I was one of the last people to ever touch the decedent's hand before they were buried into the earth. Then, at dusk, I peeled off the scrubs or suit and slipped into a lacy number, piling on the lipstick. My wardrobe was bursting with sequinned bikinis, diamante-studded stilettos and 'naughty schoolgirl' costumes, yet my lounge room told a different story. Black stockings and professionally dry-cleaned suits were draped over the couch, red silk ties on almost every bare surface and shiny leather funeral director shoes by the front door.

I adored working with death. The world I was born into—the West—seemed to have an unusual perspective on death: that it should be ushered quickly from sight, which led to misconceptions and myths that still break my heart today. I yearned for people to open their minds to the beauty end of life offers.

Death enriches life.

Acknowledging mortality every single day made me a better person. A nicer person. Working as an FDA softened my hastiness in traffic. I was grateful to be alive and sitting in peak hour. I sent my grandma flowers regularly to remind her she was loved. She wouldn't be here much longer, and this fact sobered me every time I touched the hand of a dear old lady in her coffin.

A lover of history, I remember reading that back in the time of the Caesars there was a person whose only job was to chant the words 'Thou Art Mortal!' to remind Caesar that he, too, was only a man and lived in a mortal body. Working at the funeral home was like having my own personal assistant following me around reminding me of my mortality. Every morning when I secured a lid tight on a coffin, I heard it: 'Thou Art Mortal! Thou Art Mortal!'

My life motto became even more relevant when I began working in the adult industry to clear mounting bills as a result of a difficult divorce. Because apart from death, here was a subject with an even darker stigma attached to it: sex.

The more time I spent in adult entertainment meeting wonderful souls who powdered glitter on their cleavages after dark, the more I realised much of society judged dancers and escorts, believing they had no other choice. A lot of people felt they were 'above' exotic dancers and sex workers because they worked a 'straight' job. I think those people need a little helper too, chanting 'Thou Art Mortal'. Our lives eventually end and the way we earn money in the meantime shouldn't matter, as long as we're happy and not hurting anyone.

Death and sex are braided: sex produces life and death is the end of it. Yet they're both frowned upon. Eyebrows shot up when people discovered I worked in a funeral home. 'You work with dead people? That must be so depressing!'

When I began to confess my secret about working in adult entertainment, I was met with more astonished glances. Why? Why are death and sex so taboo? They are important fundamentals in life.

* * *

There was another similarity between my two careers.

Theatre.

As funeral directors, we shine our shoes, straighten our ties, show up with our Funeral Director Face on—an expression of compassion promising strength. We don't personally know your loved one, yet during the funeral process we put ourselves aside to be there for you.

Once eulogies are shared and the final song plays, after the funeral conductor has led the pallbearers down the aisle, I'm reminded of the dancer's stage. Following a burial, the funeral directors take a stand graveside and take a synchronised bow. Then, performing at the club, the stage show concludes with a bow before stepping out of the spotlights.

There was theatre in both the adult and death industry. In fact, one day while standing graveside in the cemetery prettied with flower beds, I realised *life* is a show.

We are all living in one big giant movie, and just like every great film or theatre production, there is always a final bow and two words looming …

The End.

PART ONE: DEATH

CHAPTER 1

CEMETERIES

'Hold your breath!' Dad called out from the driver's seat whenever we drove past a cemetery. 'It's good luck!'

In the rural area where we lived there was only the one, beside the town hospital, and I was fascinated. My lungs expanding, I pressed my nose against the window watching the headstones pass by. The cemetery was beautiful to me, the weeping figs shading the field of monuments, the ageing stonework; I especially loved how some gravestones leaned like they were sleepy. Even at my young age, I knew the place was special.

My baby brother joined our clan of four when I was seven years old and my sister only a toddler. He was unwell for the first few weeks of his life and not able to come home right away. We spent a lot of time at the hospital during this time, and while my sister was content with colouring books and the television in the waiting room, I grew restless. I spent the first decade of my life on a farm, and it wasn't unusual to explore the sprawling, green property on my own. Mum and Dad trusted I wouldn't go near waterholes or climb trees too high, so the same went when I begged to play in the cemetery next to the hospital. As long as I stayed clear of the road and was away no longer than an hour, I was free to explore. Excitedly, I danced around the graves, creating stories for the names etched into the granite. As bottlebrush flowers from the nearby tree were placed on graves, the dead were kept company by a young stranger in scuffed joggers and neon scrunchies in her hair. One of these playdates led to the discovery of the name Emma carved into a headstone with the birth date matching mine. I decided we'd be friends and once home, my thoughts were of her, hoping she was okay wherever she was. The anticipation of returning to the hospital, not only to see my baby brother but to visit my new friend, was immense.

* * *

With my youngest sibling home and healthy, there was no need to visit the hospital in town anymore. Not able to visit Emma or the pretty headstones, I began to build my own. Hours were spent exploring the paddocks, and when I came across a dead animal decomposing in the long yellow grass, I dug a shallow grave. Creating a headstone from sticks and rocks, I'd then regularly visit their place of rest. Pets had died in my short life so I understood the carcasses found in the bush were no longer alive and was drawn to keeping them company.

While death and gravestones fascinated my little brain during the day, it was a different story in the quiet of night. As my sister snored peacefully on the bottom bunk, I'd toss and turn in my Strawberry Shortcake sheets. One day my parents would die; *I* would die. Visions of my own body lying in an enclosed coffin kept me awake until the bird chorus of dawn. It was so hot on the farm, how stifling would it be underground? Would I know I was dead? Would it hurt? I was stuck somewhere between being curious about death and being completely afraid of it.

Apart from the fascination with graveyards and nightmares about coffins, we lived a regular Aussie farm life. Growing up on the farm on the Mid North Coast of Australia has been one of the greatest blessings in my 30-something years of life. Mum, Dad, my two younger siblings and I lived in our own little grassy bubble, complete with dandelion fluff and black-and-white spotted cows. Our closest neighbours were over the hill and far away; communication with them a yodel through cupped hands, our echo dancing on the hot breeze anticipating their reply. Weekends were spent fishing for tadpoles in waterholes, moving them to our backyard ponds, and we watched in wonder as they grew legs and turned to frogs. We helped dad chop firewood. Fed pet chickens. Farmed honeybees. Dad's friends from surrounding farms joined us in our backyard for barbecues, the aroma of snags and onion blending with freshly slashed grass wafting on the breeze. We indeed lived the simple life. In hindsight, I realise we may not have had much money at all. We never ate fast food. Our staple meal was noodles and mashed potato. We rarely wore new school uniforms. Dad built our bed frames with bare hands and a hammer, and it was like falling asleep in his arms. We may not have been financially wealthy but I felt like the most loved kid on the planet, and I thought I was extremely rich.

The country town's primary school had a total of 150 students, shoes were optional and we had more cows in the schoolyard than monkey bars. I remember a book as thick as a dictionary tucked on the bookshelf, an A to Z directory with every occupation you could enter when you grew big and tall. I tried to find Funeral Director but it wasn't there, so I assumed people who worked with death were in other countries, not Australia.

Imagine my excitement when I discovered that there was such a thing as an Australian funeral industry. Unfortunately, it took the death of my beautiful nan to learn this.

* * *

Most of our relatives lived on the Gold Coast and when the country bumpkins visited, it was quite a big deal. The Queensland family prepared lavish dinners for us, pool parties and endless trips to surrounding theme parks. But one particular stay on the glitzy coast didn't involve rollercoasters or visits to toy stores the size of our farm. We were staying with my grandparents because Nan had fallen ill. The house was bustling with family I hadn't seen in years, distant cousins, aunties and uncles. Adult chatter echoed in the kitchen while the lounge room was kept lively with kids playing board games and watching TV. Despite the noise, I heard Dad answer a phone call. It was the early nineties, when phones had a coiled cord, and I could see it transmitted bad news to Dad as his farm tan faded, teary eyes levelling with mine. He shakily returned the chunky mustard-coloured receiver to the base of the phone, and the grown-ups in the kitchen began to scream. The volume of the cries rattled my sternum. I'd never heard anything like it. I crept close to Dad and heard him tell Mum he was heading to the hospital, following him outside just as the black-and-yellow cab pulled into the drive.

I said 'I'm coming with you', looking up at him beneath the glow of the moon. He nodded, taking my hand, and I noticed he was cold. My dad and I shared a close relationship, in fact I considered him my best friend. I knew he would let me ride in the taxi that night. He needed me to be there with him, the way he was always there for me. My name was tattooed on his arm in the middle of a love heart after all.

I was still wearing my day clothes and shoes; I don't think we'd even eaten dinner yet.

That unforgettable evening was the first time I rode in a taxi. The motor was quiet and smooth, unlike the rattle and groan of Dad's Commodore, and the dashboard was illuminated with buttons I'd never seen in a car before. The details from this taxi ride are etched in my memory: the driver listening to a radio talk show in a foreign language, the scent of hot chocolate, Dad's faded blue jeans and how he squeezed my hand so tight I lost feeling in my small fingers. I peered up to see if he had begun to cry like the other adults had, but only the outline of his face was visible in the light of streetlamps and traffic passing by. If there were tears, they were unseen in the shadows. I shuffled in and rested my head on his chest, his racing heart beating down my eardrum.

We had visited the glary, white corridors of the hospital many times but outside visiting hours the place was eerie. A light flickered above as we moved down the sleepy corridor hand in hand. I decided I'd have to be strong for Dad as he started to get upset as we approached the room that had Nan's name on the door.

'How did this happen?' Dad shouted at the nurse as he blasted into Nan's room. I'd never heard that tone of voice from Dad before. Growing up I heard my parents argue from time to time, but this was different. His voice was weak even though it was loud. Shaky. 'Mum was fine when I left her this afternoon! How did this happen?'

As the nurses led Dad around the corner, my eyes fixed on Nan lying in her hospital bed. A dim light glowed above her head and a daffodil was tucked in her veiny hands entwined across her chest. As if propelled, I sat myself down in the empty seat beside the bed and watched her, even though she wasn't doing anything. Nan had always been well put together, and even in death she was glamorous. Her perfume overpowered the scent of the flower in her hands, her hair combed in place and fastened to the side with a silver clip in the shape of a butterfly. Her lips were blue, but dressed with gloss. I now know as an adult that my cousin had been in the room before I arrived to apply light makeup to Nan's face, just the way she liked it when alive, and comb her hair. I reached forward and touched Nan's lips. They were cold and I wondered why. I knew that someday, somehow, I would know why her lips weren't like mine anymore.

Dad returned with the nurse and he didn't seem to mind that I sat by Nan's bed. He looked calmer now, apologising to the hospital staff.

My curious eyes returned to Nan and her blue lips.

* * *

The day of the funeral, family gathered outside the chapel by a large jacaranda tree. Shaded from the Queensland sun, I observed my relatives as purple flowers let go of branches and floated around us like confetti on the breeze. A metaphor for letting go, I would think many years later. My aunty, who I'd never seen without a smile, sobbed loudly. Mum's and Dad's eyes were hidden behind dark sunglasses, and my cousins the same age as me looked afraid and confused. I wasn't as scared, knowing what lay ahead. I knew Nan would be buried in a grave now and the grass would grow above her. I'd miss her but took comfort in hoping she'd be kept company by those who visited her headstone.

Once Nan was buried, my little family returned across the state line and normal life resumed, but something in me had changed. Death visited my dreams more than ever: open graves with tree roots swirling in and out of the freshly dug soil, creating a sort of tapestry in the empty burial plot. I had noticed the men and women in suits at Nan's service. They were beautiful, so poised, standing emotionless by the gleaming hearse. I wondered what it felt like, to be standing there watching everyone cry but not be able to cry too. I decided they must have been the strongest people on the planet. Stronger than any superhero I'd seen in movies.

And what happened once they hopped back into that long shiny car and drove off? Did they touch the dead bodies? Who dressed them if the dead people couldn't move anymore?

Little did I know that one day I would conduct funerals. And not only would I discover why Nan's lips were so blue that night at the hospital, I would learn how to fix them.

CHAPTER 2

COFFINS AND CASKETS

The new millennium saw the Sydney Olympic Games on almost every television screen in the country, my Britney Spears CDs replaced by Limp Bizkit and my hair drenched in the trendy lightening spray, Sun In. The year 2000 was also the year Mum and Dad moved us from the country to the big smoke to complete high school. Eventually, memories of grassy paddocks and pet cows gave way to apartment living and Christian Louboutin heels dazzling in city lights.

My early twenties were spent studying beauty therapy and working in the makeup department of a pharmacy. By day I smashed sales targets selling beauty creams and puffing blush on cheeks in the makeup chair. At night it was espresso martinis with the girls. The single life suited me. Eating leftover Chinese takeout for breakfast, watching *Six Feet Under* re-runs and indulging in ice cream for dinner, life was perfect. Until a gorgeous wealthy man walked into the pharmacy one day and asked for my hand in marriage.

Well, there were a few dates before the proposal, but it was a whirlwind romance that turned into a wedding dress and 'I do'.

Life went from movie tickets for one to spending almost every minute with another person. I was 24. Life hummed along nicely for a while, cooking for hubby, working, making love. I enjoyed my role as a cosmetician, but a longing lingered. A sort of homesickness, but not for a place. When I saw a hearse in traffic, I found myself staring, wondering … *What if I could finally achieve that childhood dream?* I know people keep a secret or two from their spouses, like a guilty love affair with a daggy band or an embarrassing drunken experience, but my secret began to weigh me down. It wasn't that I no longer wanted to work with makeup, in fact the desire was stronger than ever; but I didn't want to apply it to the living anymore, I wanted to share my artistic talent with the dead.

So why didn't I just go for it? Well, my husband was sort of fancy. I imagined the horror on his friends' faces during our many pool parties if I became a mortician.

One particular day stands out to me during this time. It took place in a salon chair as the hairdresser styled my locks for a dinner date with hubby. Flicking through a tabloid magazine, I came across an interview with a famous actress.

'If you weren't acting, what other profession would you have chosen?' the reporter had asked.

'I would have been a funeral director,' the celebrity replied. 'When I saw my father at his funeral, I was not happy with the mortician's work and from that moment I wanted to do the work myself.'

Well thank goodness she made it big in Hollywood. Who would want to be a funeral director? Creepy! the journalist had written.

Later, over lobster, I decided to slip the subject into conversation.

'So I saw an interesting documentary on television today,' I chimed, dipping some fleshy seafood goodness into thousand island dressing. 'It was about funerals.' (The documentary had been on the Vikings, but hey, it touched on Viking funerals so I wasn't entirely lying.) 'It was actually quite intriguing. It had me thinking, it could be a great job ...'

'No way!' he spluttered over his Bloody Mary. 'Working with stiffs all day? No place for a pretty girl like you.'

And that was that. I'd contribute to the household selling scented creams and mascara but with a quiet ulterior motive. I hoped my knowledge of makeup and anatomy could be a ticket to the mortuary someday.

* * *

Funeral Director required for our team of dedicated professionals. Previous experience in a funeral home necessary.

No experience. Next.

Hearse driver required. Must be able to drive manual and have great road directory skills ...

Definitely next.

My husband was working late and I found myself surfing job websites to kill some time. This had become common practice, like window-shopping but rather than pining over dresses in the store window, I longed to apply for a job as a funeral director. But how did one even become a death professional? There was no funeral college or university degree in Australia that led to a funeral home that I could see.

Administration position available. Transfer your customer service skills to a unique industry. No experience necessary as full training provided.

I sat upright with what I imagine were twinkling eyes.

The following morning, I phoned the number and within the month was seated at the front desk of one of the largest funeral companies in the city. My job was to take phone calls and transfer them through to the funeral director in his/her private office, as well as data entry. While the role mainly entailed answering the phone, I believed I was helping the world in some small way just by answering the call. Clacking at the computer keyboard entering the personal information of the dead, I wondered about their *life*. Not the generic questions requested by Births, Deaths and Marriages, but the guts of their character. What was their favourite colour? Favourite song? Did they love lobster as much as I did? Silly question. No one does. While I sipped coffee at the desk, aware of the honour it was to be seated there, I wanted more. *Needed* more. I knew there was a whole lot of death taking place downstairs where hearses were parked and bodies prepped. I longed to be a part of it and my ears were pricked, listening for opportunities to get me down there, even for a moment.

The husband didn't mind that I'd become a receptionist, even if it was at the funeral home. He said I came home buzzing, and at first he was happy for me. A daily pang of guilt lurked inside, knowing one day I'd rebel against his wishes that I not progress further into the funeral home, but I could ease him into it. Explain that the funeral home wasn't so different to a beauty salon. There was lipstick and moisturiser cream after all.

One day I overheard two funeral directors discussing a position available for an FDA—Funeral Director's Assistant. Dashing from my chair, I approached my manager, Rose, in her swanky office and expressed my interest in the position.

* * *

The morning began in the coffin showroom. A small group of eager applicants, we took our seats by coffins so shiny they mirrored our nervous reflections. Sitting so close to them was both haunting and exciting, and I realised how beautiful coffins actually are. I was about to learn the names of them all. Enchanted by the blonde funeral director at the front of the room, I scribbled notes as she shared the exciting new information we were expected to know by heart. The less expensive option was a plain timber coffin called the Fassifern. For a few extra bucks a family could upgrade to the glossy Oxley made from dark stained pine. The Macquarie Single Raised Lid coffin had a reddish tone to the wood and like the name suggested, a raised lid amplifying its classy appearance. The Swan was pure white and popular with the ladies. And the Amethyst coffin became my favourite: painted lavender with specks of glitter in the paintwork. There were personalised options, photos wrapped seamlessly around the coffin with a high-gloss finish. The images ranged from football teams to fishing boats. The Creswick coffin I dubbed 'the Banana' as it was yellow, and the Grecian Urn was not a cremation keepsake like the name suggests, but a top-of-the-range casket with a plush interior fit for a queen. I also learnt the difference between a coffin and a casket. A coffin has six sides and is basically the shape of a person. Widened at the shoulders, slim-lined at the legs. In Australia mostly coffins are used, in comparison to, say, the United States, where they mainly use caskets. Caskets are rectangular in shape, and unlike the coffin they contain a hinged lid that is not completely removable.

Following a quiz on coffin names, it was time to move on to 'role play'.

Pretending a coffin was occupied, our mentor played a distraught family member and we were each offered an opportunity to show what we'd do if dressed in a funeral director's suit for real.

'But Mum doesn't *look like Mum*,' our faux mourner exclaimed. 'She has a purple tinge to her skin and she is so cold!'

The first guy had obviously worked with the dead before, intricately explaining the science of the decomposing body. I remember thinking *how uncomforting*, a funeral director describing livor mortis to a grieving family member. I decided upon a softer approach, offering a gentle smile and touch of the arm.

'Mum is no longer here with us. Her soul has left the body and this is why you can no longer see *her* here.'

The training officer smiled.

On completion of the group interview, we were taken on a tour of the area I had longed to visit ever since I'd set foot in the funeral home. The sacred space where hearses were parked side by side like the gleaming new cars in a showroom; where coffins and caskets were stacked almost to the ceiling and the smell of pinewood blended with chemicals from the mortuary.

Excitedly, we followed our leader towards a whiteboard hanging on the wall listing surnames in columns. I assumed this was the roster for staff members and our trainer was about to announce which of us would be added, when a huge sliding door to our left hummed open. A girl around my age wearing medical scrubs and pink goggles on her face offered an animated wave.

'Hey guys!' she said, seemingly as surprised to see us as we were to see her.

She's the mortician?

She looks so young and pretty! Aren't morticians meant to look creepy?

Wait … are they … dead bodies?

Looking past her, I caught a glimpse of slimline shelving occupied with frumpy body bags, a puff of grey hair escaping a zip and fluttering in the arctic fan-forced air. This was the fridge where dead bodies were stored and the whiteboard on the wall wasn't a list of funeral home staff, it was shelving allocation of the deceased. Black spots mutated my vision just as the cheery brunette wheeled a gurney loaded with a coffin towards us. An elderly lady lay like a mannequin inside, tucked in snugly with silk drapery.

Dashing from the group, I located the restrooms and frantically splashed cold water on my face. What was I doing here? Did I really want to work with dead people? I'd longed to work with death all my life, but nothing prepares you for the first sight of a room filled with the dead.

I finally gathered myself, expecting the group to have left. Someone else could have snatched my dream job, but when I returned, not only was everyone waiting, the curious applicants were huddled around the coffin looking down at the corpse.

'Are you alright, Emma?' The trainer peered up from her clipboard.

'Yes, thank you. It just got hot in here.'

Joining the others by the Oxley coffin, I summoned my eyes to the necrotic face. She clutched rosary beads between her stony fingers, and I wondered if her hands felt as cold as they looked. *So, this is it, hey?* I thought to myself. This is where we're all headed. We live our lives studying, falling in love, paying bills, only to end up as a number on a shelf with our surnames scribbled on a whiteboard. I suddenly felt foolish for spending a hundred dollars that morning on a pair of stilettos. Sure, I embraced death as a kid, but staring down at the first dead stranger of my life, I realised we are more resilient when we're kids than we recall. Because right then, gazing down into the satin-finished coffin at a lady who was likely baking scones or tending to her garden a week earlier, I felt incredibly insignificant and afraid, more afraid than when I was knee-high. My hang-ups about my zitty chin and bloating tummy, *idiotic.* The regrowth visible in my bleach-foiled hair, *selfish.* My own impending years as an aged citizen, *frightening.* Face to face with death, I unexpectedly missed my husband. Was the overdue electricity bill worth the heated argument before he left for work? What if he was killed on his way home? The outstanding amount in bold red print seemed of paramount importance over breakfast, but now I was panicking at the prospect of never seeing my spouse again. His habit of leaving used tea bags in the sink frustrated me but dammit, I'd start *asking* him to do it, grateful that he was alive to annoy me.

CHAPTER 3

FORMALDEHYDE

Attention Operations Staff!

- No smoking where human deceased are stored or prepared.
- Always wear shoe covers before entering the mortuary or coolroom.
- Always place a head block under the head of the deceased. It is important to elevate the head above the heart to prevent discolouration.
- Please apply barrier cream to the face and hands of the deceased to prevent dehydration while stored in the cold room.
- Have you recorded the deceased in the mortuary register?
- Relocating an occupied coffin? Check you have completed the Coffin Movement book.

This room becomes sacred when a family entrusts us with their loved one. Please conduct yourself as though the family were present at all times.

'Emma. Emma, earth to Emma …'

It occurred to me my work colleague was calling out my name and I was staring zombie-like at the laminated sign stuck to the front of the body coolroom door.

I was finally here. I'd been successful at making my way from the office with plush carpets and battery-operated candles, to the operations facility below. And I'd just performed my very first transfer from a nursing home, paired with a veteran of death named Harold.

'Sorry! I was in my own world there for a minute.' Smiling, I joined my colleague by the van.

'You sure were!' Harold laughed, removing the stretcher from the back of the white Mercedes vehicle. These bulky vans, typically used as courier vans, were used here to transport the dead from place of death into the care of the funeral company. The back of the vehicle was fitted with stretchers, complete with storage compartments for gloves of all sizes and body bags.

Harold reached for the barrier cream secured to the wall, just outside the mortuary fridge where the dead lay on metal trays until it was their time to be prepared by the mortician.

'While I pop some cream on his face and hands, I want you to take the transfer paperwork and record Mr Frederickton in the mortuary register. Write that he was wearing a *yellow*-coloured ring. Whatever you do, don't write gold. Never write gold, silver, or diamonds for that matter. If there's a rock, you simply write that there is a stone. Silver is described as *white* around here. We have to cover our arses. Funeral directors can be the first suspects if any valuables go missing.'

I'd assumed lifting the dead into coffins and learning to reverse a hearse would be the greatest challenges for me in my new job. Now I was beginning to think it'd be completing the valuables receipts, writing multiple dates on wrist tags, and signing the deceased in and out of the mortuary register. Writing *yellow-coloured* rather than *gold*. A great deal of paperwork is involved when someone dies. Later in my career at a Christmas party, I overheard someone ask one of my colleagues, 'So what is the hardest part of being a funeral director?' The funeral director answered, 'Paperwork'. The curious inquirer pressed on: 'And what's the scariest thing you've seen?' I laughed to myself when I heard my colleague answer once again, with 'Paperwork'.

As part of the operations team, I'd be required to do … well, everything. From spritzing tyre shine on hearses and nailing nameplates onto coffin lids to carrying out the transfer.

'One minute you'll be cleaning hearse windows, the next you'll be transferring a dead guy from the toilet,' said Harold as we climbed into the van and headed towards the aged care facility. 'Hope you like cleaning. Oh, you have a strong stomach, yeah?'

I followed on Harold's shiny-funeral-director-shoe-heel when we arrived, down the winding corridor that smelt of mashed potatoes and urine.

'It's not the best one in the city,' he whispered to me over his shoulder as we approached the nurses' station. The RN welcomed Harold with a hug as if they'd been friends for years.

'He's in room 12, honey. Here's the life extinct form. Oh, a new girl?'

'Emma, Tania. Tania, Emma.' Harold introduced us.

'Follow me,' the nurse said, smiling, and we did.

Mr Frederickton was thin beneath his bleach-hardened sheets, his hands curled at his chest as if clenching while taking his final breath. I stood frozen a moment, suspended between intrigue and fear. The faces of the deceased are nothing like you see in the movies. There's no smile suggesting peace, and the eyes are partially open. I was to learn that most aged care facilities make adjustments to the deceased so the family can say goodbye; for example, a flower in their loved one's hands or a rolled-up towel propped beneath the chin to help lift the slackened jaw. But on my first transfer, there was no strategic dim lighting. No gentle music, not a flower petal in sight. Mr Frederickton's mouth was gaping like he had seen something horrific on the ceiling above him as he exhaled his final breath.

'He is wearing a ring,' said the nurse as calmly as if she was telling us the time. 'I'll leave you to it and be back with the paperwork.'

She left Harold, Mr Frederickton and me, surrounded by items that represented a life well lived; walls graced with framed photographs of a smiling family, finger paintings by grandchildren, trophies on the cabinet by the piles of mystery novels.

'Right, so we will open the body bag and tuck it beneath him. Using the pat slide we'll transfer him from the bed to the stretcher …' said Harold, straight to it.

His directions became muffled, like when you press your ear up to a wall trying to make out words from the other side. All the while, I was unable to lug my eyes from the photographs, the knitted blanket on the armchair by the window, dentures in a glass by the bed.

I reached forward and touched his hand.

He was warm. He still felt alive. Nan's lips had been cold.

'He only died a couple of hours ago,' said Harold, as if reading my mind. He held the open body bag waiting for me to join him.

'Ready to tuck?' he asked, motioning towards the dead man.

I nodded, and took the body bag in my hands.

* * *

While the sight of Mr Frederickton initially frightened me, in the months that followed I found the dead body less intimidating prior to being prepped. The mouth in a silent scream, the hands curled in rigor, felt natural. I preferred the messiness of recent death over frocks and hairspray. The bodies, when made up, appeared eerie to me; perfect makeup, hair in hot roller curls. Which is why I felt so very blessed to be the first point of call when someone took their final breath.

* * *

The coolness cloaked my face as I stepped inside the cool-room. The baby in my arms wrapped in a blanket felt warm in comparison and I didn't want to lie her on a metal shelf I knew was frosty. All alone except for the dead occupants in their shelves, I tightened my embrace and allowed a tear to tickle my cheek. 'You'll be safe here,' I whispered, pressing my lips against the chilly forehead poking from the woollen bonnet. The little girl was my first infant. I'd been allocated the transfer on my own since it was a straightforward transfer from the hospital morgue. No stretcher was needed, rather a handheld carrier we called the 'baby capsule'. The veterans told me the best way to transport her was to strap the capsule into the stretcher, but it felt wrong to load her into the back so she rode in the front with me. I sat her on the passenger side and for the entire drive from the hospital I rested my hand on the carrier as if to comfort her. Just as I raised the little baby corpse to place her on the shelf, the heavy door leading to the mortuary slid open.

'You right down here on your own, mate?' The towering mortician blinked behind his see-through PPE mask, remnants of a lettuce leaf in his teeth. Lewis was on duty. A strange-looking man who had adopted the nickname Lurch from the gothic TV show *The Addams Family*, he had a deep voice, long face and crooked mouth, the walking stereotype of a mortician.

'Yeah, I'm okay,' I stammered, wiping the tear I hoped he hadn't seen. Aware of my pounding heart, I calmly placed the baby in her shelf as if it didn't bother me at all. She looked so tiny, on the adult-sized tray.

'Sorry for startling you! I heard it gave you the creeps down here, that you didn't like coming down on your own.'

'I'm okay now.' I straightened my posture. Brave girls stand tall. 'In fact, I think it's quite interesting.'

'Well then, would you like to come in and see?' he asked, motioning me towards the bright lights of his workstation. 'We have an embalming if you'd like to watch how it's done. The embalmer has already got it underway.'

'Sure.' I had to look keen, didn't I? Enthusiastic? I *had* to show them that I could do this, though I doubted myself. I retrieved a pair of shoe covers from the box hanging by the door. You cannot enter the reverent space without a pair of these little plastic pouches over your shoes. I followed his squelching gumboots inside, punched in the face with chemical fumes. Laid out on one of the three mortuary tables was a middle-aged man, naked with a cloth covering his genitalia. The embalmer stood by the workstation wearing large goggles and an even larger smile.

'Hi there!' He waved, blood dribbling down his wrist. Thankful I hadn't eaten yet, I stepped closer. Bloodied water flowed freely down the sides of the mortuary table, spilling into what appeared to be a lavatory. Inserted into the side of the dead man's neck was a chrome implement, connected to a valve and clear pipe, fluid swirling through the tube like mango juice. I'd one day learn the names for all the equipment: femoral tube, hypodermic injection set, packing forceps. Little did I know the aneurysm hook would one day become one of my favourite mortuary instruments. But right now, my head was woozy. I focused my eyes on the charts of human anatomy on the wall. I'd learned the muscular system in beauty school, and to keep from fainting I narrowed my eyes on one of my favourite words. *Sternocleidomastoid.* Don't faint. *Sternocleidomastoid.* Don't forget to breathe, Emma Jane. *Sternocleidomastoid.* Calmer now, I noticed a small vase was propped in the corner of the big bright room, withering black roses in water dyed red like blood.

'Aah, don't worry about that,' the embalmer said, acknowledging my wide-eyed stare. 'Morticians are a funny bunch.'

I returned my eyes to the dead man as the embalmer pressed down on the neck close to the implement. More blood streamed from the incision.

'Right now I'm replacing his blood with preserving chemicals,' he chimed as he pushed and pulled the skin, the pale flesh turning lifelike pink. 'Pretty cool, huh? If you come and look closely, the jugular vein … it looks like fettuccine, yeah?' *Well, there goes my idea of carbonara for dinner.*

'So, you've emptied him of … blood?' I stammered.

'Not quite, he's a bigger guy. Will take a little while, and I still need to aspirate his organs.'

I decided not to ask what he meant by this, although a decade later I'd find myself driving the trocar into the abdomens of the deceased myself.

Moving even closer, I suddenly felt unusually connected to the dead man. He'd spent his life creating memories with family, worked a job, had a home out there somewhere, yet here I was by his side as strangers emptied him of the blood that once helped keep him alive.

'Emma Jane, you down here?' I heard a voice call out from beyond the mortuary doors. 'What's taking you so long? We have a nursing home transfer!'

'Well, I guess I best be going,' I said. 'Thank you for showing me … what you do.'

'If you ever want to come in and learn some stuff, just knock,' said Lewis, looking up from the elderly lady he was washing down with suds and water on his mortuary table. 'I'm happy to show you. It's pretty cool in here.'

'I will,' I nodded.

'Hey, before you go, can you pass me that sandwich over there?'

CHAPTER 4

THE END

'What's so wrong with it?'

'It's weird!' my husband bellowed. 'What is it with you and your fascination with death?'

'I like helping people! At the end of the day I feel like I have really made a small difference in this world!'

'You smell like dead people,' he grunted.

Conversation over. The man I married was a stern man. This particular fight had me approaching my manager's office on Monday.

The door was ajar when I knocked.

'Come in!' Rose, the pretty former paramedic, sat at her desk, her makeup perfectly applied and blonde locks curled like Marilyn Monroe.

Working at the funeral home enriched my life. I had fallen in love with *being alive.*

And I was about to give it all away.

'How was everything today?' Rose switched off her computer, offering undivided attention. From the day we met during my interview for the company, the vibrant blonde had inspired me. Prior to becoming state manager for the funeral company, Rose worked as a paramedic driving citywide saving lives and, as I was later to learn, she was poignantly affected when resuscitation was unsuccessful. So, she crossed over. Medic turned funeral director, taking care of the departed instead. Not only was Rose inspiring professionally, we shared plenty in common from makeup to seafood. 'Oh, you live in Bayside?' she'd exclaimed when browsing my printed résumé in her jewelled hands. 'I love the Sea Shack there. Best seafood platter in the city!' And for the next five minutes we chatted about fresh lobster rather than the job I applied for. Not only was I about to resign from my position, I was about to lose the coolest manager ever.

'Are you okay?' She studied my face as if counting the spray of freckles across my nose.

'No, I'm so sorry Rose,' I sniffled. She handed me a tissue from the novelty coffin-shaped tissue box. 'I can't work here anymore.'

Rose's pretty blue eyes glazed over. 'It's too much for you, isn't it?' She leant back in her chair, crossing her arms across her bosom.

'Yes,' I lied.

'It was the decomp that scared you off, wasn't it? I told the transfer crew you were too new for that. Look, I know the death industry can be hard, but it's very rewarding.

Some days are harder than others, but please, can you not give it some more time?' she pleaded.

I never wish to leave! I wanted to scream. *I love being the shoulder for the families to cry on when a loved one has left this world!*

'I just can't do it.' I began to cry.

'Oh sweetheart.' Rose dashed from her chair and around her desk, and pulled me into a hug. I could have rested my sad little head on Rose's shoulder forever, not even wiping the snot leaking from my nose and onto her blouse.

'Look after yourself, kiddo.'

It was oddly therapeutic when Rose called me *kiddo.* Her words provided comfort, like it wasn't all over just yet.

I dragged my feet from her office towards the locker room to retrieve my things, when I decided to pass through the trim room. The trim room is a sacred space, where coffins are kept and modified with handles, nameplates and other symbols requested by the family. The coffins arrived at the funeral home from the manufacturer as a shell, and whistling while they worked, funeral directors hammered and drilled all add-ons with love, care and precision. This practice is called 'trimming' the coffin. The trim area was very different to the soft lighting in the offices, the tranquil music and soft speaking. Tools were scattered on shelves, wood shavings covered the floor, but the trim room still held as much heart for me because it reminded me of Dad's work shed on the farm when I was a girl.

I remember watching him hammering away, carving and measuring, wood shavings fluttering to the floor. Now it had been his daughter, hammering nails into wood.

Inhaling the coffin-pine air, I ran my fingers along the dusty shelves storing small metal crucifixes and 'Rest In Peace' emblems. Once my locker was empty, I trudged past the refrigeration unit, resisting the urge to pop my head in and say goodbye to the bodies. Passing through the garage I waved casually—so as not to draw attention as it would just increase the waterworks—at the young lads cleaning the hearses, slipped into my car and cried all the way home.

I searched for jobs in a beauty salon the following day, changing my profession from *mort*ician to *beaut*ician to spare the embarassment to my husband and others who thought I was morbid and/or weird. I would greet my husband each day smelling of aromatherapy oils and scented creams, not death. And that is where my story in the funeral industry was supposed to end.

* * *

Even though I'd left the funeral home, my marriage continued to fall apart. If not for my time in death care, I could have continued baking cakes, preparing dinners and cleaning the house, gone on making love to a man who didn't seem to love me. Wiser, I knew the scythe could strike at me next. And there was no way I was going to live out my days in battle. Nor should he. The wedding celebrant had announced we'd be together until death do us part. And indeed, death did part us. I chose death. I knew more than ever I wanted to be a funeral director but first I'd have to leave my marriage.

One blustery winter's day only days before my birthday, I slid my wedding band from my finger and placed it on the marble kitchen bench. Details of this day are clouded, as if my brain would prefer the memories didn't exist. A blubbering mess, I threw blankets, pillows and a few items of clothing—including a suit and aspirations to return to the funeral home—into the only car I had keys for, the heap of metal Toyota RAV4 parked in the giant driveway. The custom-built garage was brimming with vintage cars worth more than some superannuation funds. All I had was a bomb that spluttered at the lights. I fitted the key into the ignition and the glowing gauge indicated the fuel tank was full and I pressed the accelerator to the floor. In the beginning, I slept in the back of the SUV. With limited access to funds, I lived this way for about a month. I knew I had to find work, so I checked into darkened internet cafés among gamers and backpackers, searching online for job opportunities at funeral homes. I printed out my résumé and knocked on funeral home doors. I was mostly turned away, asked to email my CV instead. I refused to give up.

Yes, I should have better prepared my exit from the home, but the morning I headed out that door, I'd reached the end of my tether. Life was precious. Death was looming. Having no money to my name was the lesser evil to crying myself to sleep.

* * *

The following months were not bright. This was not like me. I'm usually the positive, independent one, the blonde social butterfly everyone wanted to be around. *'You know, Emma Jane, the one with that huge smile!'*

During this time, I read a book about an artist who admitted himself to the psychiatric ward, and was given opiates and taken care of for months. I wanted that.

Take me away! Get out your straitjacket!

I admitted myself to hospital.

I must have looked a danger to myself as I was seen to immediately. Catching a glimpse of my reflection in the glass separating the triage nurse's desk and patients, I was taken aback myself. Hair all over the place, mascara-streaked cheeks, dehydration lines. Things had to change. Not tomorrow. Not next week. Now.

Following an hour of interrogation, the big guy from Mental Health had reached his conclusion: I was mentally sound.

'Go somewhere you can relax, buy a coffee and just take some time out,' said the man in an oversized white coat with a name tag reading *Mental Health Psychologist.* I needed something a little more profound than coffee beans and a fishpond, I thought to myself.

And just like that, with a pat on the back I was sent on my way.

Moping towards the exit, rather upset I wasn't at least offered Valium, I scanned the waiting room of the sick and injured: sneezing patients, a man nursing a bleeding elbow staring blankly at the TV screen suspended down from the ceiling. There were babies screaming and a tradesman who appeared to have a black eye. I felt insanely guilty.

There is a scene in one of my favourite rom-coms, *The Holiday*, where Kate Winslet, portraying a heartbroken journalist, turns up the gas and leans in to inhale the fumes from her stovetop. Reaching her senses seconds later, she slaps herself across the face. 'Low point!' she scolds herself. 'Low point!'

Stepping outside and peering up at the sunset, I realised I'd reached my low point and needed a damn holiday, that was for sure. But more than anything, the longing to sit in the plush seats of a darn hearse was stronger than ever. To touch the cold hand of the dearly departed, polish a coffin. I had given away my dream for a man, and I sure as hell would never do that again.

CHAPTER 5

A TOUCH OF COMFORT

I leaned down to check my reflection in the window of the funeral home. I'd cried so much my Botox had worn off, but in my best black suit, a red necktie and matching lipstick, I looked the part. A deep breath in, posture upright, I pressed my manicured finger onto the doorbell. They needn't know I'd spent my last fifty on a French set to impress. No one would suspect I had dressed in a McDonald's bathroom and had been living on two-dollar cheeseburgers for weeks. *Showtime.*

With white painted brickwork, stained-glass windows and flowering vines, the building was an outcast among the city skyscrapers. I felt a sense of home already. A lady with a pointy nose tended to the knock with a smile.

'Good morning, ma'am. I have a job interview with the manager at ten.' The smile across my face was the first in months.

'Welcome. Come on in.' The lady motioned towards the two-seater couch by the administration desk. 'Take a seat, she won't be long.'

'Thank you.' I nodded politely, turning my attention to the *Australian Funeral Director* journal on the coffee table. I narrowed my nervous eyes on the advertisement for the latest Batesville casket to keep from trembling. I pretended to read the history of the American casket company, when actually, I wished I could crawl into one myself and be buried. Six feet under would save me from this interview. It's not that I didn't want to be there. In fact, it's *all* I wanted. I just wished I could've magically skipped to the handshake confirming my place on the payroll. Interviews make me sweat profusely; tremble as though my bloodstream's injected with an electrical current. I can write books, *actual* books. But verbal skills are not my strength. When nervous, someone could ask, 'When is your birthday?' and I'd answer with, 'Fine thanks.'

I crossed my ankles, held my head high. Phoney confidence. My life depended upon this meeting. I wiped my hands on my trousers just as a tall, lean woman appeared.

'Welcome to A Touch of Comfort Funerals,' she said softly. 'Please ...' She asked that I follow her down the hall. We passed a darkened coffin showroom, the sunlight creeping through the blinds with specks of dust dancing on the light beam like glitter. It was a touch of comfort seeing the coffins; I felt warm and fuzzy inside.

Most interviews at a funeral home take place where funeral arrangements are made. The walls decorated with funeral director's awards, the shelves brimming with cremation urns and *Your loved one has died, what's next?* brochures, a box of tissues in the middle of the large table next to a jug of water.

I slipped into the seat like the many bereaved had before me.

That day, the entire can of hairspray taming my curls into a corporate bun and the perfectly applied makeup were my disguise. I would ace the interview and start my new life.

One hour later, I walked out of that stunning building with my name on the roster.

* * *

A Touch of Comfort funeral home was independently owned, and its head office was housed in an amazing nineteenth-century building, one of the few surviving pieces of the city's bygone history. It was originally built by a wealthy citizen for his family, complete with gardens and views of the city centre. Over the centuries, the building was used for various purposes. Later during my employment, as I innocently stood at the back of the chapel overseeing the funeral taking place, the funeral conductor joined me and whispered, 'Wanna know a cool fact about this place? This place used to be a knock shop. Bordello … you know … a brothel.' *Nice.* I suppressed my chuckle.

Period furniture transported visitors and staff back in time, with carpets selected to match the history of the business. The building truly felt like a grandparent's home, providing comfort and stability, hundreds of years of hugs and support. A Touch of Comfort funeral home stood proud and confident, despite the urban renewals of cookie-cutter high-rises turning the area into a modern bustling city.

None of the 'dirty' work was conducted here. The operations facility was on the north side of town, a large warehouse where ten gleaming hearses were kept, with towers of coffins and the sterile clean mortuary.

I was hired to work full time from the operations facility. The day I slipped back into a funeral director's suit, I was reminded there was no love that could be given by a man (other than my dad), no wedding cake, no fancy refrigerator filled with camembert cheese, that could bring me joy the way working with the dead did.

Two pay cheques and I was able to rent a small cottage in the suburbs, quaint and ageing, tucked away in a quiet street far enough from the city to indulge in wearing odd socks and watching unlimited Netflix in peace, but conveniently close if I ever craved a midnight kebab. With ants scurrying along the window sill and garden beds hugging the backyard, my new home was the perfect place to begin my healing journey. Swapping king-size satin sheets for minimum thread-count cotton and a mattress where my feet hung over the sides, I was serving the dead again and the size of my bed no longer mattered to me. I didn't mind eating two-minute noodles rather than lobster. I *chose* to start over from scratch. I didn't go back to the house to collect belongings, so I made do with the few things squeezed into the car the day I left. A friend retrieved my Maltese puppy, Cupcake, from the house so I had company and cuddles.

At night, I stared into the blackness; sometimes I wailed hysterically, others I screamed anger into my pillow. There were more peaceful nights, thinking about my childhood on the farm and how it had prepared me for the transition from married woman to sleeping on my own. Unbeknown to me, Mum and Dad had survived week to week yet they'd provided my siblings and me with the happiest of childhoods. Alone now, I appreciated my childhood. Growing up in a mildly poor household taught me that a bit of poverty wouldn't kill you, not in our nation anyhow.

I don't even think I missed my husband, rather I grieved my role as wife. I loved grocery shopping for our little family, potting plants (badly), baking bread (to a crisp), assisting my stepson with his homework (googling answers to his math questions), enjoyed date nights in the city.

But my longing for the funeral home surpassed all of that. And now the 'on-call' phone was tucked beneath my pillow, ready to be there when someone exhaled their final breath. I closed my eyes and thought back to the lonesome nights that I had cried myself to sleep in the spare room of our marital home, begging to a higher power to help me.

If taking care of the dead and serving their families is not a prayer answered, I don't know what is.

CHAPTER 6

TRANSFERS

Funeral directors can change clothes multiple times a day. We'd start the day in something casual, but suitable. We didn't rock up in singlets and sandals, but something comfortable enough to wash hearses, nail handles on coffins and move bodies about. When a transfer came in, we dressed in our suits, and of course for funerals we were to dress sharp with shoes so shiny we could use them as mirrors.

When helping in the mortuary, it was scrubs and gumboots while assisting the head mortician in removing IV lines from the dead, bathing them and washing their hair, cleansing weeping sutures post-autopsy and beautifying their cold faces. I helped remove remnants of foreign materials from chest cavities and scooped faeces from bottoms. I cleansed dirty toenails, and helped repair cuts and wounds.

Next, I'd assist the funeral directors with their paperwork for the services the following day.

Had the flowers been ordered?

Was the correct hearse booked? (It is common that a white hearse is requested for a female and in our fleet of gleaming death cars, half were white and half black.)

Would the funeral end with a burial or cremation? If cremation, had we removed the pacemaker?

If a burial, was the cemetery plot booked and paid for?

Paperwork completed, it was into casual shorts and a polo shirt to wash down the hearses for the funerals the following day. Then if the phone trilled and a body collection was required, it was into smart slacks and tie and out on the road.

* * *

The transfer. My favourite role as an FDA. The transfer is the process of taking the deceased from place of death into the care of the funeral home. To me, the transfer is the backbone, or perhaps the heart of the funeral home. Out on the road visiting hospitals, retirement villages, living rooms, kitchens, bedrooms and garden beds—yes, I've collected a green thumb who died while watering her roses—is when I am most proud to be wearing my funeral director's suit.

Living in the lofty Himalayan peaks, Tibetans place their teacups upside down before going to bed, aware they may never wake to use them again. When they wake the next day, they are grateful. This is how I felt every morning I opened my eyes. Some mornings were harder than others during my divorce, but then I'd remember, somewhere out there in the big city someone had not been as lucky as I to open their eyes, to experience heartache, to stir sugar into a coffee. And this thought helped me soldier on with my life.

Some funeral directors groaned when a transfer came in, but I was eager to get on the road. In fact, I once overheard my manager telling the head mortician that she allocated transfers to the staff who were slacking off, implying it was a punishment. 'Get them out of the lunch room and out on the road!'

After hearing this I'd pretend to be lazy so the task was allocated to me.

When that phone rang in the early hours of the morning I'd curse and wish it was me who had died, but once I'd spritzed hairspray in my top knot and climbed into the van, I was challenge ready. Yes, that's right: we were rostered to be on-call 24 hours a day on a rotational roster. Once a week we took the work phone home and ordered takeout, because the moment we sat a pot on the stove someone would pass away. Funeral homes are called homes for a reason: we may as well live there.

On the road day and night, we were bound to encounter scenes that made us laugh, especially during transfers. From getting lost in the middle of the night, to my on-call partner blowing wind at the most inappropriate times, through no fault of his own. *It's when I eat bread,* he'd say. Transfer partners became the best friends. Humour aside, heading out into the night side by side with one another and the dead, we laughed, we cried, we wiped blood off our trousers. One case that comes to mind as I write is the day my transfer partner at the time, David, and I were called to a decomposition case. Decomp kit (a kit containing face shields, heavy duty gloves and long-sleeved cuffed disposable suits to be applied over our clothes) aboard, we took off to a suburb by the seashore surrounded with trees that bend down as if the leaves want to drink from the bay for themselves. A fair drive from the city, the caravan park was a rural echo, with cowboy boots and ute trucks in driveways, but with a sea-sprayed twist—seashells on the patios or a surfboard leaning against front doors. We drove around the premises several times in search of cabin 5, residents sipping tea on their verandas looking rather confused as to why a huge white van was circling them. We finally located the dwelling where a deceased lady awaited inside. As soon as we climbed out of our van, Dave and I shot one another 'the look'. The look to say, '*Oh dear. I can smell it already.*' The caravan floor creaked beneath our feet as we made our way through the tiny lounge room to the bedroom, where I stopped in my tracks. The bed moved with well-fed larvae wriggling and writhing within the yellowing sheets. There was also a bag of Allen's Snakes lollies and a shopping list. While Dave collapsed the funeral cot to below bed level, I read the dead lady's list of groceries to see her handwriting, bring her back to life in the moment before she'd deteriorated to blackening sludge. This decaying lady was a daughter, a friend. No one ever deserved to be found like this and I was determined to paint a picture of her in my mind before we carried her away. She needed eggs, butter, milk and apples. I looked up at Dave and couldn't help but laugh at him, his face shield protruding from his head, and in that moment we shared a smile. Together right then, we were experiencing something that most people will never see.

'A lolly?' he joked, his voice squeaky from the mask pushing down on his nose. He pointed to the bag of glucose snakes by the dead lady.

I reached for the pile of magazines to make room on the bed; I'd have to climb aboard to successfully reach her. She was awkwardly positioned, as if she had sat on the side of her bed trying to catch her breath and instead it escaped her forever. Stepping up onto the mattress, I felt insects beneath my feet, and discovered a whole other family of maggots beneath the *New Ideas* and *Woman's Days*. I gently placed her magazines to the floor. The smell made me mad at her neighbours; they were metres away! Why did it take over ten days for them to notice? Decomp cases were close to my heart, feeling reserved compassion for them because they usually died alone. Somehow this comforted me. I wasn't the only one alone.

All that was left of the lady's character was a puff of grey hair on her shrivelled corpse; like something from a horror movie but this was no Hollywood blockbuster, this was my life. The mattress squelched beneath me as I approached her, kicking chubby larvae out of the way. Nothing mattered now other than moving her safely to the body bag. In one synchronised movement, we wrapped the lady in the soiled sheets; we'd use them as handles to move her. If we'd picked her up by her limbs she'd have fallen apart in our hands.

'One, two, three!' David called out and together we heaved. As a funeral director and mortician I discovered surprising strength in dismal circumstances. Once the task was completed I'd reflect a moment, congratulate myself with a mental high-five then once home couldn't even unscrew the lid off a jar of soup. We zipped up the bag, and carried her out of the caravan on the stretcher.

Once back out in the fresh air, we snapped off our masks and I noticed a maggot on Dave's shirt. I'd wait until we were back in the van to alert him; his reaction would be the best part of day. It was his weakness, maggots. I didn't mind them. I hated the flaky foot skin when tucking dead feet into shoes in the mortuary. Nothing worse than sitting down to lunch and discovering heel skin on your pants. Decomp slime any day over a neglected foot. We took our time heading to the funeral home; it was almost lunch. There were leftover catering sandwiches from the funeral that morning and timed well we'd be back at base in time to share them with the others. En route, the stench wafted from the back of the van to the front and the odd fly made its way to the cabin of the van, buzzing about the dashboard.

We were born to do this.

That afternoon while shopping, I grabbed an extra tub of butter and two extra apples. Jane Doe would not leave this world without her groceries. Before the lid on her coffin was secured, I snuck them in snug and hoped that she felt less alone.

* * *

With every transfer, every corpse I bathed and dressed, my heart slowly began to mend. I've read in dating columns that most girls reach for chocolate, wine and wearing down high heels on dance floors with champagne flutes in hand. 'The best way to get over someone is to get under someone else!' Oh, how often I'd heard that phrase …

Not me. I found healing in the dead, throwing myself wholeheartedly into their stories, the eulogy, the flower arrangements representing their life. When a young man arrived at the facility due to a drug overdose, I was grateful to have chosen work over cocaine. When a suicide victim was brought in from the coroner, my inner strength was affirmed. When the elderly were loaded into hearses complete with extravagant flower displays, I was reminded of the many years ahead to begin a brand-new story. I can hear writers of break-up blogs screeching, *'You find solace in working with dead people? Have you not seen* Bridget Jones*? It's supposed to be ice cream, cigarettes and wine!'*

No, I didn't need blocks of chocolate and one-night stands. With every coffin, every dead hand I was privileged to touch, every lipstick shade applied to cold blue lips, my broken heart was mending.

Okay, there was a stash of ice cream in my freezer, but you get the idea.

CHAPTER 7

FRIENDS IN SUITS

'Macca! Have you put the wrong flower arrangement on the coffin? I told you to double-check the paperwork!'

'Murray! Did you vacuum the hearse yet?'

'Who put salt in my coffee instead of sugar? That's not funny!'

Morning havoc around me, I stood by a hearse and smiled to myself. Monday mornings were always hectic at the operations facility, as hearses were loaded and paperwork cross-examined. The operations team scurried about the place as if the end of the world was near and there was no place I'd rather be than among the chaos.

Mags approached a colleague and myself with the familiar paperwork required to transfer a deceased person, and within minutes we were out of our casual clothes and into our suits. I jumped up to the passenger side of the body van and Macca flew into the driver's seat.

Macca and I had become great friends since I'd started at A Touch of Comfort. Tubby, with small eyes and oversized spectacles, Macca had been a funeral director long before fancy lowering devices and in-house florists. He was also my teacher, educating me on not only the history of the funeral profession but foreign music and cooking. When we were together we laughed, shared banter and recipes. We could hang out and offer the odd cuddle without either of us getting the wrong idea. Skinny blondes were not his thing and big round bellies weren't mine.

During my first month at A Touch of Comfort, Macca and I were on-call together for an entire weekend and were summoned to eight transfers in 48 hours. Macca brought along his beloved CD collection. To the sound of saxophone we bonded and from that weekend Macca continued to introduce me to musicians I'd never heard of. Today it was an African-American soul star, Charles Bradley.

Macca slid the shiny disk into the stereo as we drove off towards the horizon.

* * *

Mags had asked us to deliver ashes to a widow before heading to the aged care facility to conduct the transfer. Normally, the family would collect the ashes from head office in the city, but the widow was frail and lived alone with no car. A Touch of Comfort offered to hand-deliver the container of remains in person. Nursing the box of cremains in my lap, I thought, *Only days ago this man was sleeping by his wife's side. Now he sits as ash in my lap.*

We arrived at the unit block and Macca pulled up into the car park as if he was visiting an old friend and had driven here many times before. We got out and began our stroll past units with front yards of flower beds dancing in the rain. We didn't mind that the soft rain dampened our suits. We were alive. Carrying the container tightly in my hands, we located unit 23 and Macca knocked on the door. I had never delivered ashes before and thought it was sad that the last time the man left this unit he was human-sized, and now I was returning him home as dust.

'Come in!' an elderly voice called out. Macca opened the door and we entered, walking over to the tiny lady dressed in a nightie moving back and forth slowly in her rocking chair. The homely scent of Vegemite toast was sobering; regular activities, like making toast, will end for us all one day. I wondered if it even tasted the same for her anymore now the love of her life was dead.

'I have your husband here,' said Macca. He took the remains from my arms and passed them to her. Her bony hands clutched her spouse, now condensed into the plastic container, and without saying a word she shakily leant down to place him by her feet on the floor. My heart ached; I just knew she'd fall apart the second we left. Her lips quivering, she turned her undivided attention to the paperwork Macca retrieved from within his suit jacket.

'Now, I need you to go over this information for submission to Births, Deaths and Marriages. This will be the official information registered, and I can give you the original death certificate within a week or two,' he said, right to it.

I gazed around at the photos on the walls, happier times on cruise ships and at Christmas lunches with family wearing Santa hats.

'Right, then,' said Macca, popping his shiny pen in his pocket. 'If you have any questions, please call any time.

Sorry for your loss.' I didn't want to leave but I followed Macca back through the door.

'A year at most. Someone married that long won't last after their spouse dies,' Macca whispered sadly to me as we headed back out in the rain.

We joined the bustling main road, people going about their day as if death was not near at all. *I just hand delivered a dead man's ashes to his widow,* I wanted to scream from the window. *Stop a moment, people, before it's too late. Thou Art Mortal! Thou Art Mortal!*

* * *

Two hours earlier, Margaret Porter had died peacefully in her nursing home bed, aged 95.

For almost a century she walked this earth and it was an honour to take her into our care. We pulled into the pristine lawns of the nursing home, respectfully lowering the stereo. We located the ambulance bay and shared a smile.

'Ready?' Macca fetched his specs from the inside of his jacket.

'Ready.'

Margaret was a tiny lady.

'She was such a gentle woman,' one nurse said, hanging her head.

'Just last week she had a fall and as we caught her, she asked if *we* were alright,' sniffled another.

'We will take good care of her,' I promised.

'Poor old soul,' Macca sighed once the nurses left the room and we transferred her onto the stretcher.

Once back on the road, Charles Bradley was turned up loud and we sang.

It may seem absurd that we were singing with a dead lady on board. But as funeral directors, we are goldfish in the same bowl with a similar perspective on the world. Looking into dead faces and shrunken eyes daily, we knew our lives could end at any moment. In a split second it could all be over. No more blue skies. No more sunsets and the sound of rain on the window late at night. No more plane-gazing as they take off to faraway lands, no more whiskey and no more hugs from family. Our lives are transient and of this we were reminded every single day.

So we sang blues and soul at the top our lungs.

Margaret didn't mind. In fact, I reckon she would have been having a little dance.

* * *

When arriving to the operations facility with a decedent in tow, one of the first steps to be carried out is measuring them. The measurements were then passed on to Mags to ensure the correct-sized coffin was in stock for the body. Once Margaret was measured and placed in her shelf in the body-holding fridge, it was time for morning tea.

Fun fact about funeral directors: they *live* for tea breaks. During meal breaks the staff room would overflow with laughter, jokes and political debates. Tea was brewed, microwave meals heated and the whole crew sat around together with a fridge full of dead bodies only a few metres away.

Albert was one of the kindest fellows you could ever meet. Albert married a woman who had six children from a previous relationship, and two of them were disabled. The rare soul he was, he took on the responsibility wholeheartedly and spoke of them often. His caring nature suited his work as a funeral director, and he went out of his way to help the grieving in any way he could. I'd even seen him shed a tear when coffins were lowered into the ground. With a heart as big as his bottom, he brightened my morning when I saw him walk into work.

Then there was Murray. Murray was the real-life version of the Aussie comedy character Russell Coight: tiny (almost inappropriate) shorts, Aussie slang and never-ending advice. Except with Murray, rather than offering suggestions on how to survive in the outback he shared his secrets to eliminating bitterness from vodka and cooking the perfect bacon. A retired farmer, Murray had moved to the city with his wife following his sister's death to help provide for the family.

One afternoon it was just Murray and me in the hearse after a long, hot day. We hadn't eaten lunch and our stomachs gurgled.

'I could eat a shit sandwich if the bread wasn't cut too thick!' he announced.

Prohibited to laugh in a death car, I completely broke the rule.

Farts, banter, dancing while washing the hearses and suds fights; I had totally fallen in love with the array of characters at A Touch of Comfort.

They were a collection of jokers, but once those pressed suits were donned the guys were on their best behaviour, respecting and burying the dead with pride.

CHAPTER 8

HEARSE ETIQUETTE

- *Drive as if there is a glass of water on the dashboard at all times. Do not spill a drop!* When Murray drove the hearse, the dashboard would be 'soaking'!
- *No talking, waving or laughing in the hearse.* One time a car met with us at the traffic lights, and a Chihuahua dressed in a doggy Santa suit popped its head up at the window and I waved excitedly, completely forgetting I was in a hearse.
- *Drive ten kilometres under speed limit when loaded at all times.* ***Twenty kilometres an hour only*** *while driving through a cemetery.* When Murray was driving, my knuckles paled while holding on! As he swerved at high speed through traffic, the casket spray of flowers almost slid off the coffin lid! He was also known to pay a speeding fine or two.

- *Headlights must be turned on at all times when loaded. Keep lights on when driving through a cemetery.*
- *All hearses must be washed and polished with a chamois every morning. Ensure there is a bottle of holy water in glove compartment, umbrellas in the undercarriage.*
- *Refreshments kit must be topped up every afternoon.*
- *Fuel tank must be above half at all times.*

Hearses are the most beautiful machines to me. Each morning I paused for a moment, marvelling at the shiny fleet of the finest Mercedes-Benz vehicles parked side by side. There was no prouder moment than sitting in a hearse, posture upright and heads held high as we merged out onto the road from the operations facility, joining everyday commuters. I watched as drivers in other cars gawked, or looked away. We intrigued or scared them. And when I watched young faces pressed against the back window of their parent's Range Rover, I was taken back to the time when that was me. Except we were in an outdated Commodore.

While the other funeral directors moaned in the morning about having to polish the vehicles every day, I couldn't reverse the luxurious cars into the wash bay quick enough. Hosing down the lengthened Mercedes and spritzing the wheels with tyre shine was therapeutic.

* * *

One morning during my training period, the funeral conductor explained that prior to the service we would be doing a drive by. A drive by? Were there guns hidden in the undercarriage of the hearse? 'What exactly is, erm … a drive by?' I whispered to him, and he looked at me as if I had just asked if he would care to drive off a cliff together.

'You don't know what a drive by is?'

'Well, I am a fan of hip-hop, I know some great music artists who have been wounded in drive bys.'

The expression on his face had me wanting to melt into my polished shoes. Turned out a 'drive by' entails driving to the deceased's home on the way to the funeral. The hearse stops outside the home and the conductor places a rose in the letterbox, bows respectfully then returns to the hearse. I loved it. You had the opportunity to see their home, the gardens they once watered, the patios they swept. What an honour, I imagined, for the conductor to stand at the front of the deceased's home to place the rose in their letterbox which I'm sure was usually filled with utility bills—mail they needn't worry about anymore.

* * *

Not only are hearses the final sleek ride, they are also a giant toolbox on wheels. Half the funeral home is stored in the undercarriage of a death car.

First and most importantly, we have the church trolley. Known as a 'church truck' within the industry, this nifty piece of equipment allows the funeral director to safely transport the coffin from the hearse to wherever the service is taking place. The rubber tyres make it easy to roll over carpet, grass or any bumpy surface with dignity. The built-in handles also save our backs; we're able to pull, push or lift without causing injury to ourselves because, let's face it, not everyone is light! The church truck collapses nicely to be slipped in the compartment beneath the hearse among all other funeral supplies.

There are bookstands for the guest book, umbrellas, a portable sound system for graveside services; which also brings us to the box of CDs, and iPads and microphones. There's a box of RSL tribute poppies, baskets for extra flowers, raincoats. There are clipboards, pens, antiseptic, Band-Aids, miniature bottles of water, mints. String, needles, Panadol. Mouthwash. There are plastic cups and a picnic table in case Grandpa Sam brought sandwiches. There's a bottle of holy water. There's a big box of sand. The priest and family often pour a scoopful on top of the coffin in the sign of a cross.

Indeed, the hearse will be the final ride for us all. But we won't be arriving to our funeral alone. Funeral directors in front, supplies down below, when we die we'll be carried to our graves with the bits and pieces that help make a funeral run smoothly, just like the phones, wallets and keys that accompanied us in life.

CHAPTER 9

CRASH COURSE

Years of gruelling study, treacherous exams and knowing where every artery lies in the body: that is what it takes to become a funeral director … in the United States of America.

In Australia, you don't need be a licensed embalmer to become a funeral director.

The studies of anatomy and chemicals sure will help in the mortuary if the prep room is the place you want to work. If you want to be out in the field assisting on funerals and conducting transfers however, there's no textbook on earth that can prepare you for the work of a funeral director. If you wish to become an embalmer you can enrol, or be elected by your workplace, to undertake the three to four years of study.

Without this qualification, you cannot embalm a body.

However, in Australia embalming is not common practice. Our mates across the Pacific embalm almost every body to be buried in a grand casket, hence the lengthy study that must be completed before obtaining a funeral director's licence.

Here, mostly Greeks and Italians opt for the procedure so they can be stored in grand family mausoleums, or if a foreigner dies in Australia embalming is required for repatriation overseas.

Some Aussies may opt for their blood to be replaced with formaldehyde for personal reasons. I would like to be embalmed. Just like the regular Botox jabs in my face preventing wrinkles above ground, I would like to prolong decay once I'm buried beneath it. Sogyal Rinpoche writes in my favourite book, *The Tibetan Book of Living and Dying*, 'when alive, our body is undoubtedly the center of our whole universe. Without thinking, we associate it with our self.' Attached to my body at the rather naive age of 33, I want to preserve it for as long as possible. A bloating tummy and sunburn can stay reserved for indulgent holidays, thank you very much!

As well as delaying putrefaction, embalming opens the pathway for exhumation where diggers may find more than just a few bones. How cool would it be in 50 years time to be dug up from my grave for medical professionals to study my mummified corpse? To be completely honest though, the current methods of human disposition don't appeal to me. Both methods—burnt to pieces in a giant oven or having a tonne of dirt dumped on top of me—still give me mild anxiety when I stop and think about it too much.

In the US, you can opt to become garden compost, bypassing traditional methods of burial and cremation, but we'll get to that a little later. Let's stick to the funeral home for now.

Formaldehyde aside, the training involved to become a funeral director is rather achievable as long as you have your head screwed on, a heart bulging with compassion and the readiness to work outside normal business hours. You will be on-call … a lot. And the type of training involved depends on the position you're hired to do.

When I first entered the funeral industry, I had no clue about the various job titles. I assumed a funeral director was a funeral director.

I was to learn this is the generic label for staff caring for the dead. In a staff flow chart, Funeral Director is the underlined heading with a number of separate roles below.

There's the Operations Staff, also called Funeral Director's Assistants, aka FDAs. Although it's the lowest rung on the ladder, the FDA role remains my favourite. No two days are the same as you're the one out on transfers, helping with burials at cemeteries and able to wander the crematory while waiting for the funeral you're assisting at to start. You get to see and do *everything.* If you're lucky like I was, an FDA can also become a Mortuary Assistant, helping out in the reverent space with 'Do Not Enter Without Knocking' plastered on the door. The Mortician rarely leaves the mortuary. Their main duty is to beautify the dead. I know morticians who haven't been on a transfer or to a funeral in years. One didn't even own a suit.

The Funeral Arranger organises the funeral, from ordering the flowers to booking burial plots. The funeral arranger works mainly from the office or shop front and is rarely there on the day of the funeral unless requested by the family. The funeral arranger can go weeks without seeing a hearse. They're in the office filling out paperwork I know I would stuff up in one day if given the opportunity. Funeral arrangers are goddam masterminds, seriously. How they can organise eight funerals at once is beyond me, when I can hardly tell left from right some days. In fact, my good ol' mate Macca told me how he gave the role of funeral arranger a shot once, but it slipped his mind to book the church on his very first day, resulting in a hearse parked outside the locked cathedral and a shocked gathering of mourners. He was sent back to the operations facility within the week. Bless.

Then there's the Funeral Conductor, who, like the title suggests, conducts the service on the day. Conductors work from the operations facility as they are involved in everything leading up to the service: cross-checking the deceased in the mortuary, inspecting the flower arrangement created by the in-house florist and briefing the hearse drivers, discussing the route to the church and cemetery.

* * *

The interview process to gain employment in an Australian funeral home is as tough as an Ironman triathlon. The HR managers are often recruited from among retired paramedics, police officers or military servicemen; they can sense kookiness like a detective with fingerprint powder. Want to prepare the dead because death metal led you towards skulls and crossbones? (No disrespect. I freaking *love* Slipknot.) You won't be added to payroll if this is the sole reason you want to see a corpse.

To become a funeral director you need people skills; you'll be conversing with an array of personalities in the depths of grief. For an example, an intelligent accountant you've always considered the smartest of professionals will collapse in your arms bellowing 'Why? Why?', his eyes peering up at you through tears, pleading for answers. He may be able to count backwards from a million to zero and score you the best tax return, but death reduces even the most powerful to knees and tears.

You won't have the answers, because even death care professionals don't understand why we die, but it's our job to make the bereaved feel like we do.

I hope you have great eyesight too as you'll be taking many 1 am phone calls, and will be required to correctly write a whole heap of information down through yawns and sleep fog, and drive big vehicles decked out with stretchers, body bags and decomp kits into the night.

No study material can prep you for the human sludge that awaits you mid-summer, the carpet squelching beneath the expensive leather shoes you bought to make a good impression.

No exam will prepare you for the moment you transfer a young man from the forensic science unit, and his head collapses in your hand because he leapt off 42 stories above the city and his skull is in pieces beneath his scalp.

* * *

It was a midday death call. Makeup fresh and brain ignited with caffeine, the day was panning out nicely so far. Until the operations trainer, Mark, approached me with transfer paperwork in his hands.

'Congratulations on two months with the company.' He exposed his bright white teeth in a proud smile. 'Let's head out on a transfer, I'd like to see you work!'

The funeral professional I was becoming was thanks to this tall lean man who looked like he'd stepped from the pages of *Vogue*. From learning to level the stretcher with the pull of a lever to strapping the deceased in tightly with dignity in front of the grieving family, I was excited to prove his training had paid off.

One of my favourite tips I had learnt in transfer training was to use a cotton body bag at a home removal, as the blue plastic bags we also had on board for messier cases, to conceal blood and bodily fluids, made a confronting crumpling noise. This isn't exactly comforting to someone who has just lost a spouse of 40 years.

It's the small touches that make a funeral director great.

Mark took the driver's wheel as I filled in the paperwork from the passenger seat. Rain pelted against the windscreen as we pulled into the driveway of the home where we would transfer an elderly man who had died in the hallway.

Frowning through the drenched windscreen we noticed no concrete path to the front door. Just a steep mound of sodden grass and mud.

'How are we going to get a stretcher to the front door?' I turned to him, rather panicky.

'Hopefully he's not too big and we can use the carry stretcher.'

On the count of three, we dived out into the rain to inspect the scene. Invited in, we entered to find the deceased lying face down on the floor in a very narrow hallway. The family dog barked from the back patio, baring his sloppy gums and fierce teeth. I was afraid he might tear through the screen door and eat us for lunch.

I shot a side-glance at Mark, who appeared as nervous as me.

'Let's just get him out of here,' he puffed and we headed back towards the van. Rain belting upon us, we fetched our carry stretcher, but to my horror there were no cotton body bags stocked in the back of the van. I had forgotten to check.

Strike one.

I retrieved a plastic body bag, wincing.

The family were crying in the lounge room down the hall, and I wanted to hug them. Flicking rainwater from my eyebrows, I prepared the stretcher, noticing the side of the dead man's face was turning purple. The blood was pooling and the rain was worsening. We had to be quick.

CRINKLE! CRINKLE! CRIIIINKLE! The plastic could be heard over the thunder, I was sure. Together my trainer and I lifted the man into the body bag, zipped it up, and moved him to the stretcher. CRINKLE! CRINKLE! CRIIIIIINKLE!!!!

'Watch your step!' my trainer shouted once we were back out in the storm.

'I'm trying!' I cried out. With little solid ground beneath me, I became unsteady and with slippery, wet hands I tragically lost my grip. Splash! Bang! I tumbled down the steep front yard, crash landing by the van. Freshly dry-cleaned trousers now soiled with mud, I scrambled to my feet to retrieve the stretcher. Strapped in snug, the dead man was safe. I didn't know about me though. I had dishonoured my trainer. Once back on two feet, we successfully slid the stretcher into the back of our van.

'So … that went well.' Mark grinned once we were back on the freeway. 'I trained you well.'

I don't know if he was being serious or sarcastic. I think the latter.

There is no textbook training that can prepare you for the day you slip, tumble and fall in front of the man that hired you with high hopes.

And if you ever choose the career path of caring for the dead, here's a lesson for you when heading to a home removal. Always, *always* check the back of the van for cotton body bags.

CHAPTER 10

GOSH, WE'RE BORING!

'Yeah, man! Performing at Tony's Tavern tonight. Yee-ha!' Murray, our retired farmer turned hearse driver announced on a Friday afternoon. Murray had a side gig as a rock star.

Okay, so he travelled across town to pubs with bar mats reeking of stale beer and screamed into a microphone on a stage that wouldn't pass a health and safety inspection … But he lived like a rock star.

As well as misunderstandings about what takes place with the deceased behind mortuary doors, I've heard plenty of judgement in my time regarding funeral directors themselves: macabre old men with hunchbacks, warts on their noses and big bellies resting on hearse steering wheels … Okay, some have round tummies due to their love of tea breaks, but funeral directors are some of the coolest people I've ever met.

It would be wrong not to dedicate a chapter to the tall lean charmer who became one of my best friends. Phil. His alluring charm blasted him straight up the corporate ladder. Within a year of stepping into A Touch of Comfort, he had left our operations facility and become one of the coordinators at head office in the city.

Our stars aligned when I stepped out from the mortuary for a tea break and caught a glimpse of a handsome new guy polishing a hearse.

'Hi,' I said, beaming and trotting over in my glitter gumboots. I loved meeting new staff. I enjoyed showing them about the place, demonstrating how to apply barrier cream to a corpse's face to prevent dehydration in the fridge and how to record them in the register. The training officer was lovely, but after mentoring newcomers for years, she yawned when conducting the tour and had lost her spark. *They won't last anyway* was her philosophy, which was moderately true. Most left within the month after dropping a body or because they were too afraid to touch one. So when a new face appeared, sometimes pale with fear, I'd skip on over to them and hopefully help ease their discomfort.

'This is where we keep all the crucifixes and nameplates for the lid of the coffin,' I chirped, leading Phil around the operations warehouse. 'If the family request a crucifix, you must also nail a Rest In Peace emblem down by the feet. Now, we don't use outside florists,' I rattled on proudly, leading him to the florist area with petals scattered across the floor and stems piled in a bin. 'Our wonderful flower artist prepares all of our casket arrangements right here. When a family arranges a funeral, they are given a questionnaire designed by our florist so she can understand the life of the decedent before expressing their personality through petals.'

Phil nodded and *aahed*, rubbing his chin.

'Now to the mortuary …'

A tomboy on the inside, I get along with guys well. I may look high maintenance with shiny shellac nail beds and red lipstick, but I'd rather joke around with the boys than gossip over the latest issue of *Marie Claire*. I was one of the only girls at the funeral home who lent a hand with the woodwork and could reverse a hearse out of a cemetery without knocking over a headstone. With Phil there was a connection like two buddies in the schoolyard. We shared a routine of a cold beer at the tavern across the road after work in no time.

* * *

Those who officiated at religious funerals knew how to enjoy themselves, too. Three of these reverends were particularly fun. I'll name them Burgers, Harley and Pasta.

Burgers was around my age and of Indian descent. He had cheeks as round as coins and Burgers' laughter was LOUD; heard by the dead and when he released these giant outbursts of happiness, his entire body thrust forward. Funeral conductors always asked him to *tone it down please. We are at a funeral.* But I thought it was beautiful that he was always chuckling as if someone was constantly tickling him.

One morning I stood by the front of the church handing orders of service to guests as they arrived to the funeral. The door of the sacristy burst open and Burgers stepped out, strutting towards me with catwalk-model bounce.

'You like?' he laughed. 'A new robe!' and he flapped his white and gold vestment as if posing for photographs.

'Very suave,' I agreed, and he offered a high-five.

Family members loved him and were never offended by his random outbursts.

Burgers had a deep love for hamburgers. There was a burger joint not too far from head office and he'd always ask about the special.

'Mind if I ride in the hearse with you guys back to the city?' he'd ask if he liked the sound of the discounted burger. 'I could really do with that burger! Yummo!' LAUUUUGH!

I always made note of the specials blackboard if I knew I'd be seeing Father Burgers.

He also referenced superheroes during his homily. Some reverends recited their homily word-for-word every service. But in two years I never heard a word repeated during Burgers' presentation. He believed the deceased to be superheroes and likened them to Batman, Superman and *Star Wars* heroes.

Then there was Harley. I didn't get as close to Harley as I did with Burgers, but I would have liked to. Because Harley looked like Michael Hutchence from the Australian rock band INXS, arriving at every funeral on a shiny black Harley-Davidson.

As funeral directors we often arrived at the church before anyone else, including Father. We'd set up our table by the entrance with water, tissues and mints, prepare the memorial book for mourners to sign and ensure our suits looked perfect.

Vrooooom, vroooooom!

The Harley-Davidson roared up the driveway and the young priest climbed off the seat, releasing cascading brunette curls when he removed his shiny jet-black helmet.

'G'day,' Harley greeted us, carrying his helmet beneath his arm with his Bible.

'He's ... so ... dreamy ...' I'd gurgle, watching after him as he strode into the sacristy.

Following the service, Father arrived to the interment on his Harley of course, parking it up beneath a gum tree by a headstone, striding on over to the grave with swagger.

Last but not least, there was Pasta. Pasta left Italy as a young man, and had been conducting Italian funeral services all over Australia for decades. These services were grand and more like a fashion show.

Pasta was ageing, but if you've ever met a middle-aged Italian man, you know their olive skin is free of wrinkles and the grey in their beards or receding hairline is the only tell-tale sign of age. Pasta was rather handsome. Think, a dark-skinned George Clooney.

Father Pasta and I connected over penne talk one day in a cemetery while waiting for mourners to arrive.

We stood by the luxurious mausoleums beneath a sky busy with birds and sunshine.

'There is no pasta like pasta in Italia,' he announced blowing a *bellissimo* kiss onto the breeze.

'Oh, I do dream of tasting authentic Italian pasta, Father. Gosh I'd love to visit Naples.'

'I take you one day, my child.' He grinned, his blue eyes twinkling. 'The pizza in Naples not like the pizza here.'

I was sad when the mourning cars arrived. My tummy grumbled.

From that day on, if I wasn't present on an Italian funeral, Father Pasta sent his best wishes to me via the funeral directors, along with his promise of handmade Italian pasta one day.

* * *

One Saturday night with a bottle of champagne in our systems, I dragged Phil to one of the only places left in the city that played nineties pop music. A cheap-looking disco ball hung from the ceiling and drinks were served in plastic cups you'd expect to see at a kid's party. Phil, the innocent and suave funeral director by day, was now topless on the sweaty dance floor spinning his shirt above his head. That night, I learnt priests love a party, too. As we danced like no one was watching, a disco light paused upon a familiar face to remind me people *were* watching; the Catholic priest who conducted many funeral services for A Touch of Comfort. My drunken excitement had me slithering through the crowd and leaping onto Father sipping his cocktail, almost unrecognisable without his robe and Bible.

The three of us danced on until the bleed of sunrise.

* * *

The following Monday afternoon while I was gridlocked in traffic, the radio-show hosts were chatting about funeral directors. I cranked the volume.

'I was at the casino over the weekend, and there was a funeral directors' convention taking place upstairs.' The announcer howled with laughter. 'Can you imagine? That has to be the most boring meeting ever to come together, a bunch of sombre fellows all together in one room. I was outta there. What if I ran into one of them?'

I couldn't help myself. I reached for the bluetooth and dialled the studio number. 'Hi. I'm actually a funeral director!' I chimed down the phone line. 'I just wanted to say I'm currently nursing a hangover after partying with funeral directors and priests all weekend. Gosh, we're boring.'

I had never heard such dead air.

CHAPTER 11

UNSUNG HEROES

The latest in today's news, it's revealed funeral directors are crooks and only in it to take your cash …

Macaroni dropped onto my Peter Alexander pyjamas.

> *A whistleblower in the industry has revealed to Gold News that grieving families pay top dollar for a casket, while their loved one only ends up in a makeshift coffin to be cremated in. We had undercover journalists investigate a local funeral home today, where we bring to you footage of a funeral director trying to upsell a coffin …*

I set aside my bowl of Mac and Cheese to focus on the news report on the television. It had become quite popular for the media to report on the funeral industry. One negative story followed another, yet no one in the industry set the rumours straight. Why? Privacy. You're sworn to secrecy when employed by a funeral home. Before you take a seat in the hearse, slip into a suit or polish a coffin, you're required to sign a privacy statement promising not to discuss, reveal or even think about talking to anyone about what goes on behind funeral home doors while working there. I understood this was to protect the privacy of the grieving, but I also believed this was one of the reasons for all the myths and misconceptions. And why I still get asked to this day: 'Is it true you cremate people in a massive burn-off?'

If we weren't under such strict obligations and were able to talk about what we do, maybe people would start to honour and respect death care professionals the way they do nurses and paramedics. Okay, we can't save lives but we *do* work 24 hours a day, seven days a week, put our own lives on hold to serve the grieving and spend more time beautifying the dead than we do ourselves. The general public has no idea of this and instead they assume funeral directors are crooked, creepy and cremate grandma in a huge oven with many others.

While employed with A Touch of Comfort, I kept an anonymous blog, in an attempt to inform people about the exciting and special profession of death. While I was petrified that I'd get found out as it would cost my job, I longed to share how precious the industry truly was—not to mention the exciting stories that came with it. I changed locations, descriptions and even my age. I didn't feel I was doing anything wrong by sharing my stories, as I never revealed names of the deceased or their families. If anything, I felt as though I was helping people by relating my experiences. The news report that played on the television was proof that there were far too many misconceptions lurking out there, and my writing, I hoped, would one day quash them all. It broke my heart that most Australians believed funeral homes performed mass cremations, swapped coffins and were only in it for the money. Breaking news. The cremation retort is built to accommodate one coffin at a time and following cremation, the fragmented bones are laid on cooling trays with identification and this is very strict practice. It *is* your grandma in that keepsake urn on your fireplace.

Just like any industry, there have been unfortunate cases and this bad practice fuelled the stigma attached to the profession. But in my experience, 99 per cent of funeral directors care for your loved one like a member of their own family. I've worked on services where staff almost faint, suits stuck to sweating backs like jellyfish on a leg while serving in a cemetery mid-summer. I know a funeral director who paid for a butterfly release out of his own pocket, also staying back one night and missing the start of his daughter's birthday dinner so he could conduct a viewing. Following a transfer from a home, we leave behind a pouch of soothing potpourri on the pillow after removing the deceased and apply moisturiser to their skin with care to prevent dehydration from the frosty coolroom. Most people don't do this to their own face before bed!

I've assisted a mortician on a case where the body was in no state to be viewed or dressed due to not being found for some time. Respectfully, she placed his suit over the top of the tightly sealed body bag as if he was wearing it. She didn't have to do this, no one would ever see him again, but this is the kind of respect and dignity practised by funeral homes.

Hearse drivers will study the route for the service the following day in their own time over their dinner plate while their children beg to be read to.

Yes, there are fees and big money involved when arranging a funeral, but it's not so the funeral director can go and jump in his Porsche parked out back. The general public doesn't realise what goes on behind the scenes. There's the after-hours transfer crew sacrificing sleep and family time, removing a deceased loved one from the sheets they shared with their spouse while neglecting their own. Some funeral homes have contracted embalmers, costing hundreds when a car-crash victim has family wishing to view them. At A Touch of Comfort we were lucky to have a very talented embalmer working on site. Outside the mortuary there are hearse cleaners and media professionals who create the photographic montage of memories. These people need a wage to support themselves and their own families, the hearses need regular servicing and to be filled with fuel, and that's a whole fleet of cars! Look how expensive it is for us to have our own on the road. Imagine up to 12 vehicles. There are the flower orders, staff uniforms pressed professionally … the list goes on.

Funeral directors genuinely care for your loss and are there for you 24 hours a day, seven days a week. They are not out to get you or profit on your grief. In fact, they even make the best of pals. Because who wouldn't want someone who sacrifices sleep, food and sometimes even their love life, as a life-long friend?

CHAPTER 12

FUN NUNS

'I'm really starting to think there might be some truth in the whole God thing.' I reached down to fetch umbrellas from the undercarriage of the hearse. I reached up and handed them one by one to Macca, who was struggling to see clearly through his rain-splodged spectacles.

'What d'ya mean, love?' His bushy eyebrows furrowed as he peered up at the sky.

'Well, the nuns, the sisters …' I straightened up and closed the side door of the hearse. Together we wandered through the headstones towards the open grave. 'There must be truth in what they spend their life preaching. They all live for a century! Bloody hell, Joan was 101!' I nodded towards the glossy coffin hovering above the earth on the lowering device, the crimson roses against the backdrop of stormy sky. Inside the coffin, Sister Joan rested peacefully in her veil, her lifeless hands clasping rosary beads.

The sisters arrived in pairs, crosses around their necks and all glowing cheeks as they sang hymns and prayed.

'God has nothing to do with it, love.' Macca chuckled under his breath as we approached the holy crowd with umbrellas. 'They don't marry, they don't have kids, they're bloody geniuses, I tell ya!'

Smothering my chuckle with the sleeve of my suit, I handed an umbrella to an elderly sister, shaking with arthritis but able to raise her hand to squeeze my cheek.

'God's child,' she said, her big blue eyes sparkling. If only she knew my secret desire to become a showgirl, I thought to myself. I cringed.

The sisters' chorale gives me goosebumps every single time. Dry beneath the canopy provided by the cemetery staff, the sisters sang at the top of their lungs as the rain battered down upon the hundreds of headstones around us. Macca and I stood side by side on the grave's edge, the umbrellas not quite keeping the rain off our suits as they blew about in the wind. Watching these greying women who'd spent their lives serving Christ, I felt incredibly blessed.

I peered to my right, and sensed Macca was not noticing the beauty around us as he flicked water from his moustache, his tiny, round spectacles foggy.

'Oh, look! A rainbow!' a voice announced from beneath the canopy. We all looked upwards to find a bright stream of colours blasting across the sky and the rain suddenly began to ease.

As the sun managed to break through the clouds, the final car pulled into the cemetery and a man in an Akubra hat joined us graveside holding an acoustic guitar. He attached a microphone to the collar of his flannelette shirt and began to play.

He looked familiar, I was sure I had seen the singer before.

Convinced my brain was saturated, I shook the thought from my mind and held out the basket of rose petals to the queue of sisters.

The guitarist sang an iconic Australian song as the nuns took the petals from the basket, releasing them onto the breeze, the colours spiralling and landing on the coffin as it slowly lowered into the ground.

On the final strum of his guitar, the service concluded and the country singer ducked off among the headstones.

'You know that guy is famous, hey?' Macca whispered.

'I thought so!' I screeched as a sister appeared behind me.

'Yes, dear.' She trembled as she spoke. 'Joan was his aunty. A crazy lass, she was. A wild one! The many times I had to save her from falling into a campfire at those bush parties on the farm. That is where he wrote his first song, and Joan helped him write most of his work.' Walking stick in one hand, umbrella in the other, she hobbled off with the other sisters dispersing in the cemetery.

'Back to what I was saying …' Macca cocked his head like he was a rooster fluffing his feathers. 'They have the best lives. They just don't tell anyone about it!'

I watched the cemetery staff fill the grave with soil.

We all have secrets, I pondered.

Even the holiest of us.

CHAPTER 13

FORGOTTEN SOULS

'Rob?' I called out, moving in closer to the cremator. The sooty-faced cremationist attended to the thunder behind the steel doors that rose at the press of a button, revealing a skeleton glowing in flames on the chamber floor. In his neon orange protective wear, Rob raked the remains about like leaves on a yard in autumn. 'Nothing to worry about love!' The door lowered and he returned to the lunch room.

The cremator has an unnerving grumble to it that I could hear all the way from the crematorium chapel. And while none of my colleagues claimed to hear it over the celebrant's speech and funeral music, the faint rumble rattled my sternum. The funeral guests likely had no clue, but I knew a cremator door had opened, another body succumbing to flames.

On this particular afternoon, we held a service for Mrs Jefferies in the crematorium chapel. Following the funeral service, Murray and I headed to the funeral director's lounge, where the coffee machine supplied warm caffeinated goodness, and took a seat with a view of coffins in line to be reduced to granules. Mrs Jefferies, our tiny 95-year-old lady, was the final soul for the day. Her eulogy was touching. She sacrificed marriage and motherhood for a career in nursing, wearing the old-style uniform in the montage of black-and-white photographs.

We'd barely finished her funeral service when Rob fetched her coffin from behind the curtain and loaded her onto the hydraulic lifting trolley. I felt it was too soon; her family were still mingling outside. I didn't want Mrs Jefferies to leave just yet. Some funerals stay with you, the eulogy ringing in your ears long after the celebrant has chanted, 'Dust to Dust!'

It wasn't up to me however, and Rob was already pushing the green button on the vacant cremator. The door raised and I pretended to grab a drink from the nearby water cooler so I could be with her. Plastic cup at my lips, I watched as she disappeared into the chamber.

At this point of my career, cremation frightened me. It wasn't the fire that confirmed my wish to be buried. Nor the trays of bones left to cool side by side. It was the 'cremulator', a large grinder used to pulverise the ivory fragments that used to be a person to dense powder. I winced when the cremation staff flicked the switch, tibia, fibula, cranium pieces and rib bones crackling and crunching to shards inside. Following cremation in Japan, the family pick the bones of their loved ones from a bowl with porcelain chopsticks, placing pieces of the sacred skeleton into the urn themselves. No blitzing and blasting there. No fear towards the remains; it's food utensils, whole pieces of bone, and love.

Perhaps if we didn't spoil the bones in the death-denying West, I wouldn't be so hesitant to surrender my body to the retort.

Some argue, *You won't know, you're dead!* But what did our skeleton ever do to deserve to be blitzed to tiny pieces by a savage blade?

I'd often wander the dusty restricted area while waiting for funeral services to begin; studying trays of skeletal remains, the nameplate removed from the coffin prior to cremation now indicating which bones belonged to whom. At times traces of colour could be seen within the ivory-pinks and green caused by chemical reactions within the heat. If it wasn't for the funeral I was required to assist on, I'm not sure I'd ever drag my eyes away from the framework that carried the human body through life. The bones beneath our skin are beautiful.

Close by was the bucket of foreign metal removed from the remains with a handheld magnet. Hip replacements, metal parts of leg with a bulb as the knee, screws that held limbs together. All these pieces fitted to the body, improving quality of life, were now a jumble of stranger's bits and pieces piling up in a bucket at a crematory.

* * *

Some retorts had a peephole on the door enabling a view of the coffins breaking open and a human body distorting in flames. While the whole process freaked me out as a youthful funeral director's assistant, I found the burning body fascinating. I often had one eyeball pressed against the spyhole.

However, Mrs Jefferies, our selfless nurse who had more than likely witnessed a few of those metal pieces being inserted into the body herself, was only a small lady and in a basic pine coffin. So when I peered in 30 minutes after her body was surrendered, her skull had already separated from her body, the dripping eye sockets looking right at me, her mouth gaping and charcoaled.

Rob caught me as I stumbled back.

'Can you come into the processing room?' he asked. 'I need a signature.'

I followed him into the room by the funeral directors' lounge, leaving Mrs Jefferies to idly shrink away in the chamber.

Crematoriums citywide, despite their differences, had one certain commonality: the rows of blue plastic boxes containing the cremated remains. (Or smaller white boxes if the person was rather petite.) Awaiting collection on the shelves in the processing room, they're labelled with an identification number, and dates of death and cremation.

In this particular room the number of unclaimed souls took my breath away. Floor to ceiling, shelves upon shelves of blue boxes.

Standing tall in my suit, I signed the paperwork then turned on my heel as if seeing those boxes didn't bother me at all.

I felt guilty leaving them behind. Those people had homes, jobs, families, a favourite colour, and now they were stored in a container on a shelf like a book in a library. At least the books at the library get taken home.

'Ready to go?' Murray gulped down the last of his complimentary can of Coke and burped.

'Sure.'

On went the 'funeral director face': strong but compassionate—it's an art—in case family were still present.

The crematorium gardens were prettied with fountains and fancy statues softening the impending doom of us all. The efforts didn't fool us. Murray steered the glossy hearse down the winding driveway, flowers in full bloom fluttering as if waving goodbye. In united silence, we veered out onto the freeway buzzing with life that could end for either one of us in any moment.

CHAPTER 14

OUTSIDE THE 'BOX'

'I think it's going to make it!' the conductor called out the window. I peered up the hill to find the tubby funeral conductor bouncing about in the seat of the transfer van as it lurched about on the uneven dirt driveway.

'You sure we won't get bogged?' I ran, meeting him at the driver's window. The ageing service conductor wiped his specs, breathing heavily. 'I'll try to get down a little closer, then we will carry him the rest of the way.' He popped his specs back on his nose and continued hobbling down closer to the grave. For today's funeral we weren't able to use a regular hearse. Our deceased wasn't coffined. He was strapped in a stretcher. This funeral would be like no other.

At a regular cemetery there are roads paved through gravesites for hearses and cars to glide through, to allow processions to take place; even the gravedigger can drive his tractor about the grounds effortlessly. At the Scrubland

Cemetery there were no roads. There weren't even headstones. Just trees, long grass and wildlife. A kangaroo took off among the trees as the van came to a halt close to the grave. The 'Green Burial' site is tucked away in northern New South Wales. To be buried in there, there's to be no metals or laminates and bodies can't be prepared with chemical preservatives. Bodies are laid to rest wrapped in a shroud or timber coffin, which is why we were trying to get the van as close to the grave as possible. With no coffin, we had no handles to hold onto. Mr Anderson was in late stages of decomposition, to add some razzle-dazzle to our already challenging task. The perfume of decay wafted to the front of the van the entire trek to the regional town.

'Ready?' My conductor opened the back of the death car.

I took Mr Anderson's feet, while he carried the deceased under the broad shoulders. I'd never worn gloves to carry a deceased person to his grave before; it felt rather odd. Bodily fluids bled through the fabric of the shroud, pitter-pattering onto our shoes as we stepped over rocks and branches. We made it to the grave safely, leaning in and placing the man into his final resting place, only the shroud separating his rotting corpse from the soil. His family would arrive shortly for the committal.

'Righto, I'll take the van back up top.' The conductor rolled his gloves outwards, careful not to splash his face with body juices, and left Mr Anderson and me alone with the birds, the dragonflies and the whistling of the wind. I've been left alone in cemeteries before, but with a grand flower arrangement on the pretty coffin and plenty of movement all around, from tractors to visitors attending to graves, it's easy for it to slip your mind that there is actually a dead person lying only inches from you. This day, I could smell him, but with the richness of the soil and the freshness of the gum trees all around, it blended into the most wonderful perfume. I was able to see the shape of him, wrapped in the cotton shroud. His legs, his arms crossed across his chest, his head resting on the dirt at the bottom of the rather shallow grave. A splinter pierced my skin through my thick stockings as I sat waiting on the log. But I didn't mind, as I inhaled the air, closing my eyes to absorb the peaceful moment.

The cemetery could be mistaken for an overgrown paddock and as you looked for others who had been buried there, you had to keep an eye out for snakes. The burials were located using a GPS tracking service and a stone. When families buried their loved ones there, they were offered a rock from the pile by the entrance, painting the name of the dearly departed, left to sleep forever deep within the wild.

* * *

Mr Anderson would never have a headstone. On the drive back to the city, I thought about the similarity of the Scrubland Cemetery to the graves I dug on the farm during childhood. I'd made their headstones from rocks myself, just like the green-burial site in Lismore. Later in my career I would come to call this the 'stripper burial'. Naked. Stripped of clothes, modifications and chemicals.

The bare human body in its natural form, the way nature intended.

* * *

There are three main methods of disposing of the human body after death in Australia: fire cremation, ground burial and vault burial. Australians rarely choose to be secured in a vault; it involves embalming and a shitload of cash. It's popular with Italians, who can spend most of their life earnings on regal mausoleums, resembling marble apartment blocks within city cemeteries. We are lucky to have vast land here in Australia, however many overpopulated cities in the US and Japan are running out of room for their dead, and measures are being invented to combat the war between the corpses and breathing inhabitants.

In a number of US states you can be cremated by water. Well, it's not exactly water. Alkaline hydrolysis, BioCremation, Flameless Cremation, Aquamation are all terms used for the process of liquefying the dead. Basically the body is placed inside a steel vessel filled with water and potassium hydroxide heated to astronomical levels. Rather than boiling, a blend of pressure and chemicals breaks the body down over a course of four to six hours until all that is left are the bones, as at the end of fire cremation.

Then there's the eco-friendly trend of pods, where you can be popped inside a biodegradable pot and planted as a tree.

The method I'm most curious about is 'human composting'. In the United States, rather than cremains being returned to family, you can opt to be handed back as a handful of composted fertile soil that can be used in mum's garden. Also referred to as 'recomposition', the method suggests a gentler alternative to brutal flames or alkaline. Over the course of several weeks, with the body covered in natural materials including woodchips and straw, your mortal vessel breaks down into soil. Oh, and apparently this process will take place in a large facility with many others in the room sleeping in makeshift garden beds by your side, so you'll never be alone, as you would be in the dark chamber of a fire cremation retort.

Down Under remains untouched by the alternative funeral movement taking place in more progressive countries. The green burial is about as rebellious as it gets for the time being, where kangaroos can sleep above you as you decompose in a cotton shroud … But maybe, just maybe in your lifetime, you'll be offered less confronting and creative ways to leave this world once your deeds are done.

CHAPTER 15

AFTER DEATH

A dead body gurgles.

And the living body, close to crossing over, rattles.

This is called the death rattle.

This 'gargling' sound when someone is dying is due to fluids accumulating in the throat and upper chest. Working with the dead only, I have never heard the death rattle but my friends in the medical field say it's a noise you never forget.

This can be quite disturbing for anyone who is observing life seep from a mortal body. I have often said that the medical staff and/or loved ones who watch a person die are far worse off than the funeral director.

Woody Allen once said, 'It's not that I'm afraid to die—I just don't want to be there when it happens.'

Neither do I, mate. Neither do I.

So Death strikes and the body is tucked away in a body bag.

What happens next?

Allow me to present to you the stages of death and decomposition!

Algor mortis is the term used to describe how the body temperature drops after death.

Livor mortis is also known as the colour of death. No blood is circulating and this causes discolouration, or pooling of the blood. Livor mortis is often used in forensic investigation. For example, if the blood is pooling to one side but the body was discovered on its back, it's obvious the deceased has been moved. Pretty neat, huh?

Rigor mortis or post-mortem rigidity is the stiffening of the muscles and limbs due to chemical reactions in the dead body. I enjoy watching the transformation of the corpse as I manipulate and relieve the stiffness in the limbs. With care, massage and a hot-water bath, the body appears more peaceful and lifelike.

Eight hours after death, post-mortem staining becomes permanent without embalming. This is where it can become troublesome for a mortician if a body is placed in the fridge with the face turned on its side. The blood pools and stains that side of the face, making it almost impossible to cover with a few cosmetics. Funeral directors are trained to always place the decedent in the fridge with head upright on the head block to prevent staining and an unwelcome look for the loved ones wishing to view the deceased.

Two to three days after death, the abdomen is one of first parts of the body to turn green. As the body begins to decompose, the smell is really starting to kick in. The decaying blood cells and intestinal gas containing sulphur is filling the air.

Seven days after the person has died, discolouration spreads over the entire body. Blisters form all over the corpse and the skin begins to peel off in large pieces. This is called 'skin slip'. To combat the skin sliding off the remains, we commonly wrap the slippery areas with plastic food wrap and bandages. There have been times I had a bucket by the mortuary table peeling off skin like on a really bad sunburn, only sloppier.

* * *

Face to face with bodies in various stages of decay, I became grateful for the wrinkles forming on my forehead. I embraced my curly hair. The decomposed bodies did not scare me, rather they taught me to appreciate the body I inhabited. I'd stop a moment and ponder grudges I held. I cancelled my expensive online makeup orders. Nothing, and I mean *nothing,* matters when you're staring down into the decomposing face of a human being. Handling decay spurs love for life (and promotes savings as I realised makeup and clothes really don't matter much at all).

It happens to all of us. The lipstick fades, the hair falls out and we become sludge. Unless you choose to be cremated, of course.

There are dead bodies all around us. We live alongside the dead. From the cemeteries passed by on the work commute to the hospitals with morgues lurking below the wards taking care of ill loved ones—we are sharing the land with corpses.

Have your drains been rather stinky lately? Maybe it's time to call in the investigators. There might be a corpse right under your house!

Ha!

Just kidding!

Maybe.

CHAPTER 16

BE AN ELEPHANT

The city morgue is where autopsies reveal secrets, diagnose mystery illnesses and assist law enforcement in solving crimes. It looks much like a hospital from the outside, and most city locals have no idea what goes on behind those tall walls.

There is a known fact within the funeral industry: if the deceased is brought out from the morgue's refrigeration in a black body bag, *don't open for identification.* The body is either in parts, decomposed or burnt beyond recognition. When the black body bag is wheeled out into the collection bay, we put the identification wrist tags back into our pockets. There will be no arm to secure the name to.

When the body bag *can* be opened, we never know what awaits us. At times, it's confronting—gunshot wounds to the skull, stab wounds to the chest or rope marks deeply imprinted around the neck and bleeding eyes.

* * *

The morgue has a smell that punches you in the face as soon as you step inside. Like cut flowers left too long in stagnant water, mixed with soggy socks in muddy tradesmen boots and the first poop of the day after a big night on the booze, you can smell it on your skin for days.

I'm yet to come across anyone who can describe the scent of decomposition. The unforgettable stench tickles the back of your throat, yet there is a sweetness in the smell.

During my very first week as an FDA, my transfer partner helped me slide the rather large body we'd collected into a shelf in the cooling room, just as the mortician poked her head around the door.

'I have a decomp!' she trilled. 'Wanna see?'

I'd never seen a decomposed body before, but had overheard my new colleagues chatting about their 'decomp' experiences.

I once went to a home in the middle of the night. The lights had blown, so we followed the smell using the light on our mobile phones. We felt movement at our feet and looked down to discover kittens! Tens of them! The lady who had died must have bred them, and what was left of her decomposed body, the kittens were eating!

It's a smell you'll never forget. You'll smell it in your nostril hairs for days!

My time had come. With one eye closed I peeked inside the mortuary. Muffling my squeal with the sleeve of my suit, I was met with a greenish corpse lying on the mortuary table, the face completely disfigured. It wasn't the maggots dropping onto the mortuary floor that caused me to squeal; it was indeed, as warned, the stench. Larvae and bloating aside, I actually felt very lucky to be in that moment as many forensic students would kill to be standing where I was.

And it was true; once having worked with a decomposition case, I'd smell it in my shower for a day. My shoes smelt of it, my blankets and lounge cushions.

'Breathe that in!' said my on-call partner during our very first decomp transfer together. He nudged me playfully, I dare say to break the trance I was in staring at the mess on the floor.

A man had died mid-summer in bed and undiscovered for over a week. Oh, he had also pooped himself. I was afraid of hurling my breakfast onto the floor.

'Be an elephant! Be an elephant!' my partner cried out as I heaved into the sleeve of my suit.

'Did you just call me an elephant?'

'Yes! Be an elephant!'

I knew I'd put on some weight but this wasn't the time to remind me!

My transfer partner told me later—while wiping the dead guy's faeces from the soles of our shoes—that elephants don't vomit. The reference to the animal was to encourage me not to spew, not a stab at my increasing waistline.

'Wait 'til you fart.' He laughed at me as I wiped corpse juices from my $300 shoes. 'You'll smell like him for a day!'

And he was right.

Inhaling the gases of a dead person affects your own bowel movements. You smell them following you about the house with every emission.

It was gross at first, but eventually it became quite normal for me.

My house sometimes smelt of death.

While decomposition cases and those requiring a coroner's inquest became a focus of mine, let me clarify it wasn't a morbid interest in rotting organs that fascinated me. It was the story behind the mess. For a body to arrive at the funeral home in such a state, there was usually a sad story attached. Sometimes the person had no family and wasn't found for a month, which pulled on my heartstrings. Others took their own life in remote locations, so I made a point of spending extra time with them before they were buried or cremated. I was drawn to their stories. I knew a decomp entered the facility the moment they arrived, and if I wasn't already out there investigating the paperwork, the funeral directors soon chanted my name: 'Emma Jane! One of your favourites has arrived! The body bag is moving!'

The body bag is moving is not a term used to describe the corpse having risen from death; rather it was moving with insects.

The decomp became special to me. With the person usually leaving this world in a state of loneliness, and feeling lonely in the depths of my soul for so many years, I wanted to be there for them. Not only would I flick the maggots from their body bags, I took the time to pray for them, speak to them and let them know they were no longer alone. I would be there for them.

CHAPTER 17

SPONGE CAKE AND FAT FIRES

Hair shampooed and pores cleansed of mortuary chemicals, I slipped into my favourite pyjamas, poured a herbal tea and lit my scented candles.

Raindrops patted a tune on the tin roof as I sank into my couch. Cupcake bounced up to join me, licking my toes.

Any funeral director knows however, that as soon as you are ready for bed, the universe has other plans for you.

My Britney Spears ringtone sent Cupcake jumping off the couch and scurrying to my bedroom. *I must change that*, I winced.

'Hello?'

'Emma, it's Albert.'

'Albert?'

'Yes. Albert. You know, the fat balding man you work with eight to five every day.'

'What's up? Did I leave the mortuary door unlocked or something? Has a body managed to escape?'

'No, but if that was why I was calling, you would be happier than what I am about to tell you. We need an extra set of hands. Macca and I are on a transfer and the lady who has died …' a moment of silence, '… is rather large.'

Lucky I hadn't poured that wine.

'Shoot me the address mate, I'll be there in 30.'

Half an hour later, I pulled up outside a large home in the hills, overlooking the twinkling city lights. Mesmerised, I had to remind myself, *I am not here for social media snapshots of the skyline.* I'd been called upon to collect a deceased person.

A slick of lip gloss and hair pulled back, I jumped out of my car and trotted towards the house. In ghostly moonlight, palm trees cast shadows across the manicured lawn.

I knocked on the door and Albert answered, sweat beads dripping down his frown. He looked as though he wanted to hug me.

'Thank you for coming, Em. Follow me.'

I followed my colleague across the marble floors, passing a grand piano and a sparkling chandelier. I followed Albert into a bedroom and almost tripped over my jaw. Lying on the bed in a floral nightie, was the biggest lady I have ever seen.

There was a slice of sponge cake on her bedside table. A scented candle flickered.

After plenty of heaving, lifting and grunting, we finally had Mrs Cake strapped in on one of our stretchers and it took all three of us to wheel her out through her magnificent, shiny home towards our van. As we approached the transfer vehicle, I could feel the stretcher beginning to tremble, as if it was about to give way. And then, it did. The stretcher collapsed and smashed to the ground. Thankfully, the deceased's family were still inside—not to worry, no decedents were harmed. The stretcher was lying on its side on the grass however, and we had one big challenge on our hands. Together our team heave-ho'd, we perspired and ached as we lifted her into our vehicle and secured her into the back of the van with extra straps.

Wiping the sweat from my face, I took a deep breath and gazed back at the doorway, to find the daughter huddling into her husband, crying.

I walked over and offered my condolences, which they returned with a hug and a thank you. *This is why I am here on earth.*

* * *

On the way home, in memory of the large lady who loved cake, I pulled into the service station and bought an iced slice. My waist had expanded a little with the divorce. Wine and cheese had become my staple meals. But as chocolate flakes dropped into the lap of my suit, I thanked my somewhat speedy metabolism.

I was trim enough that it wouldn't take three people to transfer me if I were to die tonight.

* * *

Okay, I take it back.

My suit buttons felt tighter the following morning. And on the topic of big bellies, I was spending the day at the crematory, and a man who had enjoyed too many buffets while alive cloaked the doorframe of the cremator retort with smoke. Mr Smith, a food lover in life, was now a fire hazard. The excess body fat caused a melting oil pot and tremendous heat that almost sent the crematorium up in smoke. He was departing this world with a 'smoking hot' mark, like a graffiti tag announcing 'I was here'.

'We aren't actually allowed to call them fat fires anymore!' said Ben, the cremator operator as he extinguished the flames that flickered from behind the doors of the cremator. 'It's politically incorrect. We must call them pressure fires!'

'Big Ben', with his bushy beard and belly laugh, had been a retort operator for over 15 years. He didn't mind that between funeral services I followed him about the place.

'Does this happen often?' I asked, my jaw at my knees.

'It's not uncommon.' Big Ben chuckled, taking off his hard hat and wiping the beads of sweat from his face with his forearm. 'The obese need to spend a day in the crematory rather than read diet books. One look at a fat fire, er … excuse me, I mean a pressure fire, would turn them right off that next Chinese buffet!'

Pressure fire under control, I continued my crematory lesson on Big Ben's heel, watching skulls break open in the heat and cremated remains being swept into the collection tray. I watched bones transition to dense grey powder and people who were walking down the street only a week ago get poured into sparkly urns.

With the funeral I would be assisting on about to start, I headed towards the swanky chapel when I was derailed by the cremation urn showroom. Just when I thought I had seen it all, I noticed three giant seashells. Too large to sit on a shelf, they were on the plush-carpeted floor leaning against the wall.

'They're new, just in.' Big Ben startled me. He grabbed one and held it out to me.

The blue seashell seemed to be made of foam.

'They're for families who want ashes scattered at sea. Instead of flying all over the place when you set them free in the wind, the ashes are put in a plastic bag and then put inside the shell. It's then thrown into the water and after a few hours, it dissolves. Pretty neat, hey?'

Thud! Bang!

'Shit!' And off he dashed to the cremator to save the day. Well, the crematory grounds anyway.

I wandered around the room brimming with keepsake urns; some built of Himalayan salt, like the salt lamps that glowed in every corner of a crystal store, others thumb-sized for when families wish to share the ashes, a portion for all. Some dazzled with a golden finish, others bright pink and covered in glitter. *If I was to be cremated, I'd choose that one.* I smiled. I wondered if there was such a thing as a glitter coffin for burial. Then the funeral conductor poked his head into the sacred room.

'You ready, Emma Jane? We're about to kick off.'

'Sure thing.' I nodded, and took one last glance over my shoulder at the array of different ways the cremated body could be disposed of. Once again, for the zillionth time that week, I was reminded I was lucky to be alive.

CHAPTER 18

CATCH THE BRAIN!

'Isn't it fucking amazing?' Brenda exclaimed. The head mortician's eyes were wide with glee as I held the human brain in my gloved hands. I nodded, my trachea constricting. This veiny organ, bloodied wet, once kept someone alive. It was the storage space of memories, a personality.

The hairs bristled all over my body as I cradled an entire life in my hands.

The body had arrived post-autopsy and Brenda was teaching me to unstitch and cleanse the cranial cavity then put it all back together using calvarium clamps.

The calvarium is the top part of the skull that covers the brain like a lid, and right now it was lying upturned on the mortuary table. To lock the piece of bone back into place once we were finished, we'd be using the clamps … and a screwdriver.

Tightening clamps on a skull with a screwdriver.

I was holding a brain.

I'd never imagined, in my childhood dreams of becoming a funeral director, that the role consisted of this.

I held the brain up in the bright mortuary lights.

'I just can't believe this is inside my head. This is what we are,' I said.

'Bloody beautiful, isn't it.' Brenda blinked, her top knot loosening and falling forward towards her pretty face. 'Okay, place it down and I'll show you what we do next.'

I followed her instructions, placing the brain on the mortuary table by the calvarium and leaning in closer to the vacant skull. Jolting me, Brenda screeched.

'Catch the braaaain!'

My eyes followed her panicked ones to the organ, sliding down the mortuary table towards the adjoined sink like it was off on a joy ride.

I leapt, clasping the brain like a football player saving the ball from scoring an opposing try.

Brenda and I stared at one another for a moment, not sure whether to laugh. I climbed to my feet and handed the brain to Brenda.

* * *

When you hold a body organ that once kept someone alive, you're never the same again. In a positive way. I've touched the intestine that once fed a ballerina. Held a blood clot that caused premature death to a young man wearing odd socks; and touched part of a cancer-stricken liver post-autopsy that struck down a middle-aged mother.

I studied the piece of diseased organ, shocked at how pretty the cancer was. It resembled my leopard-print handbag at home.

'Disease can look so … pretty?' I turned to Brenda who was half-smiling in agreement.

One afternoon a motorbike rider was brought into the facility. He'd intentionally wrapped himself around a tree. His body was torn open, his bowel now neighbouring his heart. Poop spilled out into the body bag, his face hanging by a thread of muscle. I remember staring in both shock and awe, taking in every organ.

Growing up we study human anatomy charts, learning which organ is where doing this job and that. To see it in person, you discover a newfound appreciation and wonder how, without making a sound, all of this keeps us alive.

CHAPTER 19

HIGH PROFILE

Nothing quietens the busy operations facility like the arrival of a child who has died.

When a young person is removed from the back of the transfer van, hearse polishing ceases. Staple guns securing drapery onto coffins stop clacking.

Banter disappears and hats are removed.

If we're out at funerals, sometimes funeral directors don't know a child has arrived until we hit the tea room and it's the sad topic of conversation. I know right away, however, because as soon as we get back, the first thing I do is check the mortuary register to see who has been brought in while we were out.

I always go straight to the age rather than the name. My heart pains for ages under 30. A life cut so short, often leaving a spouse and young children behind.

But when an age is recorded beneath ten, I actually cry.

* * *

One night I was licking my bowl clean of Mac and Cheese—again—when a news report flashed up on the screen about a young boy allegedly killed at the hands of his uncle. Police had set up a crime scene around the two-storey home located only streets away from the inner city.

The man had reportedly returned home after a night out and drunkenly headed to his nephew's room. Never did I expect to touch the tiny hand of the boy myself.

When news caught hold at the funeral home that the high-profile case would be taken care of by our company, frowns sprouted on the faces of all the funeral directors. And when he arrived we all took a place by the stretcher, looking down at his tiny sunken eyes. He was still dressed in his SpongeBob flannelettes, his delicate autopsy incision peeking through the open top button.

In silence we decorated the back of the hearse with stuffed toys from the collection kept in the storage room for times like these.

The day before the murdered boy's funeral, I was honoured to see my name on the day sheet hanging in the lunch room.

The morning of the funeral, although the place was busy, it was unusually quiet. No jokes shared, no water fights while cleaning hearses. With adult-sized coffins loaded into death cars, we knew too well that at midday we'd be loading one much smaller.

When it was time, everyone gathered by the hearse and shared a moment of silence as the child's blue coffin was lifted into the back of the hearse. I sat in the back seat behind driver and conductor, my head inches from the boy. Only a thin plate of glass separated myself and the eight-year-old who allegedly had been strangled by a man he trusted.

* * *

We arrived at the church, and could not park in the designated area for hearses due to the sea of news cameras. News reporters crowded the windows, bright lights flashing in my eyes.

'Please, please, give them some space!' The priest appeared, flapping his hands at them. 'We have a funeral to set up! Give us space!'

The news crews dispersed to the other side of the road, as we carried the small coffin into the church. We placed the boy on a makeshift bier, as the regular-sized one at the altar was far too big for a child.

We had turned our backs only a moment when we heard the click of cameras. A journalist had snuck inside and was literally on top of the coffin, snapping photographs of the nameplate on the tiny coffin lid.

'GET OUT!' Father bellowed, racing down from the altar. The journalist, in his skinny jeans and Converse shoes, had never run so fast I'm sure.

The boy's family had tricked the media, placing a mock notice in the papers to steer them in the wrong direction, away from the burial site. It was easy to shoo away cameras from a church, a little harder in the large open space of the cemetery. As we approached the cemetery I held my breath hoping no camera crews were waiting by the gates.

There were none in sight and I released my breath. It would be a quiet, private burial after all, as the mother had requested.

As the hearse approached the grave, the barefoot mother collapsed into another woman's arms.

I had overheard her telling my conductor she was not wearing shoes as she wanted to feel the grass by her son's grave beneath her feet. And that she hoped that would be okay. Of course it was.

The coffin was placed on the lowering device and I stood by the hearse loaded with teddies.

'May I have a toy?' the dead boy's brother asked, tugging at my skirt. He could have any he wanted, I said. He could have them all. I didn't even care if I got into trouble for giving them all away.

'Which one do you want?'

He pointed to a blue bunny. I fetched it and handed it to him and he hugged it, running over to his mum crying by the grave.

I often wonder if the little boy kept that toy.

* * *

As time went on, I found myself a part of many high-profile death cases. A Touch of Comfort did not have the police contract, so there was some time between coronial inquests and the arrival of the deceased.

When someone dies by suicide, murder, vehicle accident or any death requiring investigation, the funeral home granted the police contract provides the crew who attend to the scene. They are the ones who carry bloodied body bags from roadsides, crime scenes taped off with police ribbon and even small aircraft disasters. They are contracted by the government and their role is to take the victim to the city morgue. Autopsy and investigations completed, the family then choose which funeral home they'd like to make the service arrangements. When a death was reported by the media, I'd wonder if our company would be the ones to take care of the poor soul. A highly respected city company, we usually did.

The more I learnt about the funeral industry, a professional dream manifested to work for a company with the police contract, to be there at the raw moment of bloodied death.

I was to achieve this dream, in the future. But that's a whole other story.

* * *

At A Touch of Comfort, we took care of other murdered children. We dressed famous sports stars. We dyed the hair of a local celebrity who had owned restaurants frequented by the stars. Her famous sons insisted she be buried without regrowth peeking through her blonde.

I'd dabbled in journalism in my younger years, thirsty for the excitement of the media, but when it came to death, the scrutiny of the camera upset me.

Please let them rest in peace, I'd silently plead as I stood by headstones and watched the coffin photographed like a superstar.

Please just let them Rest in Peace.

CHAPTER 20

A PINK CARDIGAN

When back in the public sphere after working on a child's funeral, I felt compelled to turn around to all the whingers complaining about the tiniest of misfortunes and blast, 'I buried a nine-year-old today! Be grateful you made it to your age!' I never would. And I never meant to get so angry. I'd made it past 30. How lucky was I?

The death of a baby is close to me; it's not just the tiny cold hands. The little eyelashes resting on a small cheek. The tiny little feet and tiny little clothes.

I lost a little tiny one of my own. Some years ago, suffering an ectopic pregnancy was one of the most physically and mentally challenging experiences of my life. A tubal pregnancy occurs when a fertilised egg becomes lodged in a fallopian tube en route to the womb. If discovered in time all can be saved, except for the undeveloped baby. However, if undetected too long, the condition can be fatal to the mother. My symptoms arrived too late, and it wasn't until I woke late one night with frightening bleeding and pain warranting an ambulance, that I discovered it was happening to me. Rushed into surgery, I had half of my reproductive system removed and I've never felt quite the same again. It's an ongoing feat, as I'm reminded of the tragic ordeal every time I shower and clean my belly button where the scar slits my tan.

I remember the first baby I cared for following my ectopic.

My colleague carried her, strapped in the baby capsule; the inconspicuous carrier used to transport newborns from the hospital morgue into our loving care. He left me with the infant and his orders: the family requested she remain in the outfit she was currently wearing for the viewing the following morning. Her tiny autopsy incision had leaked and blood soiled her jumpsuit around the neckline. Her fragile neck was bruised where the umbilical cord had choked the stillborn, her *oh so small* face bright red. Her bonnet covered a scalp still forming. If I could suspend my disbelief, I'd imagine she was only sleeping. I cradled her delicate head carefully; her entire body, from head to tiny toe, fit in my gloved hand. Her mother wouldn't see the bloodied cardigan. I'd protect her from such a sight. The end of the workday near, I decided I'd take the pink knitted outfit home myself. I carefully slid the baby's frail arms from her first and last outfit, smuggling it into a small plastic bag along with some gloves. 'I'll bring it back for you tomorrow,' I promised, placing her on a frosty tray, my pounding heartbeat a metronome which set the tempo for each movement.

* * *

Gardening Australia echoed from my neighbour's television that evening while I retrieved the newborn's clothes from my bag. Their kettle squealed at regular intervals as I washed the pink jumpsuit and cardigan by hand. A crimson coil swirled down my drain returning the wool to its original pink with each swish of soapy water. Its heart-shaped buttons sparkled beneath the bathroom light. I hung the cardigan on the vanity to drip-dry then retreated to bed. Listening to the palms in the backyard rub together in a haunting song, I pondered life's contrasts. Coconut trees, coffins. Pizza, war. Baby corpse. Stars. Blood.

Later I sprang from sleep and struggled to catch the breath my nightmare had stolen from me. Half asleep, I stumbled to the bathroom where I caught a glimpse of the infant's cardigan. Relief washed over me; I hadn't endured an ectopic pregnancy at all! My baby was alive, her clothes drying on my sink. *Phew!*

Gradually waking completely, I remembered; the clothes belonged to the dead.

Dead as can be.

I'd always taken pride in my professionalism as an FDA. I'm thick-skinned. I've taken care of teenagers, victims of suicide, women my age who lost their battle with cancer—without tear or fear. But sometimes a case makes its way into your life, rattles your heart valves, and visits your dreams. This baby didn't quite make it to the world. She'd died in the womb; life cut short by the body that carried her. It wasn't her mother's fault, but it was her body that killed her. The pain she'd endure for the rest of her life would be disabling.

I knew this was true. I was living it.

CHAPTER 21

HEELS AND HEARSES

It all began the night I almost fell to my death.

I crawled into bed and tucked the work phone by my pillow. The rotating on-call roster had reached my name, and I hoped the night would be uneventful.

Ring! Ring!

My eyes snapped open, staring into the blackness.

Ring! Riiing!

Fine! I threw my pillow at the wall and was summoned to a home removal. As I've said previously, I consider it a privilege to be called upon when someone takes their final breath, but some nights it truly is the last thing you want to do.

I met my removal partner at the funeral home so we could attend together in one vehicle.

After chatting about what we'd had for dinner (I had eaten garlic and he could smell it), turning down three wrong streets and almost knocking over a letterbox, we arrived at the house. The porch light exuded a sleepy glow. Someone had just died in that house and relied on us to take care of them.

I slapped on some lip gloss, adjusted my tie and jumped out into the night.

The removal was going smoothly so far, despite the yawns cracking my mandible. I hugged the widow, assuring her that I would take care of her husband, checked the deceased for valuables, and collected the life extinct form completed by the attending doctor. I patted the cat.

We decided upon the carry stretcher as the bed was in an awkward position, sandwiched between the vanity littered with pill bottles and a chest of drawers covered in family photos. If it wasn't for the wrist tags I secured around Mr Wilson's wrists to identify him, I wouldn't have believed he was the same man in the happy snaps. He was thin now, jaundiced, his eyes looking past us. I wondered where he was now.

With the deceased safely strapped in our stretcher, we began our journey through the cluttered home. The family remained at the other end of the house, thankfully.

My butt hit a table, the vase danced from side to side then came to a stop, without smashing to the floor. I almost tripped over a pile of *Time* magazines and books. The cat meowed beneath my feet.

We made it around the tight corners, making it to the porch unscathed. *Only a few more metres to go*. Walking backwards, each of my steps cautious and slow, I somehow bloody tripped. As if in slow motion, I fell backwards and I squeezed my eyes shut as if doing so would soften the landing.

This is it. This will be the end of me. I will land on something sharp with this large man on top of me.

Astonished, I landed … in a chair! The best-placed chair on the planet. There I sat with my end of the stretcher in my lap, looking up at my partner with what I imagine was a shocked look across my face.

'Take a load off,' my partner chuckled quietly. 'Take a seat!'

Once Mr Wilson was locked in the back and we hopped into our seats, we broke into hysterics.

'If only we could tell people our stories,' he said, shifting gears, and we joined the living, cruising along the highway.

'No one would believe a word of it.' I'd often thought about creating a blog, sharing what happened behind the closed doors of a funeral home. One day, a friend who worked in traffic control had texted me with the most shocking question, reminding me how clueless most people really were about the death profession.

I was chatting to my colleague here at a traffic incident, the text had read. *We were just wondering, what happens when a head is decapitated for a viewing? Do you sit the head there and cover the neck area with stuff?*

I remember my mouth gaping as wide as a dead guy's. Did he really just ask me that? Did people truly believe we would do such a thing?

* * *

Following the transfer that night, just after 1 am in the glow of my Mac screen, *Heels and Hearses* was born. The title came to me with little thought: I collect heels and love hearses. I envisioned the title catching the reader's attention; that's right, a fun-loving funeral director who wears heels and pink lipstick! I'd never created a blog, but it only took me an hour to work my way around the free website. All I had to do was choose a font and get writing. My fingers glided across the keyboard so fast they disappeared in a blur. I laughed to myself, reliving the moment the chair caught me, not expecting anyone to ever read the words. But if they did, I hoped I'd make them chuckle.

I fell to sleep in the early hours of the morning grinning to myself, anticipating the end of the workday when I could get back to my computer.

* * *

Over the coming months, I recorded hilarious adventures, heartbreaking moments, devastating causes of death. Writing anonymously, I wrote about the time I almost fell into a grave. I wrote about the crematory, my colleagues. I designed a logo and sent it off to a graphic designer, and paid a fee to upgrade the blog from the basic text on the screen to a fancier template with a bright pink background.

The day the logo arrived in my email inbox, I squealed with glee. It was perfect! A high-heel shoe blending into an image of a hearse.

Not only was the blog looking great, writing every day after work was a great debrief. A glass of red, crackers and cheese by side, I was the writer I always dreamt I'd be.

I had one thing missing.

Readership.

How did you get someone to read your little words in the busy universe of the world wide web?

I created a Facebook page for the blog, freely adding my credit card to the social media platform. I was clicking OK on the boost button as often as I bought a skinny latte, boosting the post to reach unsuspecting social media lovers.

Writing under a pseudonym, I couldn't tell many people about my new story-writing venture except my family, who read each blog post every time I clicked *Publish*. My sister had a great suggestion.

'You need to start an Instagram page,' she said excitedly. 'For those interested in your blog but who don't have the time to read lengthy posts. You can engage them with photos, and add cool captions about the funeral profession. Use the right hashtags and I reckon it would blow up!'

Instagram was a platform alien to me since photography is not my forte. It sounded like a fabulous idea, but I barely knew how to open Word on my computer and add a few Facebook posts, let alone start creating a gallery of photos for the world.

I decided to give it a try. But what would I add photos of? I couldn't exactly dance around the funeral home snapping shots of corpses in all their glory. I could take some photos of the gorgeous coffin showroom, the chapel, but then what?

I created an account for *Heels and Hearses* on Instagram, and searched hashtags like #mortuary, #mortician, #hearses, #funeralhome. This opened up an incredible world I'd had no idea about. Hours and hours were spent scrolling through shots of funeral homes all over the world, like-minded morticians posting pictures of themselves in their PPE wear and yes, photos of the dead was a thing.

I began following morticians from Africa to Las Vegas and they followed me back. Before I knew it, I had hundreds of people just like me at my fingertips to communicate with and get ideas from. I had one problem though; my feed was empty.

* * *

I wanted to incorporate heels into the theme, since the logo had a bright pink one in it, and I was determined to stand out to attract readers to the blog. So, what did I do?

I began to take my sparkly heels for photo shoots in cemeteries. I'd position my favourite high heels on top of ancient headstones, the sun catching diamantes and casting twinkling rainbows in the cemetery.

Cemeteries deserve sparkle too, I wrote beneath one photo.

Turned out Instagrammers loved the unusual take on the cemetery and death profession, and adding a link to the 'bio' on my page, I had paved the way for a whole new stream of traffic to the *Heels and Hearses* blog.

After a few months of snapping shots of stilettos in graveyards, I took the plunge and posted a few photos of the deceased in the most respectful way. Faces unseen, photos of their hand in mine or toes with the morgue tag attached.

* * *

One morning, my email inbox was flashing with messages from a journalist and a radio host informing me they loved the blog and asking if I'd take part in an interview.

I had remained anonymous for a while now, and knew the funeral home would be *dead* against me talking about what happens behind mortuary doors, so I declined, continuing to write in secret with my heart incredibly content, fulfilling my two dreams: serving the dead and writing every day.

A couple of years later, the blog gained readers from all over the world and my evenings were spent not only writing stories, but responding to emails written by budding funeral directors and those curious about whether dead bodies actually do sit up. (Yes, I got asked this question ... a lot! For the record, they don't.)

I had a spring in my already bouncy step each morning as I entered the funeral home. I was Miss *Heels and Hearses*. I was now not only helping the dead, I was helping the living.

I began to accept interviews. I had no idea these would go viral and I would be dubbed 'Australia's most outrageous mortician'.

I took the plunge and added my face to the blog, believing (and hoping!) the funeral directors had better things to do with their free time than navigate social media. But before too long work discovered it all. Presented with an ultimatum—quit the blog or quit caring for the dead—I clicked the *Delete blog* button, grateful for waterproof mascara. Just like a life, it was here one day, gone the next.

If I wanted to continue helping the dead, I'd have to stop writing.

CHAPTER 22

FUNERAL PLANNER

From the back of the chapel, my jaw gaped in horror. The service was open-casket, uncommon in Australia, and the deceased's family leant in to open the dead man's mouth. *The mouth suture! They'll see the thread.* I panicked, turning to Macca. 'It's okay. They've seen it all before,' he assured me, polishing his specs as if this was totally normal. Well, to the Hindu family it was. They were feeding him; this guy wouldn't leave this world hungry. Oil was anointed on the deceased's face, incense burnt and traditional Hindu food was placed in snug around the body. I nibbled my new shellac manicure nervously. *Would the dead man catch on fire with all that oil and incense?* and *Look at all that amazing food!* Would the guests mind if I popped up to the lectern and grabbed a buttered roll? I'd skipped breakfast.

As the celebration progressed with song and prayer, the more I wished the West could embrace death the way this beautiful culture did. In Australia, it's common for the family to be afraid of even touching the deceased. And here was a family making sure their loved one had snacks for the afterlife.

Food forever. Now that's love.

The second part of the Hindu celebration took place behind the scenes next to the cremator. The area usually reserved for staff had been tidied and cooling trays of bones covered. Four members of the immediate family would complete the service here, while the rest waited in the chapel. I quickly realised someone was being cremated beside us. Would they notice?

With a haunting song, the family members poured a bottle of vegetable oil over the deceased. *The mortician's work, ruined!*

To conclude, fire starters were placed in the coffin and set alight by the family to represent the spirit freed. When it was time, the retort doors rose revealing tiny embers twinkling on the cremator floor like a dancer's diamond earrings. The cremationist pushed the coffin into the flames and the mourners howled, holding onto one another. When the door lowered, they oddly stopped crying as if understanding their loved one had gone to a better place now, shook our hands, and returned to the chapel.

The Hindu service is a reminder that funerals don't need to follow the common structure. There's no cookie-cutter way of saying goodbye.

You want a barbeque as guests arrive? Go grab that bain-marie and start loading up stuffed potatoes! Want to have a bubble machine set up as mourners depart? There are no rules!

Sure, there are some detailed logistics that need to be thought through prior to the day of the service, so don't go ordering the daiquiri machine and jumping castle just yet. A heads-up on a few things to consider: during the arrangement, confronting questions are asked, and while you think you have all the information you need as you drive to the funeral home, the moment the funeral director offers their condolences, you may fall to pieces and forget it all.

A Touch of Comfort funeral home had a wonderful in-house florist. I found it touching she provided a checklist for the family prior to creating the floral display. Using this list of hobbies and passions, the artist brought to life the deceased's personality through flower petals.

Just like her bullet points, here's my checklist:

Does dad really want to wear that suit he hasn't worn since 1969?

Dad may look strapping in his tux, but did he prefer wearing shorts, enjoying a cold one while fishing? We've dressed people in their hobby clothes from football jerseys to tutus. Feel free to provide a can of beer. I've heard it called 'One for the Road'.

Do you really need to pay for a newspaper obituary?

A newspaper notice is a great way to invite friends of your loved one to the service as you may not feel like making all of those phone calls while embarking upon the frightening grieving process. These days Facebook is a popular way to announce to family and friends where the funeral will take place. And if elderly relations aren't on social media, at least notice can make its way to a phone call or official invite without the expense of a printed newspaper notice.

How can one personalise the farewell?

One funeral that has stayed with me was a simple graveside service. No celebrant or priest present, the son conducted the entire service himself. In closing, he offered everyone, including the funeral directors, a greasy drumstick from a fast food bucket. As the sun belted down upon us, we chomped at the chicken in memory of his father who apparently was rarely seen without one in his hand.

What music would you like to include in the service?

Music is an integral part of life for many people. There is no rule you have to play a sombre, tear-jerking tune. Did your loved one enjoy Elvis Presley? Why not play a little rock'n'roll? One of my most memorable moments in death care was pallbearing to the Rolling Stones.

You could even start thinking about your own service. It's not morbid, in fact I believe it's healthy, relieving your loved ones from the duty.

Some funeral directors know every fine detail of their big day, right down to the song they want played as the pallbearers carry them down the aisle.

I haven't planned that far ahead, but here's a few ideas. Friends take note!

- I must be buried in my favourite pyjamas and fluffy socks. Oh, and my favourite knitted throw from the couch I practically live in when watching Netflix.

There could be Netflix in the afterlife too, you know. I need all of my favourite books tucked in around me like a huge hug.

- Fairy lights in my coffin in case there *is* an afterlife and I don't find myself in a dark coffin deep under the ground. Hopefully I discover the afterlife before the batteries expire.
- Champagne on tap.
- Sparklers and a bubble machine.

Most funeral directors have a similar view: *Celebrate my life! Make it a goddamn party!*

I believe it's because we witness many sombre services day in day out, and crave a farewell complete with party poppers and tacos at the wake rather than standard sandwich triangles.

CHAPTER 23

FOREVER

'Would you like to take communion?'

I must have looked confused.

'You're free to take communion,' the conductor pressed on. 'I'll go first, then when I get back, I'll take over the music controls so you can head down.'

I hesitated, not sure what to say. I hadn't taken communion since high school, plus, I was working! Was it appropriate to approach Father at the altar as he offered the Body of Christ to sobbing mourners? Besides, the aisle in this city cathedral was a hundred kilometres long. I doubted I'd make it to the end when it was time to acknowledge the coffin and exit, let alone walk the distance twice.

I nodded. 'Yes. Okay. I'll take communion.'

* * *

My memories of church date right back to the days of my grandma on the Gold Coast. Nan attended church every Sunday of her life, expecting the rest of the family to accompany her two times a year. Anticipating our return to overfilled Christmas stockings or uneaten Easter eggs, us kids would trail on Nan's heel in our best clothes and take our seat in the pew. The wooden donation plate was passed around the crowd and we placed the coins parents had given us. I truly believed this was pocket money for God. I spent mine on notepads and pencils to write stories; did he share his with Rudolph the reindeer, who lived in the clouds too? I believed my shiny two-dollar coin would be hand-delivered to God in the sky.

Dad was obliged to remove his Akubra, which he laid in his lap as hymns were sung, and I was proud I knew the lyrics because I attended a Catholic school. 'The Lord is my Shepherd' was my favourite, as it sang of green rolling hills and sheep and I thought it was cool that God grew up on a farm too.

When it was time to kneel, Dad never did. He remained seated in his pew, the muscles in his jaw twitching. My little kneecaps on the floor bench, I held my hands together in prayer and told God that Dad had bad knees 'so don't hold it against him'.

As a kid, I believed Nan had a second boyfriend that Poppy was okay with. Photos of Jesus graced her bedroom walls whereas family photos sat at our home on the farm. Crucifixes crowded every spare space and a plastic bottle in the shape of the Virgin Mary sat by the kitchen bench filled with holy water. Nan blessed herself every morning before making her toast.

So I did too. I even drank it once, thinking it would do something awesome to my insides.

Nan's house had an eerie feel to it, despite the scent of beauty creams, coconut and banana trees. In fact, my sister and I both claim to have seen white fog lurking in the hallways at times, and now grown up we still chat about it, sure it was our childlike imaginations taken with the size of the sprawling house and all this talk of God and the Holy Ghost.

* * *

When I was seven, Nan and Poppy lived with us on the farm for about a year while building a new home on the Gold Coast. They didn't share our farmhouse; they lived next door in a caravan.

During this time, I caught a cold. This cold turned into the flu and this flu turned into pneumonia. Bedridden, not only did I miss school camp, but my first mini deb ball was only a week away, an important event in our country town. With only six girls in my grade fighting for country waltz partners, missing the dance meant you no longer had a boyfriend. If I didn't get better soon, I'd be forgotten.

While this was my major concern, Mum's was that I could die. I'd heard her crying one morning as I sweated into the sheets. During the day, I camped on the couch so I could watch daytime TV and be with her.

One afternoon a dream pushed its way through a fevered headache and remains in my memory forever.

I slid down the flimsy slippery dip beneath the gum trees in the backyard, and looked up into the sky to see a handsome young man sitting on a cloud. He was God,

I knew, but he had no beard in my dream; instead he had an impressive pair of sideburns.

I'm sure 'Greased Lightning' was his theme song, as he soared down towards me and met me at the bottom of the sun-tarnished slide.

He took both my hands and held them tight.

'Hello,' he said. Close up, he definitely looked like Danny Zuko. 'I am God,' he said.

'I know,' I replied.

He squeezed my hands tighter, his fingernails digging into the palms of my hands.

'You're going to be okay.'

'I hope so. My mum is very worried. She keeps crying.'

'You will be,' he said.

Puddle Lane on the television set, I woke from my dream and shot off the couch as if the cushions were made of nettle.

'Emma Jane!' I heard Mum call out as I sprinted across the front lawn into Nan's caravan to tell her I'd met her true love.

'Nan! Nan!'

'What is it, dear?' she asked, looking up from the peanut butter cookies she was baking in the tiny kitchen.

'I met him. I met him!' I puffed.

'Who, dear? Who??'

'God! Look!' I uncurled my hands to reveal the half-moon-shaped nail marks in the palm of my hands. I'm sure I created the marks with my own little nails in my sleep, but he'd helped, I was sure.

She looked into my eyes and smiled.

I was back at school two days later without a cough.

* * *

We never attended church as a family, but Mum sent us to the best school in town, where not only did we attend church twice a week, we had an entire period dedicated to God.

At home, there was no grace at the dinner table. The sheep on the farm had nothing to do with those in the Bible. God-talk wasn't forbidden. It just wasn't thought of in between chores, homework and routines.

When writing this, I asked Mum why she sent us to Catholic schools if we weren't religious. She answered: 'So you wouldn't lose your tuckshop money.'

Apparently the hills we grew up in were riddled with petty crime, including school bullies who beat you up for a meat pie from the canteen unless you attended a school with a monument of Jesus Christ at the front gates.

* * *

It's safe to say I'm not a religious person. But I do believe in a God. Who is he? Does he really have a beard today's hipsters would envy? What's with the robe, it's bloody hot these days.

What if our God is actually a lifesaver in red budgie smugglers and a fantastic tan? Maybe the Lord is a woman? No man loves bread and wine the way a woman does.

Religion doesn't have to be followed by the book. Dad taught me from a young age that you can believe in God without dusting your knees on the ground. There may not be such things as angel wings, halos and grand golden gates. But my time in death and Catholic schools has me believing there is something else out there besides our little mortal bodies scurrying about. We won't know exactly what it is until our own death rattle, but in the meantime, there's no harm in whispering prayers before sleep, just in case.

There's no need to clutter the walls with framed photographs like my nan.

There's no need to preach.

Take communion once in a while. Confess your sins occasionally. Trust me, these dark cubicles are solace in a busy world. Take a coffee. It's bliss.

CHAPTER 24

GHOSTS

DO NOT ENTER WITHOUT KNOCKING.

'Who is it?' the bubbly mortician called out.

'It's just me, Emma. I have some paperwork for you …'

I knew the rule written in capital letters plastered on the door didn't apply to me since I was in mortuary training. Out of respect, I still knocked, waiting for Brenda to laugh and say, 'You don't have to knock silly! It's for those bloody funeral directors who come in poking their noggins about while I'm trying to focus!'

I pushed open the door and froze at what I saw. The dead man's face was rolled down, his skull cap removed and resting upturned next to him like a porcelain bowl.

Brenda, the head mortician, was not only a cosmetician to the dead, she had a degree in forensic pathology and when the forensic science unit was busy she was qualified to investigate and remove organs. Skull caps. Brains. The pink organ was placed in a dish on a trolley close by.

'Mr Hansen's mortuary care forms,' I choked, heading over towards the bench where Brenda kept her files.

'Thanks hon. Can you read it out? I don't think I'll be touching anything.' She held up her soiled gloved hands.

'Sure.' I coughed to clear my throat.

Brenda returned her focus on wiping out the cranial cavity with Dryene, a sort of topical embalming fluid, but noticing my awe, she invited me closer. 'Sometimes the head post-mortem suture isn't perfect,' she began. 'So right now I'm tidying it up. See all this fluid? We can't dress him while his head is bleeding like that. Once the cavity is cleaned out, we'll put the skull back together and then I'll suture the scalp.' She looked up at me, her blue eyes smiling through the goggles. 'You'll be doing this soon.'

Staring at the bone, flesh and hair drenched with blood, I was dizzy.

'Do you believe in an afterlife?' I stammered, passing her implements as she worked.

'No, I don't,' she said, matter-of-factly. 'This is all we are. Skin and bone. There's nothing else, hon. When we're gone, we're gone.'

My faith was shattered just like that. A lifetime of believing in some sort of heaven was sucked right out of me. Brenda was right: it *was* impossible for a soul to survive such brutality.

That night I tossed and turned in the dark, my mind haunted. Blood, skull, the flesh, that bloodied hair … but it wasn't the physical mess that had me crying into my pillow.

I'd believed in a higher power my entire life. Surely we were more than a biological mass of bone and flesh. Once released from our mortal vessels we continued living, able to visit the moon and New York in a flash! There had to be more to this mess. The world was one giant yin and yang; war, crumpets, mass shootings, cake, brain tumours, the ocean. The glorious mix of pain and beauty couldn't be a coincidence, could it?

Was I wrong?

Could it be that everything I believed was all a load of crap and everyone else was right?

Maybe I was crazy after all.

Maybe we are born, live, then die, and that's it.

* * *

The greatest unsolved mystery of all time is life itself and how it ends; what happens to us once we take our final breath remains unknown.

Is there an afterlife? Is there such a thing as ghosts? Not the sheet-like apparitions booing in dark hallways of medieval castles, but invisible forces watching over us. Preferably not while we showered.

When writing my blog I discovered there is huge public interest in what happens when we die.

I read somewhere the dead can sit up due to gases…is it true???

Do dead people poop?

Do you cremate ten bodies at a time?

I'd be answering dozens of emailed questions while neglecting dinner and bed.

I've never met a person who doesn't ask questions.

But rarely did someone ask about the spiritual side of things. I have only been asked once, *Do you feel a presence in the funeral home? Have you ever seen a ghost?*

I was surprised at the opposing views of the funeral directors; half believed it's lights out and there's nothing more, others claimed to see spirits hovering over coffins at the front of the chapel. I worked closely with a lovely man who strongly believed in a world where we all hang out together when our deeds are done. He collected books about spooks and whenever I visited on weekends he had documentaries on the afterlife playing in the background.

I'd agreed with him, but with what I witnessed at the funeral home, I became ambivalent. It's hard to believe there's an afterlife when scooping intestines from the chest of a motorbike victim. They resembled roadkill on the Nullarbor, making it hard to believe a soul survived such an ordeal. Working alongside science-minded morticians who believed there was no heaven at all stung my own spirit if I had one, or whatever it was that made me uniquely … me.

'I've been working in the biz 20 years,' an embalmer once announced, massaging the embalming fluid through a dead man's circulatory system. 'I ain't ever seen a shadow!'

'I've been doing it for ten!' his assistant piped up. 'I embalmed my own grandma and I just know she was gone.' Her eyes lowered a moment, then returned to her work. These professionals were very … professional. Prepping a frail old lady myself, I peered down at her vacant stare. My heart ached for her grandchildren. They'd created finger paintings to be placed in the coffin, believing grandma's spirit would be watching over them; she was in heaven now.

But was she?

Like a radio station stuck in between stations, my brain was confused.

Yes, there's an afterlife.

No, there isn't, dickhead.

Hurry up and dress her. You've only got 45 minutes per body, remember.

Yes, there's something else. The spare car park this morning while Nan's favourite song played on the radio, wasn't a coincidence, you know.

I curled the little grandma's hair and dressed her in her floral dress before placing her in her lavender-coloured coffin. I looked down at her one last time before placing the lid on her final bed, and wondered, *If I believe in the soul so much, why haven't I experienced anything?*

* * *

'G'day!' the bearded man sang from the driver's-side window of the transfer van. The van belonged to Nationwide Transfers, a service that drives all over the country with the back fitted out like a mini refrigerator. Curtis was strapped in the back. He was 33 years old.

This particular day when Roger from Nationwide arrived I was the only one at the facility, other than Mags who was busy in her office.

'Is it just you, mate?'

'Just me.'

'He's a big guy. I'll help you load him in but then I gotta fly!' Together Roger and I heaved heavy Curtis onto a mortuary tray. A high-five later, he was off interstate to collect the dead.

There was no need for me to open the young man's body bag. When a body arrives via Nationwide, everything is done for us. The crew complete the paperwork and secure all wrist tags.

Open me. I felt a magnetic pull and giving in, I took the frosty zip in my hand to reveal Curtis's face. His jawline was strong, deflated eyes like dark pools. Shocking me, I felt intense energy zap through me like sharp diamonds. Curtis was here. I could feel him.

I kissed my hand and placed it on his cheek, zipped up the body bag and slid him into his shelf.

I was on annual leave that afternoon for my birthday. I'd booked a solo holiday at the Gold Coast so I could write for days, read and day-drink.

I'd be away the day of Curtis's funeral.

At the end of shift I returned to the fridge so I could say goodbye to him. I placed my hand at his head. 'Bless you,' I whispered and pulled shut the heavy door on Curtis … forever.

* * *

'Hey, Emma Jane!' My colleagues saluted, slapping high-fives when I returned a week later. 'Welcome back!'

Refreshed and suntanned, I slipped into the passenger side of the hearse as Murray, out of his tiny shorts and in pleated trousers, locked a coffin in the back. He joined me in front, and we were off to the church.

Mid-chat about meter maids and the Hard Rock Café, something hit my foot as we veered around a corner. I reached down to retrieve a bundle of service booklets with Curtis's face on the front. There he was, alive and as tanned as my legs. His living eyes clear and blue, smile lines framing his lips.

'Oh, we were looking for those!' said Murray. 'It was such a large funeral, we had four boxes of booklets and we lost a bundle! Oh well … too late now!'

'Yeah …' my eyes trembled with the weight of tears, '… too late now.'

Curtis was with me that day in the hearse, his presence was as strong as the day I touched his cheek in the fridge.

Suddenly, the GPS beeped three times with a giant red exclamation mark blinking upon the screen.

'What the hell?' Murray fumbled with the buttons. 'I've never seen it do that before!'

I leant my head back, content. Curtis was saying hello, I'm sure. He died at 33 years old. I'd just celebrated my 33rd birthday and now the GPS flashed three times with a *Looney Tunes*–type exclamation mark, like it never had before.

* * *

No, there's no such thing as ghosts.

There's not even an afterlife.

There's simply life.

You're either living it wearing flesh, or stripped bare of it, unable to be seen with the eye.

We are all living side by side every day and you don't need objects to move around the room to know it.

It can only be felt with your heart.

CHAPTER 25

REQUESTS FROM THE OTHER SIDE

'Before you get those boots on!' Mags appeared just as I reached for my mortuary gumboots by the prep-room door. 'This morning you must take Mrs Joy to the private viewing room at head office. The family want to apply makeup and style her hair themselves.'

I could hardly contain my glee! Most families are petrified once their loved one has died, quickly handing the corpse over to the professionals. So when families request involvement with body preparation, I become rather excited. *I'm so proud of you!* I want to offer a high-five, but I restrain myself. Supervised, in a dimly lit room, the family take over the role of mortician, minus the mouth suture and cotton Webril in cavities, which take a few lessons to master.

But it can take *hours*. Letters are written, prayers and rosaries chanted, tears, just *being* by the coffin …

'Emma Jane.' Mags snapped me back to the present, shoving some paperwork into my hands. 'You can load Mrs Joy into the van now and head into head office. The family will be there in about an hour.'

Mrs Joy and I arrived at the grand head office building, met by the always cheery funeral director, Parker. 'I went on a date last night,' he beamed as he helped remove Mrs Joy from the back of the van in her coffin, placed her on a gurney and took her into the viewing room. Red velvet drapery amplified class, water sparkled in crystal jugs on corner tables and battery-operated candles flickered in dazzling candle holders. 'She's so lovely, I just can't wait to take her out again,' Parker said as we adjusted Mrs Joy's head into perfect upright position and dabbed her face with tissues. 'Anyway, I'm off to arrange a funeral. A 26-year-old.' His eyebrows pulled in the middle. 'Wasn't found for a week. How does that even happen? Here we have a family who want to apply the makeup to this lady's face herself, and then on the other end of the spectrum we have a family who don't give a shit about their kid.'

We shared a moment of silence.

'Anyway, toodles!'

Moments later there was a knock on the viewing-room door, and I opened it to find a lady with pastel-pink hair in a cropped style and glowing blue eyes. The skin on her forehead was smooth as a 20-year-old but the map of lines on the back of her hands indicated she was middle-aged. She studied my face.

'Oh, hello! Have we met before?'

'No, I don't think so,' I said, motioning her inside.

'Anyway, my name is Ashley. I am here to do lovely Mrs Joy's hair and makeup today.'

Without further ado, Ashley pranced over to the dead lady, placing a suit on the chair by the coffin. The pink-haired makeup enthusiast opened a giant leopard-print cosmetic case, bottles of foundation, eye shadows and lipsticks rattling as she rummaged about.

'No one else?' I peeked into the hallway expecting the usual tribe.

'Nope, just me!' she replied, gazing down into the coffin with adoration as if Mrs Joy was simply asleep and about to wake up and greet her. 'Hello, Mrs Joy,' Ashley chirped. 'I brought Frank's suit for you.'

At first, Ashley speaking to dead Mrs Joy did not seem unusual to me, as I'd seen many people talk to their dead loved ones during a viewing. Even *I* spoke to them from time to time. 'Sorry to interrupt,' I said in my best funeral director tone. 'Just letting you know I'll be right over there in the corner of the room, available to help at any time. Feel free to touch her, just be aware that Joy's skin is a little cool. And please, ask any questions you need to.'

'Oh, my dear!' she chimed, almost laughing as she reached for a makeup brush. 'I know all the answers, she's right here!' Ashley paused, looking beside her as if someone had joined us in the room. 'Yes hon, the suit is here. I will give it to this lovely lady when we are finished!'

Okay. This is new. Speaking to a corpse was okay, but to thin air?

I stepped back and looked away, allowing Ashley time with her friend. But the exuberant stylist had other plans. I would not be standing back during this visitation, so it seemed.

'I'm sorry about your loss,' Ashley said.

'Excuse me?'

'Your loss,' she repeated as casual as board shorts in the summer. 'You experienced a significant life change recently. A divorce?'

I blinked several times in surprise.

'I'm so sorry, love. I must explain. You see, I'm a medium and clairvoyant and I tell ya, it can be really bloody annoying. There are many conversations happening around us and it may become overwhelming for you when I start rambling away on a tangent. Here I am trying to do what Mrs Joy requested, yet she's standing over there telling me I brought the wrong bloody earrings for her burial!'

I followed her gaze behind my shoulder. No ghost. Why did I even expect to see something? I shook my head as if to clear it and focused on my shoes. While questions churned inside, I remained quiet. Apparently, there was enough noise in the room already.

'Your middle name, it represents love,' she said casually. I wasn't sure whether she was talking to ghosts, the body in the coffin, or to me. She reached for the hair curlers. 'You were meant to be here today, love,' she said to me.

On the final curl, Ashley turned her gaze from grey ringlets to my face.

'Okay, darling. Listen carefully. Frank is Mrs Joy's husband. He was buried six years ago wearing an outfit he was not happy with. He *hated* it! He's asked if you could please place his suit in the coffin with Joy. They loved dancing together and they want to go dancing tomorrow night.'

Ashley pointed to the pressed suit and black silk tie lying on the armchair. I nodded, gulping to moisten my cotton-dry throat. *A beer would be nice right about now*, I thought. *Or a shot of vodka.*

'So … there *is* an afterlife?' The words tumbled from my mouth, they shocked even me. Ashley threw her head back and laughed.

'Darling, there is more of an afterlife than the life we are living right now! This, right now, is not even a speck compared to what's over there. They love it! Now I'm not saying let's all go jumping off bridges so we can join the party, but it's a beautiful place.'

We both smiled and my heart grew like a flower.

When Mrs Joy's makeup was applied and curls set with hairspray, Ashley packed up her cosmetics and handed Frank's suit to me. 'Please, he really wants to wear this.'

'I will,' I promised.

'You were meant to be here today, I will be calling you. We have plenty to talk about.'

I wanted to call out after her that she didn't have my number, but she had already left the building.

CHAPTER 26

A FASHION DESIGNER AND A DUNNY

You learn not to head out for an eggs benny when on-call for the weekend, because the second your fork breaks the yolk someone will die and so will your plans.

So, it was a Saturday at home with laundry and Netflix. Just as I began to fold the washing, the work phone rang.

'Emma, lady on tha dunny!' my transfer partner announced. 'I can't come because of me back pain. Can you call one of the casuals? She's only small.'

'Sure,' I said, tossing my crinkled sheets back into the to-be-folded pile. 'I'll be there soon.'

Every funeral director has a story about transferring someone from the loo, from the hilarious to downright heart-breaking, but I was yet to experience a loo transfer myself.

First toilet case, I texted one of the funeral directors I had grown close to.

It's the way Elvis died, he wrote back.

* * *

I steered the body van into the driveway and we headed to the door. The distraught son answered our knock and pointed to the bathroom. And there she was, a tiny little lady with her head tilted back, ankles crossed daintily with a candle flickering by her feet in an attempt to soften the dismal scene. A blanket was draped over her legs, thankfully, as I would use this to help lift her from the porcelain bowl. She was small enough for me to lift her on my own (the casual staff member I had called in to help had only been on a few transfers himself, and looked a little afraid). I didn't mind taking the lead, so with no further ado, I slipped my arms beneath her knees and around her shoulders and gently lifted her from the toilet, carefully placing her in the body bag we had laid out on the floor. She was as light as a feather, and I did indeed have poop on my trousers.

Driving back to the operations facility, I pondered: some say it's cool to die like Elvis, but I don't think anyone should die with a soiled bum and toilet water below. Couldn't she have died five minutes later when she went back to bed? Made it to the kitchen? The lady I will name Coco was 99. She'd almost made it to her 100th birthday, passing away only two weeks before receiving a card from the queen.

'You know why so many people die on the loo?' the casual guy piped up from the passenger side. I'd only worked with him once and we'd hardly shared a word.

'Actually, no.' I thought for a moment. I had no idea. Did they push too hard?

'Well, my stepdad's a paramedic. He told me that someone experiencing cardiac arrest feels like they need to go to the toilet. They mistake a heart attack for needing to go.'

The following day I dressed Coco in a leopard-print wraparound dress with a matching headband. I thought she was the most fashionable old thing I'd ever prepped, and felt even worse that the glamour died on the toilet when she was such a trendy lady. I imagine she'd be mortified, if she knew.

'It's okay,' I whispered. 'I once had to go in the bushes while camping, and used leaves as toilet paper. Your secret is safe with me if mine is with you.'

* * *

The day of her funeral I was rostered to assist in the mortuary. I had been looking forward to the eulogy, her story of 99 years. I bathed and stitched that day with a pout.

The following week while working on a funeral, the celebrant who conducted Coco's service approached me.

'You would have loved the funeral I conducted last week! She was a fashion designer and flew around the world catering to the stars. She came home to spend her last days with family. Such an amazing story. Hey, I know what. I will print out the eulogy for you so you can have a read!'

I couldn't contain my smile. I'd been terribly disheartened about missing Coco's eulogy, yet I wouldn't miss it at all. In fact, I'd have my very own printed copy.

As promised, the following week the celebrant handed me an envelope with Coco's story folded inside. I learnt of her journeys from Paris to Milan, Africa to Sydney, her lavish lifestyle, a far cry from the dismal scene at the end of her life.

Life is all about balance. Coco travelled with the wealthy, dressed the famous. It was as if the universe was showing her it's not all expensive labels and Louboutins. Sometimes life is shit, and you can die while taking one.

CHAPTER 27

INTO THE EARTH

To bury someone truly was an honour.

Commonly, a priest was present for a graveside committal. Father at the head of the grave with his Bible and holy water and mourners huddled close by, we all stood with heads lowered; crows squawking in the distance, kangaroos nibbling grass by headstones, thunder rolling far away, the sun beating down upon us. No matter the weather, no matter the native animals observing, we buried.

Watching intently, waiting for the nod from the reverend, it was time to lower the deceased into the earth. The priest of chosen religion chanted his blessings over the coffin that rested on the strong straps of the lowering device. Fitted to the grave, this nifty piece of machinery is simple to use and lowers your loved one into the ground with the push of a lever.

'Will the family please come forward to place some sand?' said Father once the coffin reached the bottom of the grave. I heaved the heavy sandbox into my arms and offered the scoop to mourners.

Tipping sand into the grave symbolises the deceased returning to the earth. Many cultures and religions believe that we were born of the earth and return when we die.

'Ashes to ashes! Dust to dust!' the priest chimed.

Once the sand and flowers had been released into the grave, we covered the grave with a flower grate, a large metal cover used for the flowers the family wish to leave graveside, but it's also used as a safety measure. Funeral directors never leave a grave uncovered.

Once the cover was placed, we took a bow, and headed back to the hearse. If the family chose to move the grate and dive for their loved once we had left the cemetery, that's up to them, but more often than not the gravediggers were close by with the tray on their truck filled to the brim with soil. The family usually took off pretty quickly, leaving the cemetery staff to do their thing.

There were times the traditional burial routine took a slippery turn. If the deceased was being buried in a monumental grave, say, on top of their spouse who passed away decades ago, it was not safe to fit the lowering device to the ageing granite. On these occasions we performed the *hand lower*. That's right, folks. We lowered the coffin into the grave by hand. While the funeral directors moaned and groaned when they read on the day sheet that a hand lower was required, my tummy somersaulted.

To lower a coffin into the grave by hand, a strap is fed through the handles of the coffin and in one coordinated movement all four of us shuffle the straps through our bare hands at coinciding speed. It only takes one member of the team to shimmy the strap too quickly and the coffin is not level, causing the others to catch up; it's not a great look for the family watching over us. Even if we managed to tear the flesh on the palms of our hands, we hid the pain as we lowered the deceased to the bottom of their grave.

There really is no moment as raw and as sobering as placing a coffin into the earth by hand lower. As I write, I can smell the rich soil, see scars of tree roots on the sides of the grave, the contrast of the colourful flower arrangement on top of the coffin against the red earth. Reminded I was one of the last people to ever touch that person.

The hand lower is an art and one of the most beautiful forms of teamwork I've encountered. Hobbling on old stone, sometimes it felt as though I'd topple down with the coffin, but the mighty responsibility kept me focused and above ground.

When the coffin reached the earth's floor, I took a moment, gazing at the nameplate on the coffin lid. If I'd prepared them, I remembered their face on the mortuary table. From body bag to the floor of their grave, I was with that corpse to the end.

CHAPTER 28

POLICE CALLS

We've all seen it: the devastating fatality causing a lengthy traffic jam, commuters peering out the window to catch a glimpse of the distorted metal and perhaps a body.

Not many people consider the funeral director at a scene like this. Shadowed behind flashing ambulance lights, the police sirens contributing like a disco, *red, blue, red, blue*. The fire crew are on site also, with their huge vehicles and crucial equipment. But what about the other guys attending to the scene? The van with no blinking lights? Let me introduce the contractors.

Earlier, I mentioned that it had always been my dream to work for a funeral home with the police contract. I was blessed to achieve this goal around four years into my career.

Government contractors are the team who remove the corpse from tragic events involving police with care and dignity, and hand-deliver the poor soul to the hospital morgue where they await examination or autopsy. Once the body is released the family can select any funeral home they wish to conduct the service; they don't need to choose the contractors. In fact, one of the first rules while attending to the scene: we weren't allowed to mention which funeral home we were from, unless of course a family member asked. We couldn't even wear our name tags or any identifying features that gave away the funeral home we worked for. We were simply present to remove the casualty from the gully, burnt wreckage of a car, shower floor or field, side of the road or dam, or arcade game simulator. I tell ya, even Hollywood screenwriters couldn't create some of the bizarre places I was called to as a police contractor, and don't get me started on wacky causes of death.

I remember my first police transfer as if it happened only yesterday. In fact, I remember them all as if they're embedded in my brain like my family's birthdates.

I leapt into the passenger side of the van excitedly. Tony, my manager and transfer partner, took to the steering wheel. As we drove towards the house we were called to, I felt my eyes widen as Tony shared stories of the cases he'd worked on over the 15 years he'd spent working as a government contractor.

'We never know too much before we get there,' he told me. 'I've walked unprepared into homes with the deceased still hanging from the ceiling, brain matter on walls after a gunshot, a man at the bottom of his stairs half eaten by his pet. I'd had no idea that's what I was walking into. I'm not bothering you with this, am I?'

'It's fascinating,' I replied. 'Sad, but fascinating.'

'I don't want to offend ...'

'I work at a funeral home, Tony. It takes a lot to offend me.'

'Hmmm. Okay. Only if you're sure.'

I nodded enthusiastically.

'One day we collected a man in front of his computer with … a sexual device attached to his … well … let's just say he was into sex games,' he said, blushing. 'I had to collect a plumber once. He had a heart attack while fixing an old lass's pipes. Died right in front of her on the kitchen tiles by the sink.'

I soon came to admire Tony's ability to predict the incident we'd face simply by observing the houses around us. 'A lot of older people live around here,' he said thoughtfully, leaning in closer to the windscreen as we turned down our designated street. 'I betcha it will be a case where a doctor will sign off on his death. Nothing too exciting.'

I pouted.

Although no decomposition kit was needed, I was deeply moved by my very first police case. I'll name him Mr Wilson. It was how he had dressed only an hour before we arrived that touched me: in perfectly ironed trousers and a leather belt, a notepad and car keys in his pockets. Not a hair out of place, he smelt of Classic Brut. He'd phoned the ambulance reporting chest pain, the police said. His heart failed him before they arrived. Had Mr Wilson dressed handsomely out of courtesy for the hospital staff? I stood close by and watched Tony check the pockets of the body. Fluidly he removed car keys, a mobile phone and the notepad. I wondered what was written on those pages, wishing I could see Mr Wilson's handwriting for a moment. Tony handed the notepad to the police and they popped it into a ziplock bag. I was to learn that before we could remove the dead from a police scene, we searched the body for any valuables, leaving them behind; contrary to a regular transfer where we carefully recorded all valuables in the 'Valuables Book' and left them on the body. One might think this is the police officer's job, but it was usually my partner and I who rolled these bodies from side to side to check for wallets and keys. Drugs. Weapons. 'Ready?' Tony peered up at me when it was time. The courteous man's skin was warm and his limbs floppy as we moved him from the floor, and I experienced a little chest pain of my own. All I could think was, *Mr Wilson had no idea a few hours ago, that tonight he would be dead.*

I had anticipated a gruesome discovery with the call from the police.

Instead, I was moved by pleated trousers and a notepad.

* * *

We'd hardly veered out from the hospital morgue when another police call came through.

'Two police calls in one night!' Tony straightened his tie as he ended the call. He reached over and retrieved a clipboard from the glove compartment and handed it to me. 'Now it's time for you to learn the paperwork. This form must be filled out with every police call,' he instructed, shifting the van into gear and back out onto the main road. 'Since we're contractors, we don't get paid until we submit this paperwork.'

I didn't care about pay, but I wrote 7.10 pm in the column titled *Time Departed to Scene.*

The tyres of the van groaned on driveway gravel a short time later. *Distance to Scene,* 15km. I followed Tony to the front verandah where two police officers were waiting.

I could smell decomposition.

'Just down the hall,' one of the constables said, writing notes on a notepad, then flicking the cover closed and popping it into his pocket by his belt, keeping a taser and pistol close. 'She wasn't found for a week or so. Her husband's been away for work. Got home this evening to find her.'

I hadn't experienced this much police interaction since owning a V8 engine sedan, complete with custom rims. Following the *thump*, *thump*, *thump* of their heavy boots through the house, I recalled the random breath test I was pulled over for a while back. My brother, who happened to be my passenger, was mortified when I took the whole tube in my mouth like a porn star during audition.

'You don't need to take it like that!' my brother cried out.

'Just the tip, ma'am,' the police officer said, blushing.

I didn't know!

Now I was working alongside them, staring down at the little lady decaying on the linoleum floor of her kitchen. Of course I was heartbroken for the widower wailing from the bedroom. But just as a police officer can't retreat to their car and cry with every scene they attend to, a funeral director has to detach from the dead bodies they encounter, to a degree. I felt incredibly blessed to help her. I didn't mind the squelch of body juices beneath my shoes, as I lifted her from the floor.

* * *

We opened the bathroom door to discover a man had slit his throat in the shower.

'At least he was considerate,' said the police officer on my heel. 'Didn't want to make a mess on the carpet.'

The boys in blue stayed out in the lounge area as Tony and I assessed the situation and how we'd get this man from the tiles and onto our stretcher without marking the plush carpet with blood. We laid out a body bag to cover as much carpet as possible. His wife had been notified and would arrive soon, probably just as we were leaving. I'd be horrified if we'd left any trace of her partner's gloomy death in her ensuite.

'You gotta leave the knife!' a forensic investigator called out from the kitchen as he examined the suicide note.

Judiciously, Tony carried him by the shoulders and I took the man's ankles, shuffling backwards from the shower to the body bag. It was haunting, movie-like, staring down at the handle of the knife protruding from his neck, no more than a quarter of the blade visible. Dried blood clung to the injury, a stream of crimson crust traced down his neck to his chest. Together in silence, in unity, Tony and I drove the suicide casualty to the hospital.

While we were signing the man into the morgue, sirens echoed in the distance.

'Hope you don't have dinner planned.' Tony raised an eyebrow as we rolled off our gloves. 'Head home, have a coffee. I'll see you in an hour or so.'

And he was right. Before I could peel a potato, I was on my way to a car accident.

We arrived at the scene around 9.30 pm. The road was blocked off and I was oddly exhilarated when we parked in the area taped off and allocated for emergency vehicles only. I gulped some water before we jumped out and approached the emergency service staff. Politely, the team had retrieved the luckless driver from the mangled vehicle to save us witnessing the extremity of the injuries. Their efforts didn't stop the blood soaking the outside of the body bag, gravel and tar sticking to it like glue. Beneath blinding emergency spotlights, Tony and I crouched down and counted in … *one, two, three!* and heaved the slippery body bag onto the funeral cot we had lowered right to the ground. Raising the stretcher, I quickly realised the body was not whole. I felt he or she was in pieces, body parts moving around inside. When I squeezed the lever to collapse the wheels and return the cot to the van, the decapitated head rolled down and rested against my hands.

I don't think I will ever forget that scene. The bright lights and the lane reserved for police cars, fire crew, us. I can still see the police officer hiding behind a fire truck stuffing down a kebab. It'd been a long day for him. I remember the stars glittering down upon the grisly scene as if nothing dismal had happened at all.

And I will never, ever forget that head—the bloodied head severed from its body, landing against my hand.

* * *

Surely a body removal from a tragic scene would be harder than removing a sweet old thing from the pristine sheets of a nursing-home bed?

Right?

Wrong.

For me, anyhow.

I found the police transfer far more straightforward. A removal from an aged-care facility entailed a journey down numerous corridors, complete with multiple entry and exit points and disoriented aged people asking if I'd seen their friend lately. (These friends they ask after are dead 20 years.)

The process for a police transfer was easier for me because I didn't get lost a single time. The police transfer went a bit like this: we arrived at the scene, paperwork and body tags in tow. The police officers waited for us at the entrance of the scene, usually two or three of them depending on the severity of the case. They'd give us the lowdown before we entered, and family were seldom present. But if they were, they'd already spent time with the police and paramedics prior to our arrival, and rarely wanted to engage in further conversation, especially with us, the scary ones in black suits there to carry their loved one away. We may as well have been carrying a scythe.

Next, we assessed the scene to determine whether we'd require the carry stretcher or the funeral cot on wheels, then got right to it. Sometimes there were stairs, or pets got in the way. We had obstacles such as knives in necks and nooses, bloodied mess roadside, but usually, with the help of the officers if need be, we escaped the scene unscathed.

We then proceeded to the hospital and parked up in the ambulance bay. One of us would take the paperwork inside, the other waited by the van. I always volunteered to stay. We were required to open the back of the van so a doctor could come and declare life extinct before signing the decedent into the morgue. While waiting, I used this opportunity to spend some time with the dead, no matter the stage of decay or how ghastly their inevitable end. So many times I looked down at blood-soaked hair escaping the zip of the body bag, honoured to keep them company after such an ordeal. Sometimes I cried a few tears. Police calls really panged at my heart some days.

Paradoxically, it was rather entertaining to watch the doctor squirm in their scrubs. After such a draining experience removing the victim from a horrific incident, the facial expressions on the doctor upon inspection lightened the moment for sure.

With the nod and signature from the doctor, we drove the van down the ramp to the morgue surrounded by city skyscrapers and the living, passing by with no idea what we were doing at all.

CHAPTER 29

THE HUM

Each morning, I'd head straight to the mortuary register by the coolroom door to see who the crew had brought in overnight. It was my way of greeting the dead each day too, poking my head inside a moment, the arctic air waking me faster than any double-shot espresso served in the staff room. Hanging by the door of the refrigeration unit was a whiteboard with columns for surnames, given names and shelf numbers. This is a record of the deceased lying on shelves inside. One particular morning, I noticed rather an odd name recorded. Surname: Roach. Given name: Cock. Shelf: 6. Curious, I popped on some shoe covers and headed towards shelf number six. Although surrounded with the dead, I couldn't help laughing my lungs raw when I saw a dead cockroach on the human-sized metal tray. Lying on its back, its tiny legs curled up towards the ceiling.

'Hard transfer that one!' Albert laughed from behind. I turned to find him poking his head into the coolroom with his signature goofy smile across his rosy cheeks. 'Flight of stairs and all!'

Together we laughed and laughed and I stepped back out into the world of the living, pulling the door closed behind me. 'Ah, you gotta laugh.' He wrapped his arm around my shoulders and we started towards to the staff room for coffee. 'Otherwise we'd all go mad.'

* * *

Making new friends as an adult is hard enough, without throwing the word 'mortician' in the mix. When meeting new people, a common question I'd get asked was, 'So, do you see anyone? About *it*?' It, referring to death. Everyone assumes that to work with the dead there must be a part of us that is mad, and our spare time is spent in the office of a psychologist. Perhaps they're right. Maybe we are a little mad, but we're all mad together.

Funeral directors are a family. The crew at A Touch of Comfort needed no therapy because we had one another. Hugs in spades, jokes on everyone's lips to lighten heavy moments, water fights while cleaning hearses. We were a tribe with the coolest vibe.

When I first entered the funeral profession, I found it odd that so many funeral directors within the company were either married to one another or dating each other. I remember thinking to myself, *'Do they not realise there is a world outside of the funeral home?'*

But the longer I worked in the industry the more I got it. It's hard to share the events of your workday with someone who has never voluntarily stepped inside a funeral home.

'How was your day today?' is usually met with something along the lines of: *'Well, where do I start? The young boy who got run over by a tractor, or the brain I held onto while assisting the mortician with a head reconstruction?'* Even if family, friends and/or partner were generally interested in the gore, they simply could not understand the specialness of it all. It is near impossible to describe how precious the job of a funeral director really is. So I began to understand why death care professionals formed romantic connections with one another as well as unbreakable friendships.

Albert and Macca were truly very special blokes to me. Wonderful big fellows with belly laughs and a wealth of funeral industry experience under their belts, they helped shape me into the funeral director I was to become.

But as well as the funeral family, there was one other element that meant a lot to me. And it wasn't a person.

* * *

Walking into the operations facility each morning, I was met with the blended fragrance of pinewood coffins, mortuary chemicals and tyre shine, with the droning hum of the body fridge as the soundtrack. It was beautiful. Death has a smell that becomes rather sweet to a funeral director after some time. It doesn't warrant Vicks VapoRub slicked beneath the nose like you see in movies. I can't exactly describe the scent, but fellow funeral directors know the smell I'm speaking of. It becomes part of your day.

But it was the deep droning hum, the background music to the workday that was very special to me. *Hum … huumm … huuummm.* All day and night, the coolroom storing the dead hummed and hummed and hummed. It reminded the living that we were side by side with the dead, and to me, it was sacred.

Everyone is afraid of death. Even if it does transcend to heaven or endless utopia, every single one of us is damn afraid of what it's going to feel like; will we know it's happening? What if there is no heaven after all and we enter an eternity of black abyss? If we stop a moment to consider our last breath, it's frightening. And there were times while going about my day that this reality struck me and stopped me in my tracks. I may have been fastening handles on a coffin, polishing a hearse, crossing the dead's cold hands across their chest. There were moments when I remembered I was going to die and yes, I became afraid. But like a form of meditation, I'd close my eyes and listen … *hum … huumm … huuummm.* It was going to be okay. I would never be alone in death. The coolroom at A Touch of Comfort, and the many funeral homes I was to work at in the following years, stored many, many bodies at one time. I'd always have a friend. A slumber party of sorts, side by side in the big cold room.

No, we didn't need therapy. Us funeral directors, we had each other. We had the daily reminder of our mortality. We had endless coffee and leftover catering food. We had hugs. Jokes. The coolroom *hum.*

We truly were and always will be, the luckiest people walking the planet.

PART TWO: SEX

CHAPTER 30

SHOWGIRLS

Death was not my only unusual interest when I was a girl.

One humid night when I was around nine years old, the sticky heat, my sister's snoring and the insomnia I experienced growing up had me crawling down from the top bunk and creeping to the spot I frequently sat late at night with its view of the TV. While Mum and Dad snoozed on the couch, I learnt a lot from midnight television: I watched the bloodied mess of human birth on a medical show, I saw a man and woman have sex for the first time, and I developed a crush on John Wayne as he trotted through old country towns on horses.

This particular night, I was captivated by beautiful women performing on stage with feather boas and glitter rain in spotlights. The performers were naked, but the pearls and sequins were what captured my attention. *Showgirls* stole my heart. Elizabeth Berkley's lean legs carrying her across the stage were hypnotic; I wanted to *be* her.

From that night onwards, I twirled around my bedroom using scarves as boas and school caps as an imaginary tiara. I longed to be pretty like the showgirls, dancing beneath bright lights in front of an audience.

I hadn't met many glamorous people living in the country. Mum was beautiful, with her long sun-kissed hair and eyes as blue as my Barbie dolls', but she rarely wore anything other than faded blue jeans and T-shirts while helping Dad with chores on the farm.

My nan, however, wore floral dresses, had rollers in her hair and taught me a thing or two about being a lady.

'No one is born glamorous,' she would say on our annual Queensland holidays. My eyes level with her marble vanity littered with beauty products, I watched intently as Nan tapped Elizabeth Arden lotion on her cheeks and dabbed perfume on her wrists. 'Anyone can learn to be glamorous!'

Anyone. Even me?

Glancing down at my faded jeans and dishevelled sneakers covered in old cow manure, I realised growing up on a farm wasn't exactly *sexy.*

Once back in the country, I rehearsed Nan's tutorials with the few cosmetics Mum owned. Drenching my hair in lemon, I'd lie in the sun for hours as Nan told me lemon juice and sunshine were the secrets to her perfect blonde streaks. Determined to be as beautiful as the dancers in the movie, I wore red lipstick to bed believing it would stain my lips and mascara on my lashes hoping it would darken them permanently.

Dancing about my bedroom by night, I was on stage in front of an applauding audience throwing rainbows of cash at me like confetti. In my Michael Jackson phase, many of these make-believe stage shows took place to the songs 'Thriller' and 'Billie Jean'. As the pop star sang about zombies and movie-star queens I had no idea that one day, heels and hearses would be my life.

I would eventually take to the stage.

* * *

Death care saved my sanity during my divorce. Burying the dead reminded me that shiny appliances didn't matter at all, polishing caskets a daily reminder I was blessed to be alive.

However, bills still need to be cleared and a funeral director's wage just wasn't going to cut it.

Death did indeed rescue me, but so did the adult industry.

* * *

Close to the end of my marriage, I found solace in a pub among TAB punters and cheap steaks. Taking a seat in the shadows, I downed a pint without stopping. My windpipe ached from the most recent toxic fight; chilly liquid gold calmed the burn. Observing the scene around me—punters shouting as if the racehorses on the big screen could hear them, sooty-faced tradies with gravy dripping down their chin—I fantasised about placing a bet on Keno and winning a million dollars so I could disappear.

Downing my second, I saw a girl strutting into the bar standing out like red roses on a grave with her long, blonde hair and glittery heels. The bar staff pointed towards the toilets where she headed, reappearing wearing lacy suspenders and a red lingerie ensemble. Punters almost fell over their drunken feet to get to her, stuffing money into her garter.

The lingerie waitress fluttered about the pub for two hours, a schooner glass the makeshift tip jar in the middle of the drinks tray.

Why was she doing this work?

Did she have a boyfriend?

Was he okay with her doing this work?

How much money was in that tip jar? It's overflowing!

The girl didn't approach me until near the end of her shift.

'Hi,' she beamed, leaning on my table. 'You've been sitting over here in the corner all evening. Sorry I haven't had a chance to serve you, those guys won't leave me alone!'

'That's fine,' I said trying to pull my eyes from her shimmering cleavage. I wondered what bronzer she used.

'Can I get you another?' She acknowledged my empty glass.

'No, I best be going.' I climbed down off my stool and headed out into the night.

The lingerie waitress spurred a confidence within me.

Could I do that?

Maybe it was my ticket to freedom. A few secret shifts and I could escape, lacy bras and hundred-dollar bills bulging from my suitcase.

Toodles, husband!

I pushed open the grand front door of the house, his snoring from the cinema room echoing throughout the tiled bottom level. Tiptoeing upstairs, I made it up without a fight, slipped into satin sheets on the king-size bed and began my research.

I searched lingerie waitressing agencies online, and I was surprised to see so many. Femme Fatale Waitresses. Flirt Model Waitresses. Busty & Brunette, Boobs Only. The list went on and on. I'd phone one of the agencies in the morning, start saving some money in secret, pack my bags and sneak off into the night and a new life.

I woke with the sunrise feeling foolish for even entertaining the thought. I forgot all about the lingerie waitress. My silly escape plan was pushed out of my mind.

* * *

I inserted the surgical needle beneath Mrs Harrison's mandible bone and fed it through under her tongue. Driving the suture thread until her rigid jaw was closed, I was finding it hard to concentrate since I'd seen the newspaper advertisement on my tea break.

Promotional models and waitresses required for a variety of events, from golf days to private parties.

Must be outgoing, fit, and well presented.

Opportunities exist for huge money.

Call now!

Startling me, my manager flew through the door, designer glasses halfway down her nose. 'Is Mrs Harrison prepped yet?' Mags inquired, peering over her spectacles.

'I just have to style her hair. She had great taste.' I pointed to the photo of the smiling grandma in the photograph by my work station. Poor old soul. Her death certificate said she had battled cancer for almost a decade. 'The family decided they would like a viewing at midday. I'll get her coffin sorted.' My thoughts of bikini waitressing were pushed to the back of my mind as I reached for the hot rollers.

That afternoon, I dragged my feet to the letterbox and flicking through mail I came across an unfamiliar government envelope among the utilities.

Had I forgot to vote?

Oh no! I could not afford a speeding fine!

I tore it open.

It was a notice informing me my husband had not signed the divorce papers, suggesting I reapply independently, which would cost hundreds.

How much longer could I go on, barely paying rent and no fresh milk in the fridge? Why didn't funeral directors get paid more? Maybe I should consider that course in embalming like the head mortician had suggested. Getting paid a few hundred per embalming, it could certainly help.

After four years of study of course.

I didn't have four years. My credit rating was on the line. Remembering the lingerie waitress all those months ago at the pub, I noticed the newspaper in my driveway. A kookaburra cackled. Even the birds thought my predicament was a joke.

I unrolled the paper, relocated the advertisement for promotional models and without further hesitation dialled the number.

'Bikini Waitresses Australia!' a bubbly voice on the other end piped. 'Josie speaking, how can I help?'

'Hi,' I stammered, staring down at the ants scurrying in the clover patch. How did you even ask for a job in the adult industry? I was soon to discover you needed no résumé, just a smashing bikini and killer pair of heels.

CHAPTER 31

HAPPY HOUR

'Your first shift will be at the Fisherman's Tavern tomorrow night. It's a local pub, plenty of tips. You will be serving drinks in a bikini for the first two hours and selling raffle tickets for the final hour.'

'A pub?' My stomach dropped to my stilettos. The advertisement had promised luxurious golf days, sexy boat trips and celebrity-studded parties at glamorous city hotels! I hoped those shifts were to come.

'You'll be fine. It's a great first shift. The guys are fabulous, so friendly!'

* * *

My first waitressing gig only hours away, I unzipped the body bag to reveal the car accident victim. It didn't take long to realise this was the young woman I'd overheard one of the funeral directors talk about in the lunch room.

From the country of neon lights, go-go dancers and the Full Moon party, the Thai bride moved to Australia with a hopeful heart and a wealthy new husband, and now she was dead and I was washing her thick black hair. I reached for a towel and began to pat dry her slim figure. Tomorrow it was Saturday, and swapping eggs benedict for formaldehyde I'd assist Brenda with the embalming. Secured in a custom-made coffin, unbeknown to the travellers on AirAsia the young Thai woman would return home in the undercarriage of the plane on Monday.

'Everything will be okay,' I whispered as I rolled her into a shelf in the cooling room.

It had been an exhausting Friday but my bed sheets would have to wait.

'What's on tonight?' Diane, one of the funeral directors, asked in the locker room as she slipped out of her suit and into her jeans.

'Not much,' I lied, gathering my belongings from my locker. 'Just a wine and movies I reckon.'

Oh, how I wished that was true.

* * *

The pub smelt of stale beer and men were singing at the top of their lungs to a familiar AC/DC track blaring from the speakers. My bag full of spray tan and makeup, I approached the bar as the agency had instructed.

'The toilets are that way,' the bartender pointed as he served a beer to a drowsy toothless man who needed a shower.

'The toilets?'

'To get changed,' he snapped and continued serving the thirsty humans leaning on the bar. Observing the unruly audience, I felt a sudden urge to run.

'First time?' A young man strapped in soiled tradie overalls leant into me. 'I'm regrettably leaving,' he burped, slipping me a 50-dollar note. 'Hope this gets you started,' he said, and he wobbled out of the door. I looked down at the yellow note and suddenly decided I *could* do this … I *had* to do this! That was quarter of my phone bill paid in two minutes. I made my way to the toilets and fumbled for my heels and a bikini in my backpack. I hadn't seen a single female in the venue and I wondered how long it had been since someone had opened the door or windows of the Ladies. The restroom was stuffy and smelt of stale urine.

You can do this, you can do this … I chanted at my reflection in the greasy, streaked mirror secured on cheap-looking wall tiles. Thick marker stained the glass:

CHLOE 4 RODNEY FOREVER.

Fake lashes widened my brown eyes and the artistic use of contour powder thinned my cheeks. My studies at beauty school had equipped me with makeup skills; hopefully it would fool the opposite sex into thinking I was glamorous. Staring at my foggy reflection in the grubby mirror, my mind wandered to the Thai bride who was at rest at the funeral home.

'Are you almost ready?' A lady wearing the pub's uniform poked her freckly face from behind the door. 'Happy hour is starting and the boys need their waitress, pronto!'

A bell announcing happy hour began dinging from the bar, and I was reminded of church bells at a funeral. I was a funeral director! A mortician! Not a goddamn bikini waitress.

I gathered my heels and bikinis and stuffed them back into my bag and slipped through the back door of the pub. Carving tyre marks into the driveway of the pub, I sped off into the sunset.

Someone else could strut their stuff in a pub. I'd rather go without milk.

CHAPTER 32

DEBT COLLECTORS

Gas explosion on the M1.

Semi-trailer fatality.

It was just the truck driver and me, the radio playing softly in the background. I took the icy zip and opened the body bag. The charred scent slapped me in the face, taking me back to campfires and burnt marshmallows as a kid. The sweetness quickly disappeared into the stench of oil, gas and melted flesh.

The man was unrecognisable but the coroner's report informed me that he was 30 years old. His eyes incinerated to small black holes, his nose had perished and his mouth was twisted in fright. As I reached for the exhaust fan, the mortuary door sprang open. Mags shuffled in with her arm outstretched, holding the cordless phone.

'Thanks,' I frowned, taking the phone in my sooty-gloved hand.

'Make sure you disinfect that phone,' she grumbled, closing the door behind her.

'Hello?'

'Hi, am I speaking with Emma Holmes?'

'Yes, speaking.'

My legs almost gave way when I was informed that debt collectors were standing at the front door of my home as we spoke.

'Debt collectors?' I shrieked.

'Yes, ma'am, you have a rather large outstanding bill for electrical appliances you financed through our company 12 months ago. We have tried to contact you multiple times.'

'I don't have them, I left them behind with my husband!' I had forgotten about the 70-inch plasma I'd purchased for hubby. Wanting to surprise him for his birthday, I took advantage of the finance plan so he had no idea of the surprise. While I was at it, I bought a deep fryer and cappuccino maker.

'Well, Mrs Holmes, our records show they were in your name. We will need to repossess these items, unless you're able to make the total payment with me over the phone.'

'Your debt collectors will be spending their afternoon watching ants in the grass because there is nothing to collect from my home.'

Tears gathering at my chin I paid the full amount over the phone, leaving me with exactly $37.88 in my bank account.

The call and sickening payment finalised, I studied the remains of the burn victim. Poor guy. Money didn't matter to him anymore and there I was sobbing over useless televisions and a coffee machine.

But seriously, how would I eat that night? Skim milk was four bucks a bottle! And I had run out of dog food that morning. I could go hungry, but it would be cruel to starve my beloved four-legged friend.

The money could be replaced. On a funeral director's wage, however, it would take some time, plus I still had other bills to clear.

I removed my sooty gloves and dialled the number for the waitressing agency hoping for a second chance at serving drinks in a bikini.

CHAPTER 33

HOT PANTS

Rocky is incredibly short and peers up at me to order a vodka.

Rocky is also one of the biggest hip-hop stars in the world and is asking me for a vodka.

Resisting the urge to ask for an autograph on my cleavage, I nervously balance my drinks tray, heavy with empty glasses, and head towards the bar.

It was my second attempt as an exotic waitress; thankfully Josie had granted me one more chance to impress. I doubt I was impressing anyone just yet, hobbling in seven-inch heels and hot pants barely covering my buttocks.

'Vodka on the rocks,' I ordered, attempting to pull down the shorts, hoping no one could notice the cellulite on my thighs beneath the layers of fake tan I had applied frantically an hour prior to the shift. While I wanted to run out of the crowded room, at $80 an hour I decided to stay put.

The marble bar was lit from beneath and the sea of liquor bottles gleamed and sparkled along the wall. I watched the bartender pour alcohol into a glass, her manicure decorated with small rhinestones glittering in the lights as she sliced fresh lemon. Mesmerised by her pout, I wished I had the money for lip injections. She caught my gaze, and I quickly looked away and scanned the room. Other waitresses, wearing their tiny black shorts and matching midriff tops fluttered about the party, serving drinks and collecting empty glasses from tables. I recognised celebrities, their heads bopping to the smooth beats of Rocky's latest hits. The bartender handed me Rocky's drink and my seven-inch stilettos carried me to his table.

'Thank you gorgeous.' The star flashed his stunning veneers and I blushed. I managed to find myself a darkened corner, and an abandoned cocktail. I gulped it down, thinking it could have been spiked for all I knew and kind of hoping it had.

'Not your scene?' A stocky, dark-skinned man startled me. He was leaning against the wall by the window with views of Circular Quay. A chunky gold necklace caught a distant light and he smelt of Giorgio Armani.

'Australia sure is beautiful.' His accent screamed swagger as he sipped from his martini glass, peering out at the harbour. 'Ain't seen no view like this for a while. I practically live in the studio. You like Rocky's new album?'

'Sure,' I stammered. *Hurry up cocktail. Do your job!*

'Waitressing your full-time job?' He undressed me with his big brown eyes.

'It's a new thing,' I said, trembling. 'A part-time thing ...'

'Yeah? What else you do?' He sipped again, biting the corner of his full, pillow-like lips.

'Uh, I work in cosmetics,' I said, deciding to spare him the details.

'We're looking for a makeup artist. You should come back to my room after you finish work. Talk business.'

'Sure.' I offered a nervous smile, almost dropping my drinks tray. 'Sounds great.' I was totally lying—I wouldn't be going back to his room, but in that moment, I felt desirable again. The sexy American placed his empty glass on the nearby table and suddenly moved in, startling me with a kiss. His huge hand squeezed my cold bum cheek before he told me his room number at the Hilton and returned to the party.

* * *

Later that night, in odd socks eating Vegemite toast on my couch, it occurred to me that I hadn't been kissed since I'd left my husband.

The first 'post-separation' kiss was from a music star while wearing hot pants and serving fancy cocktails, and the next day I would be bathing dead bodies and driving a hearse. I could write a book about all of this, I said to Cupcake, who gazed up at me through her fluff.

Of course she didn't answer, but I thought it could be a bloody good idea.

CHAPTER 34

LACE AND LIPSTICK

I stared down into the grave as the beauty queen's coffin was lowered into the earth. Buried with her pageant sashes and heels, she was 32 years old.

When you see a beautiful young woman lying in her coffin enveloped in satin, it hits home and reminds you Death doesn't discriminate. Beautiful people were invincible to me and I envisioned them staying here forever. I trusted Luke Perry to grace my TV eternally with his good looks. I cried for a week when Brittany Murphy died. I ate my weight in chocolate when Michael Jackson passed away, and don't get me started on Anna Nicole.

A crow squawked in the distance as the coffin reached the bottom of the grave and mourners turned towards their cars with heads hung low. Another curtain closed on another life. A week earlier, the beauty queen was on a stage, flowers thrown at her as she took the crown. Now her dainty body had been laid to rest, slightly wounded by the car. I had assisted the mortician in camouflaging the bruises with makeup.

I was uncomfortable leaving her behind on her own in the ground. Unbelievably, life goes on. Whispering my farewell to the beauty, I turned and headed back towards the hearse.

* * *

That evening I was met with beauty of another kind. Allocated a shift at a strip club called the Lace and Lipstick, I'd be waitressing for a main event. The entrance of the club, known as the L&L, welcomed customers with an archway of multi-coloured fairy lights blinking like a Christmas tree. The infamous L&L was hosting Miss Pole Dancer Australia and performers from all across the country had arrived with suitcases crammed with sequins and stilettos. I watched from the bottom of the stairs as stunning dancers dragged their heavy suitcases up towards the entry doors, mustering the courage to walk in there myself.

The red-light district began to wake as if the sunset was its alarm; women in sky-high heels and mini-skirts, guys with slicked hair showing off tanned arms in tight shirts, a homeless man hurling through the garbage cans. Taxis lined the pavements. Adult stores were illuminated with neon lights, and the avenue of strip clubs opened their doors.

Glancing at my watch I realised it was time to start my shift, so I carried my feet in Converse sneakers up those stairs and into the venue.

The club was dimly lit inside, smelling of alcohol, cologne and the carpet-cleaning powder you sprinkle on the floor before vacuuming. The bartenders were preparing the bar for opening, drink glasses tinkling like wind chimes. The mirrored walls cast reflections around the room and a large chandelier hung from the ceiling in the centre of the club.

As the venue prepared for the event, I stood in the shadows unable to pull my eyes away from the performers rehearsing for the competition. A mirrored catwalk adjoined the main stage where the dancers would strut and twirl and break into the splits as if the eight-inch stilettos on their feet didn't exist. Nipple tassels dangled from boob jobs, tans shimmered with glitter, rhinestone-studded heels caught the reflection of the disco ball spinning slowly above.

Patrons began to arrive and the performers dispersed backstage. A smoke machine hissed haze towards the catwalk.

'Jimmy and coke!' A slurring voice broke my trance, pulling me back to the job I was hired to do. He passed me a crumpled 50-dollar note. 'Keep the change.' He collapsed into a seat by the stage. My naturally curly hair straightened and plastered to my scalp with hairspray, I walked to the bar in the new beaded bikini set I had bought from the adult costume shop next door.

The club was soon packed and the bartenders scurried about like ants before rain. I found a spare spot at the end of the bar. A funky remix of Michael Jackson's 'Bad' was pumping when a man who smelt expensive slipped in next to me, winking over his whiskey glass. He threw back the liquor, resting the empty glass on the bar before retrieving a bundle of the club's 'tipping dollars' from his suit pocket. Tipping dollars are strips of plastic with various denominations on them used for tipping the girls. Patrons 'buy' these and use it as real money, even to buy their drinks. At the end of the night, the dancers exchange what they accumulated throughout the shift for cold hard cash.

'For you' he said, handing 200 dollars of plastic to me. 'Give up that drink tray, you belong up there.' He nodded towards the stage and disappeared into the crowd.

* * *

One thousand and ten, one thousand and twenty …

Rain pelted against the windows of my cottage and I was grateful for the day off from both jobs. Cupcake snored at my feet while I counted my waitressing earnings in bed, snacking on brie and strawberries, champagne on my bedside. My fears about lingerie waitressing had been unfounded. I'd imagined a seedy dark world with gangsters and cocaine lines on taut tummies like I had seen in mobster films. What I experienced was a crowd of TAB enthusiasts who popped the change from their beers in my tip jar, and most of my shifts were spent chatting to the bar staff. At private jobs, a security guard watched over us intently as we served drinks to guys celebrating their favourite sports on TV. At bucks' parties held in houses, the guys offered us sausage sizzles rather than bum slaps, and the craziest drink I had been offered so far was a Vodka Cruiser Black. I felt safer working for Josie than I did walking down the street. She was only a phone call away and with safety her number-one priority, Josie organised licensed security drivers to take care of the girls and always sent more than one girl to a private job. We were never alone. I was new to the industry and had plenty to learn, but so far, so good. I had hot water, groceries in the fridge, and my rent was up to date. This was before my weekly wage from the funeral home. Shit, maybe I could even start saving for that house deposit.

I'd sorted dollars in their coloured denominations, when my mobile rang as I tapped away on the calculator.

'Yep, hello?'

'Emma Jane, it's Josie.'

'Oh, hey!'

'I'm just calling with a message for you. I'd never pass on your number so she's left hers. Have you got a pen handy?'

I reached for the closest notepad, one from the funeral home. 'Ready!'

'Okay, the Lace and Lipstick phoned. Beck, the manager, said you left something there last night. Her number is …'

I held the phone between my shoulder and cheek, jotting down the contact number for the L&L beneath A Touch of Comfort letterhead. The polarity of my life right there on paper. The words *strip club* and *funeral home* on the same page.

'Enjoy your day off, babe,' Josie chimed. 'Busy weekend ahead, you will be booked solid! Hope you like seafood. I have a boat charter shift on Saturday if you're interested, a bunch of deep-sea fishermen. Anyhoo, talk soon.'

* * *

'Thank you for calling Kings Cross's first-class adult venue, the Lace and Lipstick. Beck speaking'

'Hi Beck, it's me, Emma Jane. We met—'

'—here at Miss Pole Dancer Australia! Lovely to hear from you, thanks for getting back to me!'

'The agency mentioned I may have left something at the club last night.' I couldn't recall leaving anything behind. Oh well, it sounded like something I'd do. I didn't even know what day it was half the time.

'Sorry about that,' Beck laughed. 'I didn't know how else to get in touch with you without sounding like I was poaching.'

'No problem.' I felt a frown. Why hadn't I made that darn Botox appointment yet? And what did Beck mean by poaching?

CHAPTER 35

STAGE LIGHTS

'I'll be seeing you soon, love!'

Liquor breath cloaked my face as the man in torn jeans leant in. 'Nice tits.' Swaying into a trash can, he burped then continued to hobble down Darlinghurst Road.

'Don't let him discourage you, mate,' said a tall man coming to my side. He wore the Lace and Lipstick security polo shirt, proudly. 'We don't let scumbags like that in here. First night, huh?'

'Yeah.' I still couldn't believe I'd mustered up enough courage to accept a dancing shift at the strip club. Beck had practically begged me to take to the stage, just to see if I liked it.

'I think you have great potential,' she had said over the phone. 'The customers loved you! Please give dancing a shot. I don't think you'll regret it and the money is *amazing*!' She had emphasised the word 'amazing'. And since I needed amazing money to start my life over at an age when most have mortgages and babies, there I was about to head inside.

'Paul is my name. I'm one of the bouncers here.' My hand in his, I felt less anxious. He towered above me, and there was warmth about him that reminded me of my dad.

'I'm Emma Jane, but you can call me Em.'

'You got ID love? You know I can't let you audition without making sure you're over 18!'

Gladly, I reached into my handbag.

'I'm kidding love, I saw you waitressing here the other night!'

'Oh, right.' I felt my face redden.

'Shall we?' He motioned. Paul waved to the bartenders as we entered. 'I'll go get Rebecca for you,' he said and disappeared through a swing door by the bar. The bar staff wore black-collared shirts with *The Lace and Lipstick* embroidered in white thread on the pockets. Heart thumping, I stood by the back wall staring at the stage. I was petrified that I might twirl right off it while holding onto one of those slippery-looking poles. Within minutes, Beck bounded towards me on Louboutin heels.

'Emma Jane! It's great to see you again!' She grabbed me and pulled me in for a hug, her skin cold from the club's air conditioning and smelling of Chanel. 'Thank you for coming. I was really impressed by your work the other night when you were waitressing.'

'No problem.' I offered her a half-smile as we parted from the lingering hug. She kept her hand on my shoulder as she peered into my face. 'You ready?'

'Sure.' I wasn't sure.

'Great, follow me. And please, call me Beck, not Rebecca.' The slim beauty rattled off a brief tour as I followed her expensive scent. 'That's one of our lap-dance areas over there ...' She pointed to a room branching from the main floor with large velvet couches inside. 'There's no touching at all here in New South Wales, but you know, if they slip ya a hundred in the VIP room you can let them have a quick play of your boobs or whatever. But absolutely no physical contact in the genitalia area of both parties. There must be a 30-centimetre gap between your vag and his crotch. If the client breaks any rules or makes you feel uncomfortable at any time, they're outta here!' She pointed her shiny manicure towards the exit doors.

The size of the club was deceptive. There were rooms I hadn't noticed during my waitressing shift; the place was like a carnival funhouse with all of its mirrors and secrets doors.

'Now, babe, when you're on stage you have to dance for three songs. So, you know, take something off each track, so by the end of the last song you're only in your G-string. Your bottoms don't come off up there. Only in a lap dance ...'

Struggling to keep up with Beck's fast-paced tour, I listened and stewed on the information that landed in my hooped-earring ears.

Lap dancing! Touching! Nudity!

What had I got myself into? It sounded like far more work than waitressing. I was a funeral director who had a bit of a wobbly tummy and cellulite on her buttocks. Would I have to join a gym, too? When was I going to fit all of this into my life?

'We will get you up on the stage for a bit of a practice soon, but I'll get you a locker for your things and show you the change room first. It's going to be a busy night so we'll get this stuff sorted before the club opens.'

Beck was absolutely stunning, dressed in tight black pants and an L&L tank top revealing her highlighted cleavage that shimmered beneath the chandelier. I wondered why she wasn't a showgirl herself. Sweat dampening my blouse, I followed her into the dancers' change room, almost blinded by the body-length mirrors framed with fluorescent globes.

'This is where you will get ready for each shift. We have a professional makeup artist and hairdresser here on weekends but during the week just bring your own cosmetics. We supply hair curlers, hair dryers, and if you do happen to forget your makeup, we supply a heap of that too!' She pointed to a basket by one of the mirrors overflowing with lipsticks and powder compacts.

There was one other dancer in the change room, ginger curls cascading down her trim back. She didn't take her eyes from the mirror as she greeted me, carefully positioning fake lashes on her eyelid.

'Hey, babe, I'm Sophia.'

'This is for your locker.' Beck fished into her skin-tight pants and retrieved a key hooked on a green keyring. Locker 14. My lucky number. Had to be a good sign, right? 'The lockers are just through there in the next room. Oh! I almost forgot! What will your stage name be?'

Stage name? Stepping inside the strip club alone was a shock to me, let alone coming up with a pseudonym!

Rigor? Morticia?

The red-haired beauty was looking at me now through the mirror, as she swept lipstick the colour of her curls across her lips. She appeared much older than the dancers I had seen perform here; pretty though.

Mature pretty.

'How about … Madison?' the dancer suggested, puckering her lips. 'We haven't had a Madison here for a while. It suits her.'

'Like it?' Beck turned to me and raised her eyebrows, sending only slight creases across her smooth forehead.

'Sure,' I said, nodding. 'Madison is cute. I like it.'

I pushed back my shoulders and flashed what I hoped was a sultry smile, but I'm sure I looked more like a corpse with a poor mouth suture.

'That's sorted then!' Beck clasped her hands together. She shifted her eyes to the watch that was far too bulky for her slim wrists. 'Jesus! Is that the time? Right, Madison, I have a few things I have to get done before the club opens. Get ready and then I will get you up on the stage for a practice. I'll be back soon.' And she scurried off, leaving Sophia and me in the big bright room.

'Madison.' The dancer turned to me now, pulling her T-shirt up over her head revealing her full, round breasts that waved side to side like the Bondi surf. 'Welcome.'

I felt like I should have looked away, but I couldn't. She had the most naturally beautiful body I'd ever seen; fair-skinned, curvy. Finally, she reached for the sequinned gown sprawled across the back of a chair.

Thank goodness! Put some clothes on so I can concentrate!

'Oh, Sophia!' Beck appeared again with a Red Bull in her hands. 'When you're ready, could you give Madison a bit of a lap dance and show her how it's done? You're the veteran!'

'Of course,' Sophia leered. 'My pleasure.'

* * *

Nervous sweat streaking the fake tan I had slapped on my dehydrated skin, I stood in the shadows by the stage waiting for the song to start.

'Hurry, hurry,' Beck called out to the DJ. 'The club is open in ten!' He gave two thumbs up, positioned his headphones and nodded my way. I'd chosen 'Sexy Back' by Justin Timberlake. I cringe now looking back, but at the time it seemed fitting. Sophia passed by me as she headed towards the bar. Detecting my low-key anxiety attack, she patted my arm and assured me I'd be fine.

'Just dance as though you are making love to the audience, and you'll be great,' she purred.

Great advice, but I hadn't made love in over a year. I'd kind of forgotten what that looked like. Beck waited down where soon an audience would be, her face beaming with hope.

Please don't hold such hope for me, I thought. *I was licking cheeseburger ketchup from my car seat before I walked in.*

One pedicured foot following the other, I stepped into the spotlight and clasped the pole in my clammy hands. My reflection was unrecognisable in the mirrored back wall of the stage. *I look pretty,* I thought to myself. *I can do this …*

Closing my eyes I was back in my childhood bedroom, dancing alone with the curtains drawn and my door locked. Reopening my eyes, I was in stage lights for real, the spheres of colour turning my skin pink, blue, green and orange at fast tempo.

As the song came to an end it occurred to me I was topless, every freckle, every strand of fair body hair and tan lines on show. This was it. It couldn't be undone; my boobs were out. And I really did need to reconsider that discounted gym offer in my inbox.

'Great!' Beck was clapping excitedly. 'Love it! Madison! Welcome to the team!'

Sophia winked at me from the bar and ordered two champagnes.

Stepping down the stairs panting, I realised that while I was dancing, I hadn't thought of the bodies needing my attention at the funeral home, my divorce or the overdue electricity bill. Perhaps this could be my new form of therapy. Goodbye wine bottle!

I popped my boobs back into the bikini as the club opened. *Showtime.* My heart thudded violently in my chest as the herd of men poured through the door—*they were lined up outside already?*—but I could not wait to get back up on that stage.

I may have aced the pole dancing, but there was still one more lesson before progressing in my exotic dancing career. I needed to learn how to lap dance, and Sophia was dragging me into the VIP area to show me how.

CHAPTER 36

LAP DANCES

When you start work at a funeral home, you are taught to polish a hearse and apply barrier cream to a corpse's face. When you start work at a strip club, you are taught a lap dance.

Sophia plopped a champagne in my hands as I slipped onto a large velvet couch. The club had only just opened, so no lap dances were taking place yet. Eager patrons hovered by the bar waiting for the first drink of the night as a buxom blonde named Heaven took to the stage and reached for a pole.

'So, the lap dance,' the sultry redhead purred, kneeling in front of me, 'is not actually a dance as such. Have you ever had a sexy photo shoot, Maddie?'

I shook my head and gulped some liquid gold confidence.

'Imagine a suggestive photo shoot, moving sexily from one pose to another. Please don't ever dance as if you're in a nightclub. I cringe when I see this. Let me show you. A great way to start is to swish your hair like this ...' and she began to flick her head over and over so that her strawberry-scented mane brushed my legs. She shifted onto her back, arching her spine and slightly opened her legs. While Sophia writhed from one seductive move to another, slowly undressing, I was both terrified and turned on. Unable to look away, I watched her glide across the floor as if it was made of polished floorboards rather than carpet. How did the guys deal with this tease? I could hardly handle it myself. I also realised that I could never move as sexily as this, and hoped my great personality would make up for the fact that I could hardly arch my back at all.

'You're always being watched.' Sophia finally stopped slithering about. 'If you are too close to the man's crotch you can be fined and possibly lose the following night's shift. It's just best you perform as much floor work as possible.' I was soon to learn that floor-work moves are performed, well … on the floor, mimicking sex positions and some sort of hungry feline creature. I stayed off the floor as I had forgotten what sex looked like and had never owned a cat. 'Some girls like to drape themselves over the guy's lap,' Sophia continued. 'It's hot, sure, but if Beck thinks you're too close to the genitalia you can say goodbye to the night's earnings. Now, expect to see inflation in the pants …'

Don't laugh Emma Jane. Don't laugh.

'…try not to draw attention to it. He will already be embarrassed about the growth, especially the young guys. Just do your darn hardest to make him squirm in his seat, that's always fun. An older guy, usually the regulars will be chuffed, so just smile and call them Big Boy. You're guaranteed a big tip.'

* * *

'New here?' the strapping man asked, raising an eyebrow as he handed the bartender a hundred-dollar bill.

'It's my first night,' I confessed, biting my lip. I hadn't been this rattled since my wedding day. In hindsight, I was clearly doing the wrong thing as my sister laced up my corset and Mum polished my pearls. I'd popped a Valium and walked down that red carpet and said 'I do' to the man who wasn't right for me. It was kind of how I felt in this moment, on my first night as an exotic dancer, talking to the customer with the suit pocket bulging with cash. I *wanted* to dance and make money, but I wasn't quite sure it was the *right* thing to do. And the only way to find out was to give it a go.

'*Your first night?* Shall we?' He offered his linked arm.

'Excuse me?'

'Shall we head to the VIP lounge? A lap dance,' he chuckled, like I had missed something.

'Oh, right!' Shit. I was actually about to start writhing naked across the floor in front of a complete stranger.

To my surprise, however, my customer never asked me to dance. Instead he advised me on the industry: '*Don't trust everybody you meet, no matter how lovely they are—save your money and don't take drugs!*'

I was paid $120 to sit in the nude and listen to advice from a wealthy banker.

* * *

Sunrise illuminated the sky as the stage lights were turned down. The dancers peeled off the lashes, replaced sequinned costumes with jeans, some even took a nap on the floor using their clothes as pillows. Thankfully I was far from tired; I still had an entire day of work ahead of me at the funeral home.

'She must have found Beck's stash,' a dancer muttered beneath her breath. I ignored her comment and reached for the rest of my belongings from my locker.

'Aren't you just a ray of sunshine?' A familiar face grinned as she leant against the locker next to mine. Amy, a bronzed performer with long dark hair and blue eyeshadow—which she pulled off beautifully—had introduced herself during the night. We were unable to talk for very long as I had been too busy in the lap-dance room. Every dancer had glared at me as I led gentleman after gentleman into the private dance area, but not Amy. She gave me a 'thumbs up' with every cent I earned.

'You had a good night then, Madison?' she asked, stuffing her stilettos and lingerie into a backpack.

'I did, thank you!' I beamed, pulling my T-shirt on over my head, almost dragging off my hairpiece. 'But please, call me Emma Jane.'

'No, no,' she said, flapping her hands, 'We stick to the stage names. If we all knew each other's real name it would get pretty confusing around here.'

The whole stage name thing was going to take some getting used to.

Amy's chestnut hair, worn loose down her back during the shift, was now tied back in a casual ponytail, but on her it looked glamorous. 'How much did you make?' She rubbed her sleepy eyes, further smudging her makeup. 'I made a hundred bucks on my first night, I was so bloody nervous.'

With our cash earned from lap dances held in the office until the end of the shift, I had no idea how much money I'd made, and to be honest, I was having so much fun that I had completely forgotten that I would be receiving a paycheque.

'I'm not sure!'

'Well, don't forget to collect your cash. Anyway, I'm beat and my boyfriend is waiting out front. When are you working next, Maddy?'

'Perhaps on the weekend.'

'See you then, babe.'

It's funny, I kind of missed her the second she walked away.

Locker empty, I joined the queue of yawning dancers by the office. One by one they entered empty-handed, exiting holding wads of cash. Waiting in line, I decided I'd have to make the phone call to Bikini Waitresses Australia and break the news to Josie. I would no longer be working for them. I was a dancer now.

Finally it was my turn and I headed into the small office. The walls were cluttered with posters and calendars of hot girls in bikinis and Beck's desk was littered with empty cans of Red Bull.

'Great job tonight.' She ticked my name off a list and handed me a swollen envelope. 'Your money is inside. So … will we see you on the weekend?'

'Absolutely,' I said, smiling.

Walking back through the club towards the exit, I counted my bundle of green notes.

Three hundred … four hundred … five hundred … six …

'How did your first night go, Emma Jane?' asked Paul, the friendly security guard as he pushed open the door for me, the cool breeze of dawn tickling my face. He was the first person to call me by my real name since I'd started my shift nine hours ago.

I couldn't contain the goofy smile on my contoured cheeks.

My hand was lost once again in his as we said goodnight. I was a little sad to be leaving, and anticipated returning to the pole and my new friends already. With a week's wage earned in one shift shoved into my handbag, it was time for mortuary scrubs. I may have just worked a nine-hour shift, but I had an entire day ahead.

CHAPTER 37

'SO SEXY'

By my second week as a dancer at the infamous L&L, I'd begun to learn a few things about the place. Firstly, the nights ran like this:

7 pm – 8 pm: The dressing room is loud with chatter. The dancers discuss life outside the club while applying their makeup. Pretty girls become glamorous with curled hair extensions or sleek styles so shiny you expect to see your reflection in their mane. Plump lips shine, fit bodies shimmer, eyes are framed with precise winged eyeliner. Girls rub moisturiser and fake tan into one another's skin and shave places you probably have never contemplated.

10 pm – midnight: Champagne is sparkling and the club is brimming with patrons. The mob of horny men—and occasionally women—are tipsy, boisterous and parting with their cash.

The dancers are still eager to perform, lining up by the side of the stage so as not to miss a moment of money-making potential. The private dance area is busy, garters are full of money.

1 am – 3 am: As the night progresses, the change room becomes a gossip retreat. Dancers complain about the tubby man by the stage who won't tip and I find it entertaining to watch them lure men on the floor, then see them in the change room hiccupping, farting and checking that one another's tampon strings aren't visible. The dancers aren't as excited to perform at this hour; Beck often has to bribe them with a free drink to keep the stage from being empty.

5 am – 6 am: The lights are turned up, last drinks called. Fake eyelashes are removed, stilettos kicked off by the corner of the dressing room. Rays of sunshine sneak through the change room's aluminium-foiled windows. The girls receive their pay in fat envelopes and spill out into the real world to their boyfriends and trendy cars for a well-earned breakfast.

I reckon I was the flabbiest girl in the change room. These girls were from another planet, their curves placed perfectly like they had been designed by an artist. Well, they had been designed, I guess, by a cosmetic surgeon. The boobs were big, the butts were bigger. One dancer who had only just left high school had undergone three surgeries already. Forget boob jobs, arse jobs were bouncing around the change room like a hip-hop twerking video. The bottom-enhancement involves silicone implants inserted into butt cheeks, and with their tiny waists, these girls looked like they'd just stepped out of Rio's Carnivale. Despite my natural butt and not-so-toned tummy, I had become one of the highest-booking ladies and was viewed as competition by these glamazons. One thing I was beginning to learn about men was it's not all about boobies and bouncy bottoms. I had my cheesy grin on my side, and a bubbly personality. Beck told me repeatedly that I was a breath of fresh air, and the guys thought so too. Some of the dancers wished that air would blow right on out of the place. I could feel their venomous stares in the change room as I stood in front of the mirror applying my mascara.

Two girls who did not feel they were in competition with me were my ongoing supporters, Amy and Sophia. They assured me that there would be another new girl soon enough, and I would be a part of the locker-room family in no time. Working on alternate nights, I had a cheerleader each shift.

'Did you work today?' Sophia asked at the beginning of our mid-week shift. We shared a mirror, examining our makeup.

'Yeah.' My eyes were bloodshot. My body was fuelled with Red Bulls and vodkas at night, double-shot lattes by day. 'Looking forward to bed, that's for sure!'

I was strictly private regarding my day job at the L&L. I wasn't sure how the dancers would feel if they knew they were sharing their dressing room with a mortician. So I had told my two friends at the Lace and Lipstick that I was a makeup artist.

'I used to have a *normal* job, didn't last long. Stripping is way better money!'

There was something about the word 'stripper' that didn't sit well with me. I winced at the sound of it. Some of the dancers used the word often, proud of their stripper title. I never thought of us as strippers. We were performers. And performing didn't stop at the stage. We continued to perform when hustling the floor. When convincing a patron he should choose me for a dance, I twirled my hair, licked my lips seductively. I giggled at their bad jokes and touched their arm often. I'd never do that to a man I'd just met on the outside. It was all an act, entertaining him. And myself, to be honest. A pathetic flirt in my personal life, yet here I was in heels and sexy lingerie flirting with the best. Pretty fucking hilarious.

'Ladies!' Beck poked her head into the change room. 'Tonight we have a movie crew from Hollywood coming in! They're shooting a movie in Sydney this week and have booked out VIP!'

'Oooh!' the naked dancers squealed, boobs bouncing.

'Sophia! Madison!' Beck pointed. 'I want the two of you to dance for them. Come and see me when you're ready.'

Sophia threw me a wink as the energy of change room deflated.

'It's you and I tonight, blossom,' she said and sauntered off leaving me alone with ten pairs of eyes burning my back.

I slipped into the strappy black dress I had bought from the adult store next door (which I was visiting frequently). While my bills were up to date, most of the leftover cash I had been earning at the club was spent on outfits and makeup.

'It's an investment,' Amy assured me one shopping trip as we browsed the rack of sexy French-maid and naughty policewoman costumes. 'To make money you need to spend money!'

Later that night, this Plain Jane funeral director who lived in a tiny cottage and wore odd socks on her weekends found herself lap dancing for one of the biggest movie actors in Hollywood. It's hard to play it cool when concentrating on not falling over in front of someone you had posters of as a kid. And these guys were spending big; I had to stay upright on my heels if I wanted cash in my garter. I rolled my hips in front of the celebrity sipping his expensive scotch, his eyes small slits as he watched me move under the lights.

'So sexy,' he murmured, flicking his shiny brown hair to one side. 'Bend over.'

'Not without me.' Sophia slipped her cold arm around my waist. We shivered in the air conditioning but it was about to get hot.

'Now this is why they are paying the big bucks,' she whispered in my ear. 'Follow my lead. We will pretend to kiss.' I turned to face her seductive lip-bite. Sophia tossed her long mane over our faces, placed her chilly hand over my mouth and made out with it. We weren't allowed to kiss for real—it could be classed as a form of prostitution since the men were paying for the service.

I shadowed Sophia's movements, moving in sync with our bare breasts pressed together. She traced her manicure down my spine. I hadn't been so turned on in all my life. The two men moaned as loud as I wanted to.

'I can't deal!' the actor exclaimed. 'You two must come back to our hotel after this!'

* * *

When the shift came to a close, I was unusually shy around Sophia in the dressing room. I was attracted to her body, so different to mine. Hers was softer. Milky. Free of a belly piercing and glitter.

'You coming back to the hotel?' She reapplied some lippy.

'I can't,' I sighed, pretending to be devastated. 'I have work in the morning.'

As exciting as the night had been, I was looking forward to Vegemite toast, a cup of tea and cuddles with my dog. I had also heard that the dancers weren't allowed to visit hotel rooms after work, even for a cup of chai. The rule wasn't just club policy; visiting a customer in his hotel room after work constitutes prostitution, and soliciting from the club is illegal. The thought of Mum and Dad bailing me out of jail for soliciting sex from the club made me shudder. Sophia seemed to think spending time with the famous was worth the risk.

'Well, I'm out of here, Blossom,' she said and kissed me on the cheek, wearing Levi jeans now, effortlessly beautiful.

'Will I even see you again?' I joked. 'You might run off to Hollywood.'

'Ha!' She grabbed her backpack dramatically. 'Maybe I will.'

Grinning to myself, I swept my clip-in hair extensions into a top knot and as I secured it with a scrunchie, I noticed song lyrics, printed out and stuck to the wall. The Jacksons' 'Blame It on the Boogie'—one of the songs I'd danced to when I was a girl fantasising about life as a showgirl.

Do you ever get that feeling you are in the right place at the right time? You don't even know how you got there, but everything simply falls into place? I'd met a movie star, my purse bulged with cash, and catching my reflection in the mirror I saw that I was glowing. A far cry from the lonely woman crying in the spare bedroom of the marital home. If

I hadn't hit rock bottom, I never would have dialled Bikini Waitresses Australia, which had led to my new job as a dancer.

Well, thanks to the boogie, my rent is paid. I closed my locker and boogied my way out through the empty club and into the sunrise.

Hollywood, eat your heart out.

CHAPTER 38

BROKEN HEARTS

Body bags on board, I headed out onto the M1 towards the city morgue. I would be transferring 32-year-old Christopher who had died of heart failure. So young to have heart disease, I pondered. Grateful my heart was still beating, I cranked up the radio as I pulled up at the traffic lights. A guy in the car beside me raised a brow at the blonde in a suit driving a conspicuous van with bass thumping.

A short while later, I steered the body van into the driveway of the forensic science unit, identifying myself via the speaker by the gates. The boom gate lifted and I entered, bouncing in my seat as I bounded over the speed bumps that are in place to *stop* speeding, but I couldn't get to the big roller doors of the morgue quick enough.

I loved the morgue. I reversed the van into the parking space allocated for funeral directors' vehicles and waited for the roller door to ascend.

As I checked over Christopher's paperwork, my mobile phone began ringing and not taking my eyes from his death certificate, I answered.

'Yello!'

'Emma Jane, you disgusting tart.' An unfamiliar voice spat down the phone line.

'Excuse me?' I glanced at the screen but they'd rung from a private number and the voice was disguised using one of those voice-distorting apps.

'I saw you dancing at the club. What is wrong with you? Don't you have integrity? You should be ashamed of yourself, you disgusting stripper!'

Tears welled in my eyes. Who on earth was this? I know I sound naive, but when taking on my new career as an exotic dancer, it hadn't actually occurred to me that perhaps someone I knew would ever walk in and see my bum.

'I'm telling your parents. For your own good,' the voice growled.

'No! Wait!' I begged but it was too late. The horrible caller had hung up.

As the roller door began to rise, I thought I was going into cardiac arrest. At least I was already at the morgue. All they'd have to do was roll me out back into the coolroom. With no choice but to push the phone call to the back of my mind, I reversed the van successfully without backing into any medical waste bins or people. Trembling, I gathered paperwork, gloves and the stretcher. A post-mortem was in progress; I could smell it.

I approached the check-in window to submit the 'Permission to Release Deceased Persons' form and with a nod from the pink-haired admin lady, I was invited in to stand behind the yellow and black tape until my precious cargo arrived.

Creaky gurney wheels echoed from down the corridor, closing in the gap between Christopher and me as it approached.

'Heart attack,' said the pathologist's assistant as she handed the body over to my care. Christopher was in a blue body bag—safe to open. Once I was satisfied that the man lying before me was indeed Christopher by matching his wrist tags to the paperwork, I zipped up the body bag. Allocated the job on my own, I had to use the lifting device mounted to the ceiling. Slipping the straps under the man's knees and shoulders, all I could think about was the horrendous phone call. Once Christopher was strapped in, I stood back and pressed the button, watching him levitate. Blood seeped from his autopsy wound and his body bag and fell to the floor like red rain. With Christopher suspended in mid-air, I became faint; anxious from the abuse I had copped earlier. I didn't need this. Not now. I was doing so well. Struggling to remain calm and professional, I grabbed the multi-level funeral cot and positioned it beneath the young man so the device could lower him into place.

'See you again!' the assistant called out as I wheeled Christopher through the sliding doors towards the van.

'Have a nice day!' I replied, as if I had not received that awful call at all.

As if I wasn't about to break the hearts of my own parents.

As if I wasn't about to prep a young man whose heart had failed him.

But at least yours is beating, I said over and over to myself. *At least you're alive.*

* * *

Dad was on my mind when my phone vibrated in the pants pocket of my scrubs.

Well, speak of the devil.

Phones were prohibited on shift; I crouched down behind a wall of coffins and answered.

'Dad, hi.'

'Emma!' Dad's voice usually warms my body like red wine, but not this time.

'We have been trying to contact you! Emma, we have received a very unnerving phone call.'

The blood drained from my face. So it had actually happened. Someone actually felt the need to contact my parents and reveal my secret. Dad is an old-fashioned man. I shuddered at what was to come next.

'Emma, what is going on down there? Whoever it was that rang said you were working at a brothel.'

Dad didn't sound angry. Worse. He'd been crying.

'Dad! I am not working at a brothel.'

'Are you sure?' His voice was shaky with disappointment and fear. Oh, the fury burning through my veins. Some vindictive bitter soul thought it was their place to destroy the relationship I shared with my parents, and I wasn't sure how to fix this.

'Times might be tough, Em, but you really don't need to do this!'

Eyes landing on the power drill, I momentarily considered drilling a screw into my skull.

'Dad. I'm not going to lie. I have taken up dancing in a club in the evenings. I am broke, Dad! I'm trying to get back on top of things and on my wage alone, it's just too hard.'

Silence.

'Dad?'

'I have nothing to say, Emma Jane,' he said finally. 'All you ever have to do is ask if you need our help.'

'But Dad, I don't want to *have* to ask you! I'm 33 years old!'

Tears spilled down into the wood shavings on the ground.

'I wanted you and Mum to *offer*, just once! Or maybe fly down here and visit? I know you're busy, and flights from Queensland can be expensive at short notice, but I really have needed you guys!'

Great. Now I was blaming them.

'Nonsense!' Dad cried down the phone line, rattling my eardrum. 'You know we are here for you always!'

'I know,' I whimpered.

'I can't talk about this any longer. Just be safe. Your mother and I are very disappointed with you.'

The phone beeped in my ear.

'You okay, Em?'

Startled, I wiped my face and turned to find Murray by the tool bench in his tiny shorts.

'Yeah, I'm fine,' I lied, sniffling.

'You sure?' He frowned.

'Sure. I was, just ... trimming a coffin and I hit my finger with the hammer.'

'Jesus!' He moved closer and I stepped back.

'It's cool.' I slipped past him. 'I'll have your body prepped shortly. The funeral is at midday, right?'

'Yeah.' He nodded. I could feel him watching me as I disappeared into the one place no one could hurt me.

The mortuary.

* * *

The morning following the phone call with Dad, I distracted myself with cleaning the hearses. I hadn't slept a moment. Fighting tears, I reversed a Mercedes into the wash bay and grabbed a hose. Watching the dust stream down the custom-made windows, I wished I could wash away the pain I felt right down to my bone marrow. Suds rinsed, I worked my forearms into cramps, polishing the hearse with a chamois until the paintwork shone like mirrors.

The honour of washing the gleaming vessel that carried so many people on their final ride stopped me from breaking completely.

CHAPTER 39

NEW GUY

Freshly laundered bed linen embracing my tired limbs, I tucked the work phone beneath my pillow and switched off my lamp. I snuggled in, convinced the night would be uneventful. It had been a busy shift at the funeral home, surely enough people had died for one day.

Falling … to … sleep …

Riiiiiiiing!!! Riiing!!!

My eyes snapped open and I stared into the black towards my ceiling.

'Noooo!' I whined and squashed my pillow over my head.

Riiiiing!!! Riiiing!!!

There was no way out.

'Yep,' I mumbled.

'We have a transfer,' said my new on-call partner in his slight American accent.

Well, duh! Why else would you be calling me at 1 am?

The poor guy. Byron had only just started with the company a few days earlier and he was stuck with me. My previous on-call partner was used to my mumbling on the late-night calls, even bringing a blanket and a thermos of coffee for me when he picked me up. The roster had recently changed to accommodate new staff and I had been paired with Byron, an ex-military serviceman with biceps that threatened to break open his funeral director's suit. I muttered my address to him and dragged myself out of bed.

A puff of blush, slick of lip gloss and hair swept up in a messy bun, I slipped into my suit, kissed Cupcake on her strawberry-scented fluff and waited outside for the headlights. Before too long, the van pulled up, heavy metal blasting, and I jumped in. Sensing my grumpiness, Byron switched radio stations, smiling weakly at me.

'Sorry,' I said as I yawned, leaning back in my seat. 'Before midnight, I'm fine. After 12, you have to deal with a nightmare. Where are we off to?'

'South side,' he replied.

Over the next 15 minutes as we chatted about *MasterChef* and the soaring prices of fuel, I began to feel chirpier and by the time we reached the flashy home with porch lights glowing, I was ready to tackle our task.

A woman of Asian descent, around my age, met us at the front door. Holding onto the doorframe with tears streaming down her pale face, she pointed towards the bedroom down the hall.

'My father,' she said. 'He wasn't well for long time. He caught sun cancer from your sky here.'

Resting my hand on her quivering arm, I offered, 'We will take good care of Dad for you.'

I noticed how great Byron's hair looked even at this time of night, as we walked down the hallway, fried rice and soy sauce warming my nostrils. *He'll learn,* I thought to myself. *He'll skip the hair gel on these 3 am calls in no time.* I recalled the early days anticipating the late-night death call, my suit laid out, ready to go! Wearing a full face of makeup to bed, I looked fresh and professional at 3 am back then too.

These days the family probably thought *I* was dead when they met me at the front door. Eye bags and tousled hair, they were lucky I could construct a sentence.

We walked into the sprawling bedroom, where in a king-size bed lay a tiny man with a giant tumour growing from his face. His eyes had been taken over by the growth and all that could be seen was his small mouth, lips slightly parted and head rested to one side.

'I'll go get the stretcher,' Byron said softly. 'You do the paperwork.'

This was working out great already. Not even halfway through our first transfer, and Byron was taking the lead.

Bless.

The daughter of the deceased remained in the kitchen as Byron and I proceeded with the transfer. We fastened the name tags around Mr Quan's slim wrists, covered him gently with the sheet, and slid him from his plush mattress to our stretcher and into a body bag. As I tightened the straps around the man's chest, he gurgled loudly, sending Byron jumping back against a bedside table, knocking a glass of water to the floor.

'What the actual fuck!' he gasped. 'He's still aliiive!'

'Shhh,' I giggled, covering my mouth so the woman in the next room wouldn't hear us. 'It's totally normal.'

'Normal?' Byron's flustered face dripped with sweat. 'The dead guy is making noises, it can't be *normal*!'

GROOOOOOOOAN.

The moaning continued from inside the body bag.

'Fuck this!' Byron disappeared into the ensuite bathroom.

'Byron!' I whispered loudly. 'Come back!'

'No!'

Rolling off my gloves and tucking them into my suit pocket, I approached the new guy huddled by the toilet.

'Byron.' It was a struggle not to laugh. 'When a person dies there is still air trapped in the lungs, that is the moaning you can hear. Trust me. I promise Mr Quan is dead! Come on, let's get going, I'm tired.'

I held out my hand to the soldier on the tiles. He gulped and taking a grip, he joined me on his feet.

'I'm sorry,' he said and straightened his tie. 'It just kinda startled me. I really wasn't expecting that.'

'It's fine,' I chuckled, and together we wheeled the stretcher out into the night.

CHAPTER 40

AN UNLIKELY HEALING

I sat in my car and watched the staff car park clear out, waving to my colleagues as they skidded out onto the main road. I needed a few moments to recoup from the day before heading to the Cross. I needn't have worried about getting anywhere fast. Even with the fourth turn of the key in the ignition, the piece of shit wouldn't start.

'Dammit!'

It was about time I started stashing extra cash for a new car. I checked my reflection in the rear-view; with lines beneath my eyes, frizzy hairline and lips parched, I was far from looking like a showgirl who could afford a snazzy new vehicle. Nothing some concealer and red lippy couldn't fix. But I was tired. I considered cancelling my shift but knew a champagne and some pole dancing could do me good. I closed my eyes, said a prayer and turned the key one more time. It choked and spluttered but it resuscitated and we made it to the L&L by dusk.

Pauly was preparing the front entrance when I arrived, sweeping the stairs.

'Hi, Madison,' he said, smiling.

Madison!

Just hearing this made me smile. Tonight I was leaving Emma Jane and my shitbox car at the door. I was Madison now. With three coats of mascara, two layers of foundation and Napoleon Perdis Aphrodite lipstick, I'd paint Madison to life, take to the stage and twirl myself into character.

The stale scent of alcohol welcomed me and, to my surprise, I felt a sense of home. I hadn't worked at the club for a few nights and inhaling the blend of alcohol, perfume and fake tan, I realised I'd actually missed the place. My heart mushroomed as I approached the dressing room, hearing the dancers' chatter and hair dryers.

'Madison!' Sophia shrieked, wrapping me in a hug. 'So nice to see you! You look exhausted honey!' She tugged me towards her makeup station, a colourful spread of cosmetics across the illuminated bench. 'Let me fix that face of yours.'

Beck popped a glass of champagne in front of me as Sophia prepped my face with foundation primer.

'Big day at work?' Her mascaraed eyes gazed into mine. Her bare nipples almost touched my nose.

'Do I really look *that* tired?'

'It's fine,' she soothed. 'Hey, I have an idea! Why don't you come along tomorrow to my collagen appointment? We could smooth out some of those lines. And I'm getting my nails done …' She peered down at my chipped nails and hands callused from carrying coffins. I could definitely consider the fillers but I would have to skip the acrylics.

I longed for long nails like all the dancers, but they would get in the way at the funeral home. Drilling screws into coffin lids and feeding surgical needles through gums; long nails on a funeral director just didn't work. I did my best to hide my fingers at the L&L. Especially in lap dances. While the dancers seductively ran their glossy manicure over their bodies, I pushed my boobs into my client's face to distract him from my tattered hands.

Although I was the least glamorous dancer at the club, I was grateful for fake lashes and red lipstick. With big lashes, a red pout and a spritz of Chanel behind my ears, I felt pretty enough to share the dance floor with the others.

Conversational skills were my strength. The mandatory grief workshops for my day job had now come in handy when men cried into highball glasses, confiding in me about their personal life. My empathy filled my garter.

I never took drugs at work and limited my drinks to three during the night, keeping sharp and in control. Some dancers in the VIP lounge indulged in a few too many and the lap dance turned into a drooling nap. I didn't blame them—I was no good at lap dances extending an hour. I admired the dancers who were able to spend hours upon hours with a customer. I imagine their bank balances swelled as big as their customer's erections. I embraced the Thirty-Minute Dance. Begin with the small talk, allow enough time to strip down and show off the love-heart tattoo on my buttocks, a quick 'motorboat' and back to the stage. (Motorboat is an adult entertainer's term for shaking your breasts lightly and at speed across the man's face. Usually he makes a noise like a child does when they are playing with toy trucks, and muffled in the cleavage, it sounds like a motorboat.) I didn't mind chatting to my lovely customers but I was sure to reserve my mental energy for the funeral home. The families required my mind and heart; these guys were out for a good time and needed my bronzed glittery cleavage to forget their worries.

The less talking the better.

So motorboats all night long it is.

* * *

Waiting in the shadows stage-side, I recognised the contentment within me. The eight-inch stilettos on my feet brought comfort in the way mortuary gumboots did. Spotlights and vertical poles were teaching me there may be more to life than body bags and caskets. Taking to the stage, I twirled from one side to the other, my hair extensions fanning out behind me like a blonde shadow. The applause rattled the crystal chandelier as I climbed the pole using the strength built in my thighs from dancing. Squeezing my upper legs together, I sat at the height of the ceiling looking down at the men looking up at me. *Madison! Madison! Madison!*

'A customer booked us, for one hour!' Sophia hissed excitedly as I stepped down from the stage, holding onto her arm for support.

'Let me have a quick shower,' I puffed as she handed me the top I'd thrown into the crowd.

As the shower water sent streams of glitter down my torso, my mind wandered to my family and their disappointment with my second job as a dancer. I appreciated their concern but I had to dismiss the thought for now. My rent was ahead two months, bills were paid, not to mention the fabulous workout. I did, however, feel a stab of guilt for the bodies at the funeral home. Was I disrespecting them? Dancing at night and then the same hands that held onto a dancer's pole stitching and bathing them the next day?

I hoped they'd understand.

Dancing on stage and my new friends were becoming lifesavers.

My heart was healing with every pole trick I performed and every clap of applause.

CHAPTER 41

ADAM

A packet of Doritos and a can of bourbon were placed by the coffin. One by one, friends and family took a moment to place their special memento: science textbooks, stunt pegs and a work hardhat signed by colleagues. The deceased's beloved BMX bike gleamed at the front entrance of the chapel. Children sobbed, teenagers wailed and adults hid their eyes behind dark sunglasses.

Adam was a seemingly popular man, with over 250 mourners spilling from the chapel. He was much loved and already missed, and it was hard not to wonder why someone so loved would choose to end their own life. The overdose of heroin sucked the life right out of him, leaving behind his young wife and two toddlers.

'Where's Daddy?' one wept, pulling on the seam of his mother's dress.

With many songs scheduled for the funeral and a DVD slideshow of photos, it was my job to stay with the media controls, which I preferred on large services. This role offered a view of the entire chapel to watch the crowd. During the service, I struggled to hold back the tears when one of my favourite Australian groups, the Hilltop Hoods, rapped through the speakers. I looked away when Adam's daughter screamed out his name, making a run for the coffin.

* * *

On my way home that day, the afternoon radio presenters announced their names 12 times. Twelve times! I didn't mind their chatter really, I was stuck with it since the CD player in the dying RAV4 was broken, but their sense of their importance to the world made me think about the young man who was being cremated in that very moment. I looked at the drivers around me, barking to bluetooth devices, switching lanes hectically, beeping their horns.

Life continued as if Adam had never existed at all.

I was blessed to spend some time alone with Adam before his funeral. At A Touch of Comfort, we triple-checked *everything*, from the clothes the deceased was wearing to the coffin handles, and as I carried out this final inspection my eyes were locked to his gorgeous face and Bambi-long lashes resting on his cold cheeks.

Humble was a word frequently used in the six eulogies delivered by Adam's friends and family. *Quiet, gentle, generous and kind.*

The list went on and on.

I couldn't help but wonder … Was he told this while he was alive? Was he told how much he was loved? Admired? Cared about?

I flicked my indicator and exited the freeway, soon returning to the operations facility. The grounds were sparse and quiet. I swiped my security card and it beeped, allowing access. Once inside, I leant against the wall and cried for Adam, revisiting those horrible nights during my separation, screaming into my pillow, a bottle of red wine in my system, wishing my life was over. I wasn't brave enough to die by suicide. I've heard people say suicide is a coward's act. I think someone who decides to go ahead in that tragic last moment with a rope, gun, or by a cliff's edge, is the opposite of cowardly. I felt as though my life was over, yet deep down, my soul must have known it would be okay.

What imprisoned Adam to make him think there was no escape?

The operations facility was growing dark. I flicked on some lights and headed to the coolroom, the deep humming of the fridge warming me even though inside it was two degrees. I peered around at the 18 shelves of bodies in their body bags. Wispy grey hair snuck from the slight opening of one on the top shelf, blowing in the breeze of the air vent.

My eyes scanned the surnames drawn in marker at the head of the body bags …

Johnson …

Smith …

Peterson …

What sorts of cars did they drive? Did they have a large family? Had they died in an accident or suffered a long sickness? Did they own their homes or sip their tea from the cups provided by a nursing home? Did they get along with their spouses or struggle through divorces?

'Hey!'

'Jesus Christ, Byron!' I shrieked. 'You scared the living shit out of me!'

'Sorry,' Byron chuckled. 'What are you doing here? Don't you have a home to go to?'

'Yeah, I thought I left something in the mortuary.'

'You okay, though? You look like shit.'

'Gee, thanks mate!' I pushed him jokingly. 'Could have something to do with the fact you just almost gave me a heart attack!'

'Hey, aren't *I* supposed to be the one who is scared around here?' Byron winked, recalling the night of the gurgler. 'You're the veteran!'

'What are you doing here, anyhow?'

'I haven't left. I was on a late funeral, just doing my paperwork. It was a tough one too. Young kid, killed in a car accident.'

'Oh, I helped prep him.' I sighed, locking the fridge door on the boy. He was prepared inside and with most of his injuries internal, he looked like he was only sleeping.

'How do you do it, Em?' Byron asked as we walked. 'You know, actually *working* on them? It's one thing for me to fill out the paperwork, but the mortuary … I couldn't do it.'

'I only assist.' I shrugged, trying to act casual. 'At least I get out on transfers and funerals. Brenda never leaves her gumboots.' But maybe it *did* bother me. It was the reason I was back here after all. Because I was sad for Adam. 'Shit, look at the time!' I'd come to the funeral home to get away from the living. Not to be questioned by it. 'I gotta go, Byron. I'm really sorry. But we'll chat another time. We are on-call Wednesday night together, yeah?'

'Yeah.' He almost looked disheartened as I left. I sensed Byron liked me since catching his stare in the lunch room. And he went above and beyond for me while on night transfers, insisting on driving so I could rest in the passenger seat. Or maybe he knew how hopeless I was with road directions in the middle of the night. And there was also the Facebook friend request.

When the men at the Lace and Lipstick looked at me, I didn't mind. I was being paid after all. But outside the club, I wasn't so sure. A new relationship was the furthest thing from my mind.

CHAPTER 42

ASPARAGUS

A beauty therapist by trade, I never needed *help* with a beauty regimen. However, the lessons I learnt at the Lace and Lipstick I could never learn at any beauty school.

One Sunday morning after a profitable Saturday night at the club, Sophia and I went for breakfast in the city to celebrate. I felt fancy in Sophia's presence, wearing my oversized sunglasses and sundress as the wealthy dined around us. Pancakes were served with exquisite fruits and eggs served with champagne. Perfectly poised women with flawless manicures buttered their toast as if the condiment was worth diamonds, carefully and precisely to the edges. The glamorous diners ate their toast slowly, dabbing at their lipstick with huge, thick napkins. No paper serviettes!

'So,' Sophia grinned, her red curls swept up in a top knot. 'Let's talk pussy!'

A lady in Versace shades dropped her cutlery on the floor and coughed.

'Sophia,' I said, cringing.

'No, honey. This shit is real. Self-care is crucial in our industry. Don't get me wrong, you're hot as hell, but there is always room for improvement.'

Her French toast with a side of tropical fruits arrived as she poured us a glass of champagne and topped it with orange juice. It was breakfast, after all.

'You shave your pussy, yeah?'

'Yes.' I slunk into my seat, my cheeks burning.

'Scrap that. No more. Throw out the razor.' She waved her hands as if flapping away a buzzing insect. 'I noticed some in-growns while you were on stage. Taking you to get laser!'

'Laser?' I spluttered as the waiter sat my omelette in front of me.

'Cracked pepper, ma'am?'

'Sure, thanks.'

'Yep, a few blasts and you'll be hair-free forever. Oh! Do you use Femfresh or soap?'

That morning, to the disgust of fellow diners, Sophia taught me some beauty/body care tips that I do, and do not, recommend.

'Eating loads of salmon in olive oil' is great for the skin; *'Don't dare eat asparagus if you think you're going to have sex. Asparagus makes the vagina smell bad!'*

From pure glycolic as a facial mask to baby powder sprinkled in stilettos for fresh toes, Sophia gave me the 'rundown' on stripper beauty laws.

'Take care of yourself and you can rock that stage well into your forties, my love,' Sophia announced, nibbling on fresh mango. 'Would you believe I'm 45?'

* * *

Click!

I replaced the lid on the tube of mascara and dropped it into my makeup case. Hmmm, what else could I put on? Van had called the club ahead of my shift to book me over the phone. That's right, dancers can be booked over the phone the way you order a meal with Uber Eats. This is common practice with regular customers, who don't want to miss out on a lap dance from their favourite girl. Van had become one of my regular customers, and he was the only guy I would dance for in VIP for longer than an hour. Oddly, he didn't exhaust me like some men did. He didn't complain about his wife or his career, or boast about his money. In fact, I didn't even know if he had a wife. During our time together we chatted about T.S. Eliot, Edgar Allen Poe and our favourite band, Oasis. I made more of an effort with my makeup when Van was visiting. He was such a generous tipper and I was saving for that new car. I fumbled through my growing collection of foundation bottles, lipsticks and eyeshadows, deciding upon my latest purchase, a highlighter that smelt like fairy floss. With a dash of sweet-scented shimmer along the top of my cheekbones, I zipped up my makeup case and turned to face the change room, smiling to myself. The girls were chatting about their day completely naked in front of the body-length mirrors. A few girls by the corner of the change room were rubbing fake tan onto one another and comparing breast sizes.

'Mine are still hard!' the blonde complained as she fondled her recent additions. 'The doctor said I have to massage them every day to soften the capsule that forms around the implant.'

'I got my boyfriend to massage mine!' the brunette announced, proudly peacocking her large implants bulging from her glittery chest. 'Here, feel mine. See how real they feel?'

Two other girls had started since my name was added to the roster, and they were now the topic of conversation. Madison was old news and I was feeling far more relaxed in the dressing room. I even stood around starkers myself.

'Maddy!' Amy called out from the other side of the busy room. 'Can I borrow your mascara? Mine just ran out!'

'Of course!' I pulled up a seat next to her. We were growing closer, Amy and I. We knew every freckle on each other's figure. I guess it's only natural we bonded quickly, nestled in the dressing room among glitter and rhinestones. Side by side we painted ourselves into character in the glow of Hollywood-like globes framing the mirror. 'I remember the first time I ever wore mascara,' she said, her glittered tan shimmering. I watched as she applied mascara, lengthening and darkening the fair strands of hair that framed her piercing blue eyes. 'I couldn't believe this tiny cosmetic could dramatically change your appearance. That same day I cried, for whatever reason, and it smudged down my cheeks. How strange, I thought. Mascara can make you look beautiful, but also like a sad clown. Moral of the story: don't cry while wearing makeup.' She reached for the champagne bottle stashed in her backpack. 'Don't tell Beck I bring this in here, please! It's seven bucks from the bottle-o. They charge 40 bucks for a bottle in here—rip off!'

I'd only known Amy a couple of months, but I couldn't recall ever seeing her without a champagne flute in her manicured hands.

'I was wondering if you'd teach me to style my hair like yours?' I asked. I could apply makeup to dead faces perfectly, but I was hopeless at hairstyling. The very first day I ever had to set hot rollers in a corpse's hair, her leaking IV holes were the least of my worries. I spent an hour trying to curl the lady's hair, and even then, the head mortician had to fix them for me. I perform a killer mouth suture, but freak when the hair dryer is in my hand.

Amy clapped her hands together excitedly. 'Absolutely!'

Using a heated steel rod, Amy twisted and curled my clip-in hair extensions and sprayed what seemed like an entire bottle of hairspray on my glamorous style to set it.

'I don't even look like *me*!'

Amy laughed and I caught the first glimpse of the diamond stud in her tongue.

'Movie star!' Amy glowed triumphantly with her hands on her hips. 'Sophia!'

The red-haired beauty stopped in her tracks to look over at us.

'Yes?' She raised a perfectly groomed brow.

'Doesn't Madison look hot?'

Hot?

I looked pretty with a tonne of makeup, but hot? Wasn't that a term used to describe those gorgeous models in men's magazines? I was commonly described as cute. And I was fine with that. Everyone loves a cutie.

'Always.' Sophia's crimson lips curved in a smile as she winked at me and continued walking towards her locker.

'She likes you,' Amy whispered.

'Likes me?'

'Yeah! She told me that on your first night, she showed you how to perform a lap dance?'

I nodded.

'Well, let me just say, she really enjoyed doing so! She wants to sleep with you.'

She wanted to have a sleepover with cute pyjamas and Netflix?

'Don't tell me you didn't know.' Amy laughed, reaching for her sequinned dance costume draped on the back of her chair. 'Oh, my sweet Madison. You're so innocent and cute.'

Told you. Cute.

The friendship shared with Amy strengthened with each night at the club. The previous shift Amy confessed she naturally had very fair skin and her deep tan was thanks to a solarium that she used almost every day. Showing me a savage scar under her arm from an incident with her now-estranged father, she explained the gashes he used to leave on her pale skin were why she had become obsessed with tanning.

'My asshole father called me today,' she said, as if reading my mind. 'I hung up on him of course. I couldn't give the bastard the time of day, but you know what, Maddy?' Glass refill. 'I started today! I finally started goddammit! It's gonna happen!'

'Tell me!'

'My Gold Coast fund! I started saving! A new club opened up there. It's not a seedy strip club like the ones here. The dancers dress like real showgirls, with feather boas and headdresses—it's going to be amazing!'

'I am so happy for you, Amy.' I was genuinely happy for my friend, but couldn't deny a pinch of jealousy. I wasn't ready to lose her to the city of palm trees and ritzy avenues.

'Madison, come with me. We don't belong here. Sure, it's fantastic money, but we are wasting our talent here taking our clothes off for these drunk losers. You, me, together, we equal BIG TIME!' She shook my shoulders as if to wake me from the nap I wished I was taking. 'Come on, Maddy! You can't tell me that when you were a kid you dreamt of working in a bloody strip club with old guys drooling over your tits!'

I bit my lip.

Ummm, actually I did.

I didn't say that, of course. Well, the stage part. Not the drool on my breasts.

In that moment I really wanted to tell Amy about my day job and tell her that working at the strip club did not define me. I could barely decipher left from right when driving but I could assist the head mortician with a skull reconstruction. I didn't *fall* into the adult industry because I had no other choice. Well, okay, sort of. I was penniless and stressed, but I could have taken out a bank loan to try and clear some of my debt. I *chose* dancing because I'd dreamt of glitter, stage lights and cash since I was a young girl. Amy had no idea what she wanted to do with her life and I was genuinely a little worried about her health. She was a very heavy drinker.

There goes the funeral director in me again! Sigh.

Perhaps if I wasn't a mortician in the real world, her excitement may have come across as genuine and joyful. But I'd seen forced smiles on grieving families' faces as they arrived at funerals. I saw through those brave faces as they approached the chapel, holding themselves together but as soon as they saw the coffin or it was time to deliver the eulogy, they fell to pieces.

On stage and in the lap-dance room, Amy carried herself confidently in her heels with her lip-glossed smile, but my intuition warned me that once she went home, the smile dissolved into tears. I would know.

Looking down at my glassy stilettos, I thought, *What's the point in telling her everything? She's leaving anyway.*

'Come on, girls!' Beck blasted through the change room. In a figure-hugging dress and chewing on gum, she hurried us along to get out onto the main floor. 'There are some guys in the club already!' Her wide eyes darted over to Amy. 'Amy? Office?'

'Yes!' she squealed. 'I'll be right back, Maddy!' Amy skipped into the office and Beck closed and locked the door. The dancers noisily shut their lockers and raced out into the club just as Amy reappeared. She was noticeably moving about quicker than before and the pupils in her eyes had doubled in size. My heart sank as I realised they were obviously not counting cash in the office. They were snorting something.

Amy grabbed my arm and eagerly dragged me from the change room. 'Come on, Madison! Let's get a champagne and go on stage together, it'll be fun!'

CHAPTER 43

SOLARIUM

Amy stood at my front door in a light blue sundress just above her knees. Her face bare of makeup, she looked completely beautiful.

'Hey babe!' She blessed me with a sunny smile, leaning forward and hugging me. 'Ready for your big day?'

I had called in sick to the funeral home and Amy was taking me to her tanning salon. Working at a funeral home didn't exactly give me 'sexy skin' and when Amy rested her tanned hand on my ghost-white leg prior to fake tanning, we looked like an upside-down Top Deck chocolate bar.

The tanning salon was stifling and a loud humming filled the air, just like the body coolroom, but with no confronting decomposition, just sweet coconut and tanning lotion. The blue walls were broken up by posters of models sporting toned, bronzed bodies in swimsuits and framed autographs of body builders. Two guys, looking like heavyweight champions themselves, winked at us as they exited the salon. Even guys visited this place? I watched after them as Amy dragged me to the front counter. 'Sammy, this is Madison. Fix her skin, please!' she said to the attendant with a tan darker than her own. Sammy's blonde hair glowed like snow in the sun.

The bleached blonde smiled, flashing teeth as white as her hair.

'Actually,' I coughed. 'My name is Emma Jane.'

'I used to dance too. My stage name was Angel. Amy didn't call me by my real name for years when we worked together. It was always Angel this, Angel that, let me introduce to you my friend Angel!'

'Emma Jane has never used a solarium and we need to get her tanned and sexy. She needs to look like this!' Amy lifted her sundress revealing her slim dark thighs, lacy white G-string and toned stomach.

'Oh, I miss those days!' Sammy laughed. 'I miss taking off my clothes. I'm shutting up!'

I thought she was joking until she reached below the front counter and retrieved a small sign with *Back in 30 minutes* printed across the front. She hung the sign on the front door, turned the lock with a click then proceeded to peel off her denim shorts and tank top.

'Are … are we allowed …?' My voice locked in my throat.

'I own the place!' the bubbly blonde sang.

'Get undressed babe! We're gonna make you look like you just got back from Hawaii!' Amy tugged at my cargo pants.

Comfortable being naked at the Lace and Lipstick, I wasn't sure about taking it all off in a place of business other than a strip club. I had no choice however, as Amy tore my top off over my head. I followed Sammy's lead to a small room that consisted only of a machine that looked a giant, illuminated coffin.

'Once you get in, put on these goggles,' she instructed, handing me a pair of eyewear. 'I have set the timer, so all you need to do is lie back and relax! I will be in the solarium next door so if you have any problems just sing out. Here's some headphones, there is music connected to the solarium.' She leant into the machine and pointed to a small green button. 'Just press this when you're ready. Enjoy!'

And with that, she skipped out of the room. I took a deep breath, slipped in and pulled down the heavy lid. *I wonder if this is what it feels like to be in a coffin?* As artificial ultraviolet radiation cooked my flesh, my mind wandered. I felt guilty for calling in sick. I missed Albert, Murray and Macca, my new transfer partner Byron, and even Mags after just one day.

It didn't help that I was trapped in an enclosed, hot machine that roared loudly as it seared my skin.

What on earth was I doing, lying naked in this … *thing*, trying to be sexy?

When had looks become so important to me? I was making enough money at the club the way I was. But lately I'd wanted whiter chompers, prettier skin, mocha tan.

I chuckled to myself in disbelief, because if I didn't, I probably would have cried.

CHAPTER 44

FABULOUS TAN

'So, how's life treating you?' Byron steered the body van out onto the freeway, pat slides and stretchers thumping about in the back.

'Did you even strap the stretchers in?' I laughed out loud. 'Sounds like a party going on back there!'

We weren't 'loaded', thank goodness. Otherwise Mr Richards would have a few more bruises on his head than when he had died.

We were on our way to a hospital morgue and the sun was shining. The day had started off innocently enough, until I realised I was watching Byron change gears. *Even his hands look strong.* Since becoming a lap dancer, I found myself more attracted to this hunk every passing day. And knowing he might fancy me didn't help the situation. You know that popular phrase people use when checking out a hottie? *It doesn't matter where you get your appetite, as long as you eat at home.*

Well, I wasn't even eating. I hadn't been intimate in a very long time, and lap dancing was becoming foreplay to something that never eventuated. I found myself stupidly giddy when the ex-soldier was around. I often fumbled in his presence, placing the wrong flower arrangement on a coffin, and I never used to care what I looked like at the funeral home. Sure, I made an effort to look presentable, especially when meeting with families, but I never went out of my way to look great. Ever since Byron and I had been paired up as partners for body collection duties, I found myself adding that extra coat of lip gloss, that extra five minutes on the hair, an extra spritz of hairspray …

I was quite happy being ugly, thank you very much!

'You look great,' Byron said, smiling. 'You're glowing!'

It's the solarium, I thought to myself, darting my eyes to the paperwork in my lap.

'Are you seeing someone?' Byron teased. 'You can tell me, I'm your work husband!'

'Well, husband, you're supposed to turn right!'

'Shit!'

Byron reversed the van to the morgue roller door and in sync we jumped out and headed to the back. Byron fetched the stretcher and I grabbed the gloves and pat slide.

Byron was right. It *was* like we were bloody married! I envisioned a couple who had been married for years at the breakfast table in comfortable silence, swapping newspaper sections once the other had finished the headlines as they nibbled on their toast.

* * *

We visited morgues all over the city every day. The bigger hospitals had a morgue attendant given the high volume of funeral directors reversing in to take the deceased into their care. It was no different to the mortuary back at the funeral home.

The smaller hospitals didn't have staff sitting by the morgue roller door waiting for us. Instead, we had to lock up the van and wander upstairs to the hospital reception to hand in our 'Permission to Release Deceased Person' form and request a warden or security guard to assist us down in the morgue.

There was one particular hospital in the city I found a little unsettling. The reception desk was located on the maternity ward. Waiting in line I subtly covered the funeral home logo on my name tag so the new mothers and visitors with armfuls of balloons didn't notice a funeral director was in their presence. Babies screaming, new mothers glowing with glee; I'd observe the commotion around me. I was about to collect someone who had exited life while others were celebrating the entrance of it.

'I'm from A Touch of Comfort funeral home,' I'd whisper. We'd offer our paperwork in exchange for a death certificate like a secret drug deal. Swerving through parades of 'It's a Girl!' 'It's a Boy!' balloons and newborns, we'd return to the body van.

Pregnant bellies and balloons aside, the hospital transfer was straightforward. A brief chat to the morgue attendant, a cross-check of the wrist tags, transferring the body from the tray to our stretcher and we were done. Music turned up, we headed back out onto the busy road and returned to everyday life.

* * *

This particular day, there was more movement in the morgue than usual.

Two male wardens were standing by the morgue register. There was a hospital bed just inside the fridge to the side, a sheet covering a lifeless body. I could see out of the corner of my eye, as one of the men glanced at his watch and recorded *10.55 am* in the 'Time of Death' column. I looked down at my watch. This poor soul had died only 15 minutes earlier. When Byron and I had jumped into the van half an hour ago, the person beneath the sheet was still breathing.

The warden clicked his pen and slipped it into his pocket and they waved to the morgue attendant, disappearing back to the ward.

'Right!' The attendant snapped on her gloves. 'Who are we after?'

I handed her the 'Permission to Release Deceased Person' form with Mr Richards' name on the dotted line.

'Bed seven!' She pointed, looking over her glasses. As Byron and I rolled our stretcher into the morgue, I touched the sheet briskly as we passed the hospital bed. I could feel the warmth from the body through the material.

'Melanoma!' The morgue attendant called out as if reading my mind. 'Too young, only 40! Tanning kills ya! It ain't worth it. I hope that tan of yours is from a bottle!'

She peered over her specs at my recently cooked skin.

'From a bottle.' I grinned through my teeth.

As funeral directors we typically take care of those who died a few hours earlier. That day in the morgue was the first time I had been in the presence of someone who'd died only minutes earlier.

We approached bed seven and unzipped the body bag, identified Mr Richards, then we slipped the pat slide under the body and gently pulled him over onto our stretcher.

Before we had even left the morgue, the attendant proceeded to fill the new space with the patient who'd died at 10.55 am, who I guessed beneath the sheet had a fabulous tan.

CHAPTER 45

THE DEATH WARDROBE

What would the outfit be for today?

A suit?

A sundress?

A tutu perhaps?

I wasn't searching my own wardrobe. Each family of the dead supplied the funeral home with a final outfit for their loved one, and these hung collectively in what I called the Death Wardrobe. The Death Wardrobe had become one of my favourite places in the funeral home; dressing the dead was a special and important step in the preparation process

On that particular morning I was searching for the soccer jersey to dress a young man. I located the clothing his parents had provided, next to a bathrobe that smelt of cigarettes. *'We didn't wash it,'* the family had said, handing over the tobacco-stained robe. *'She loved her Winnie Blues and always smelt of smokes.'*

While bathing the young man, I couldn't help noticing the tan lines on his muscular body, indicating a love for the sun. My fingers lost in his thick blond hair as I washed it, I wondered if he was a surf lifesaver as well as a soccer star. The head mortician was on her lunch break, leaving the young man and me alone, the hum of the coolroom our only companion. So I spoke to him: 'I'm so sorry this happened to you. You truly are beautiful.'

Hair and skin towel-dried, it was time to dress him.

I slid the young athlete's soccer shorts up his strong tanned legs, and tucked his bottom into them using my newfound strength in my lower back and thighs. My body became a helpful tool in the mortuary. Lots of squatting, leaning and lifting; I'd never need to attend Zumba classes again.

In the bottom of the coathanger bag was a soccer ball. I'd place this in his arms once I lifted him into his coffin using the lifting machine secured to the ceiling.

I'd freshly shaven the man, so in order to prevent skin burn from the coldness of the fridge where he'd be kept until his service the following day, I saturated his strong jawline in Kaolin cream, a thick mortuary lotion.

Each outfit in the Death Wardrobe told a story. Sure, the death certificate may state that Grandma Fran suffered cancer for three years but it doesn't disclose her favourite colour.

All was revealed in the Death Wardobe. Favourite colours were unveiled, hobbies and passions divulged. One day I was required to tuck a sketchbook and a pencil case bulging with crayons into the coffin of an artist. You couldn't tell he was an artist by looking at him. The clothes and belongings in the Death Wardrobe brought a life … *back to life.*

I recall the time I was confronted with a pretty young woman who'd died by suicide. She had blue-dyed hair and several facial piercings. Expecting a torn T-shirt with *METALLICA* printed across the front, I was surprised to discover a ballerina's tutu.

Then there was the old man who had terrible mouth hygiene, his teeth loose in my gloved hand as I tried to suture his mouth. I wasn't sure what to expect when I fetched his burial outfit, but was surprised to find a Bart Simpson beanie and matching undies.

When I was married and living in a large home, the giant walk-in robe was brimming with high heels, dresses, skirts, the most expensive and stylish ensembles. A rainbow of fabrics and more glitter and sequins than at the Lace and Lipstick. I'd left the marital home with none of it because I could only fit a few things into the car, and I had convinced myself clothes didn't matter. I missed my Louboutins for a long time. All this time later, I'd never had the motivation, or the cash, to rebuild my wardrobe from scratch. You can't buy Spice Girl-inspired pump shoes anymore, anyhow. Now all I owned were piles of adult costumes reserved for the L&L.

Looking down at the soccer player, I decided maybe it was time to go shopping for regular clothes, just in case something happened to me in the near future.

The dead can't talk, so their outfits do.

And if I didn't add a few items to my wardrobe soon, I feared my loved ones would have nothing to dress me in but stripper outfits if I died.

And that would be a Death Wardrobe of its own, shocking my family into early graves.

CHAPTER 46

REAL LIVE DATE

'Call him. He will be able to help you out.' Beck winked, slipping me a pink sticky note with a phone number scribbled on it. Apparently Beck's brother was a car salesman, when he wasn't working on Wall Street in New York. Or cooking in top restaurants. Apparently Beck's brother was a chef, a banker, sold expensive cars, and was very wealthy. He had also been to the club a few times to visit Beck, and apparently I'd caught his attention and he'd asked his sister to hook up a dinner meeting with me.

'He loved your cheeky smile,' Beck giggled, pinching my cheeks.

'It's chubby, Beck. Not cheeky.'

'Just promise me you'll call him. Go out for dinner with him while he's in town. It can't hurt! He will be able to help you get a new car.'

Beck had heard my shitbox gurgle at the end of shift. And my whining.

Stuff it, I thought. What did I have to lose? I could actually go on a real live date. Those things that happened to people except me, involving a dinner table and flowers. It had been too long and I found myself missing date nights. I enjoyed getting dressed up and chatting over wine and menus, and was watching Jennifer Aniston in *He's Just Not That Into You* on repeat far too often. Turns out you actually have to socialise to get asked out on a date, but my life consisted of work. So, I found myself calling Beck's brother Stanley, and that weekend we were chatting over garlic-buttered scallops.

The topic of conversation hovered heavily around high-end automobiles and money, however, which was disheartening. I cringe when people boast about money. I wanted to hear about New York City! Did he see Sarah Jessica Parker regularly, strutting through Manhattan with her heels click-clacking on the pavement? Did diners really offer endless cups of drip coffee with burgers and fries?

Sadly, I didn't find out what a gypsy cab was or whether Madison Square Garden actually had gardens. Stan the Man kept talking about how he could help me buy a new car. My first date post-separation was not turning out to be very romantic. No getting-to-know-you questions. I wasn't even sure if he remembered my real name once I'd told him, as he kept calling me Madison.

He offered to take me car shopping while he was here from the Big Apple, insisting I couldn't visit car yards alone as I might get ripped off. And once we found the perfect set of wheels, he would help pay for it. If we couldn't find something *I deserved*—his words, not mine—he would lend me his Alfa Romeo to drive while he was away on business. No strings attached, he simply wanted to help me.

At the beginning of the evening, I'd hoped maybe there would be a few strings. He was good-looking and his cologne alone had me excited in places I'd forgotten. I really wanted to explain I wasn't interested in his money—I was craving intimacy and if someone didn't help me soon, I would end up kissing Byron at work which would be a total disaster. I imagined us sneaking kisses behind coffins and making out in the mortuary fridge. No. It just couldn't happen.

So since Byron was out of the question, and I had no other guy's phone numbers in my phone, maybe I could set my sights on Stanley. Maybe I could move to Manhattan. Wouldn't that be an unexpected turn in this story?

We had to get through our first date first though.

I noticed Stanley didn't have a single sneaky hair poking from anywhere on his body, not even his fingers. The funeral directors I worked with all had random sprouts from their ears and knuckles. And some clients I danced for had hair piling out from the tops of their shirts. Stanley seemed hair-free, except for the groomed dark hairstyle on his head. I wondered if he visited a beauty salon. I forced myself back to the present, away from picturing him naked on a waxing bed.

'So, you're a fabulous dancer,' he grinned over his champagne glass.

'Thanks.' I felt myself blush. 'It is something new for me, but I do feel like it comes naturally to me, oddly.'

'You're certainly a natural,' he smiled, reaching into his suit pocket. 'Talking of the club, I have a gift for you.'

Stanley grinned as he slid an envelope across the satin tablecloth.

'A gift?'

I tore open the envelope and four green notes dropped onto the table.

'Stanley, that's 400 dollars!'

'I know you cancelled your shift at the club to go to dinner with me tonight. I wanted to compensate for the money you could have earned.'

So let me get this straight. This guy is paying me to go on a date with him.

'Okay … well, I'm not sure I can accept this money, Stanley. I *want* to have dinner with you. I don't want you to pay me this evening.'

'I understand, my dear. But I don't want you to miss out on money because of me.'

'I really can't accept this.' I hoped I didn't offend, as I slid the envelope back across the table.

'That's odd,' he said, his expression distant as he tucked the envelope back into his pocket. 'I thought all dancers would love to take the money.'

I tried not to choke on my scallop. Was that a generalisation or what?

The poor guy. I'm sure he meant well. He was trying to be nice and helpful I suppose, but he had the wrong girl. I respected Beck, and since he was her brother, I couldn't exactly stand to my feet and leave the restaurant. My main hadn't arrived yet and I was hungry.

Hmmm. I dabbed at my lips with a napkin. Maybe I could get *him* to leave, then no one would be hurt! And his uneaten entrée looked tasty. If he left, I could eat his too.

So far, on the occasional night I did head out in the city to a bar, I'd learnt guys were either fascinated or horrified when I told them the hands holding the drink they just bought for me, touched dead people during the day. So, hoping Stan would be horrified, I decided to tell him that I had spent most of my day elbow-deep in a reopened Y-incision to help the mortician remove a containerful of blood clots from an abdomen.

Okay, perhaps I'd withhold the gory details.

'So, Stanley. *Darling.* I have something to tell you. I have a day job.'

'Oh? Well, that's great! It wouldn't surprise me you have some sexy profession once you kick off those stilettos. Let me guess … hmmm.' He theatrically rubbed his chin looking upwards, pretending to be deep in thought. 'Oh, I know! You're a nurse. Oh God! I can't even handle the thought of you in scrubs. Or a nurse costume … oh dear! Maybe we should skip dinner and head straight to dessert?' He winked.

'Well, you're pretty spot-on with the scrubs.'

'You're a nurse? I was right?' His eyes widened and he looked rather impressed.

'Darling, I'm a mortician.'

The suave waiter placed Stanley's main meal of lobster salad in front of him.

'Pepper, sir?'

Stan failed to answer.

'A mortician? Like, you work on stiffs?' He squirmed in his seat once the waiter left the table.

'Well, yeah. I prefer to call them "the deceased". But, yes. I work on stiffs.'

'Beck never mentioned that,' he mumbled, looking down at his lobster. 'Anyway, let's not talk about that.'

It didn't look like he was leaving.

My prawn fettuccine arrived and the pasta looked silky in the white cream sauce.

I gazed over at the handsome man, knowing it would be the only date we'd share. I devoured the prawns slowly, absorbed the glorious view and flowing wine. Since I'd never see him again, I had to enjoy the moment while it lasted.

I didn't need a new car that badly. In fact, I probably didn't even need a new car at all. Maybe it just needed a service.

CHAPTER 47

DATING ADVICE FROM THE STRIP CLUB

Dressed in my new flamingo pink dancer's set, I sat at the back of the club observing the scene unfolding before me. I watched Ted, one of our regular patrons, always the first to arrive right on opening time. He owned a chain of news agencies and loved to chat to the girls, although he never bought a lap dance. Some girls believed he was married and simply enjoyed the attention before he headed home to be with his wife, others insisted that no woman could love a man that resembled a goblin. He sold magazines and books for a living, so of course I found him interesting. On quiet nights, we often chatted about Charles Bukowski and Virginia Andrews, discussions I couldn't imagine having with the dancers, who preferred *Vogue*.

Then there was Charlie. Charlie was a weekend regular, and hilarious. His high-pitched laugh could be heard from within the lap-dance area, over the thumping dance music.

He had fuzzy orange hair and a small protruding beer belly he somehow carried well, and I chuckled to myself watching him amble in through the doors. Charlie also never booked the ladies for a lap dance. He stood at the end of the bar chatting mainly to the bartenders, tipping them rather than the performers. He was the guy you retreated to if you were having a tough night.

Not making tips? Charlie would tell a corny joke and make you laugh so hard you'd almost fall off your stilettos. A client broke the rules in a lap dance? Charlie'd buy you a drink, a double-shot, and give you a hug. And you'd have to linger in the embrace to hold him back from swiping the culprit. Weekends were packed and Pauly, our main security guard, was usually flat out at the entrance checking IDs and refusing entry to overly intoxicated patrons. Charlie was the unofficial bouncer on these nights. He cared for us girls like we were his family.

I watched a couple of dancers flutter around the room. It was early in the evening, not many guys to hustle, so most girls sat in the shadows waiting for the rush. I noticed two dancers in one another's laps, gazing lovingly into each other's eyes. I had seen this before, and assumed they were simply best friends, but I almost fell off my stool when Heaven and Candy started making out. I even felt a twinge of jealousy. They had more action than me and from the same gender.

Amy stepped down from the stage and headed towards the change room. I was seeking answers, so on her glittery heels I followed.

Thankfully, we were the only ones in the change room. Well of course we were, the others were too busy making out on the floor.

'So, I went on a date the other night.' I took a seat by Amy as she dabbed at the sweat beads on her face with a towel.

'You did?' She paused. 'Why didn't you tell me?'

'I am telling you, right now.'

'Tell me everything!' She plopped beside me, topless. 'Wait! I need a drink first.' She retrieved the bottle she'd snuck into the club, refilled her glass, poured me one into a random empty glass stained with lipstick, then popped the bottle back in her backpack.

'Where did you go? What does he look like? I need to know juicy details!'

'Well, actually …' I really wanted that champagne, but decided not to drink from the dirty glass. 'I actually want *you* to tell me everything.'

'How so?' She furrowed her brows, throwing back her drink.

'Maybe you can tell me why some guys only want to date dancers, and only by paying them.'

'Ohhh! Okay, first rule. Never date a guy from the club.' She hiccuped. 'When they come here, they aren't who they are on the outside world. We are their fantasy, ya know? We are paid to be a listening ear with no judgement. They pay us for a service. The club is a place to escape their real lives. You can't date a guy who came in here for a fantasy. They eventually see what you look like without the fake lashes. You will start to love him for seeing you without fake lashes, and a relationship will start to develop built on fake lashes. You see where I'm going here?'

'Umm, no.'

'Maddy. None of us are *this* out *there*. And neither are our patrons. They are paying us to entertain them! I love the guys, but really, shouldn't they be at home spending that money on their wives or girlfriends? You want to meet a guy the traditional way, you know, like on a dating website.'

'Uh, Amy, dating websites aren't traditional ...'

'And most of all, NEVER date a regular. You'll get into trouble and trust me, they stop visiting you at the club. Once you have allowed them to see you for free, the money stops rolling in from them. I've been in the game a long time. So, tell me about your date?'

'Never mind.' I kissed her cold cheek and watched her adoringly, as she tried to dress herself.

'How much have you had to drink tonight?' I chuckled, helping her with her top.

'It's my birthday week,' she giggled. 'I'm allowed to!'

'Okay, well if I help you get dressed, can you tell me why so many dancers are attracted to women? Remember when you told me Sophia liked me more than a friend?'

'Oh! I actually have a theory. I think they were gay *before* they entered the industry. That's why they are so darn good at their job! They don't mind that men can be on their worst behaviour here ... it doesn't tarnish their view of men, because they are not interested in them in the first place. Faced with naked girls and lap dances, their sexuality is confirmed, and ta-da! Romance in the locker room. Or there are some girls who may have been straight before becoming a dancer, and seeing men in their worst state has turned them off. That's the price we pay, right? We earn great money but let's face it, we don't see men in the greatest light. I can see how dancers get turned off men. It's sad though, because they forget men don't always act that way.

I salute their bravery. It must take a lot of guts to come in here, I reckon.'

She was one wise girl, but I wondered how many saw it. She didn't talk too much about her personal life, just the small snippets she offered about her estranged father. I concluded perhaps she didn't have many friends and family outside of the club. Beyond the champagne-hiccups, she only spoke with wisdom if one stopped to listen.

'Are we going back out there?' She offered her arm. 'It should be getting busy now.'

'Yes.' I tucked my arm in hers, my bracelets jangling. 'I have to find out whether I'm gay or not!'

We laughed together as we headed out onto the floor, into the glitzy fantasy world that was now a huge part of my life, and I was rather enjoying it.

My dating life may have been starving like a funeral director who has missed a lunch break, but my friendship with Amy was flourishing, and who needs a man when you have amazing friends? I didn't need a man right now, I decided, as my turn to take to the stage arrived.

I was a fantasy and I could be okay with that for the time being.

CHAPTER 48

DRESSING ROOM

The intelligence of the exotic dancers was greatly underestimated. But I could see why adult entertainers gained a stigma. Someone visiting the club for the first time might have mistaken a dancer for being a tipsy ditz, but dealing with drunk men every night was draining. A champagne or ten was warranted at times. These ladies had become my friends and I'd had enough of the taboo. I know of housewives opening a bottle of wine at 2 pm before the school run. What was the difference?

Since becoming an adult entertainer, I'd discovered those considered 'put together' in society were hiding addictions. One client of mine who worked in one of the most reputable companies in the country, confessed that some of his colleagues snorted cocaine from their swanky desks to get through the day, but their addictions weren't as 'dark' or as controversial as a stripper's.

We need to stop with the finger pointing.

My fellow dancers were *real* women, with dreams and goals and children. What was so awful about a woman realising her beauty and using this as a means to feed her child? To save for a house deposit? I dedicate this chapter to the adult entertainers.

Sugar. A blonde bombshell known as Sugar brought more to the club than fairy-floss perfume and a gorgeous smile. An aspiring fashion designer, Sugar created her stage outfits by hand. Her weekends were spent shopping at fabric stores and sewing. Changing multiple times a night to parade her talent, when Sugar was on the floor we had no chance of holding a patron's attention. The last I heard, she was accepted into design school and selling her dance outfits on social media. Go girl!

Pepsi. Pepsi was only months from graduating medical school. My understanding is, since she was not yet an Australian citizen she was not eligible for financial assistance for her studies. So she danced to cover the astronomical fees to be paid upfront each semester. It was not unusual to find her pretty nose stuck in thick medical textbooks. I even helped her prepare for exams one night in the dressing room. I quizzed her using her textbook questions; this girl was the real deal. She knew every piece of cartilage in the body.

Another dancer who comes to mind is a lady who called herself Chelsea. I had been working at the Lace and Lipstick for almost six months. I'd heard Monday nights were quiet, but there was opportunity for great money as some 'out-of-towners' would come in following corporate dinners. I hadn't worked a Monday and thought I'd give it a shot. But the floor was empty and I was scolding myself for swapping my flannelettes for glitter. I headed into the dressing room to scroll the socials on my phone to kill some time, when I noticed a new girl.

'Hi!'

'Hello.' Her eyes darted from her phone for a moment.

'I'm Madison.'

'My name is Chelsea.' The brunette smiled half-heartedly. She needed no red lipstick or fancy winged liner; sex appeal oozed from her thick mane and fierce cheekbones.

'Where are you from?'

'Far away from here,' she said, smiling.

That quiet Monday night, we chatted about what had led us to the stage at the Lace and Lipstick. We even ordered Uber Eats and ate dumplings and noodles, cross-legged on the dressing-room floor. A stripper's picnic. Nothing quite like it!

'I wanna tell you something,' Chelsea eventually announced. 'I know we've only just met, but I really feel I can tell you this.'

'Of course.'

'I don't usually look like this,' she said and grinned, patting her tummy. 'Madison … I'm having a baby.'

'You're having a baby?' I screeched.

'Shhh,' she laughed, covering my mouth with her pretty hands. 'No one must know! I am only here for a few weeks.'

'This is so beautiful!'

Chelsea sighed. 'I'm just in a sticky situation with my ex. And as well as that, I have so many things I need to buy!' She put aside her noodles and cradled her face in her hands.

I too, put down my dumplings and reached for her hands. 'Chelsea, you're going to be great. Look how hard you're already working for your beautiful bub. He or she isn't even here yet, and look what you're doing to ensure they have a wonderful life.'

'It's a girl.' Chelsea's eyes met mine, her smile restored.

I'd always considered the dancers' dressing room as the most interesting place. At the beginning of the night, I'd never expected that I'd be ending it becoming friends with a stranger and sharing Chinese, next-to-naked on the dressing-room floor.

'My real name is Emma Jane by the way,' said the beauty as we gathered our belongings at end of the shift.

'What? You're shitting me, right?'

'Ummm, no. Why?'

'*My* name is Emma Jane!'

'Oh my God! So cool!' We hugged.

I never asked Emma Jane for her phone number. I assumed I'd see her the following shift and my heart sank when I never saw her again. I attempted to find her, but with staff details confidential, it seemed she'd pirouetted out of my life forever.

'I don't think stripping is for her,' Beck said, shrugging, when I asked where Emma Jane had gone.

Chelsea was just an ordinary woman, working hard to earn money for her baby. Sugar's fashion designs will be presented in department-store windows. Pepsi is likely diagnosing the sick right now.

Dancers are just regular—actually, extraordinary—ladies who walk down the street, shop at the grocer, stand in line with us at the chemist. Just like Death, exotic dancers are all around us. I pine for the day society stops turning their noses up at the adult industry. I wish for people to not be so quick to judge a woman just because she dresses in sequins after dark.

CHAPTER 49

AMY

Amy was a terrible liar.

The sexy bottom lip bite. While hustling the club's patrons for a lap dance, her mouth would instead produce a hiccup. I'd be hustling at the same table of course, and we'd quickly down our drinks looking at one another over our twinkling champagne flutes with laughing eyes, because the drunken men hadn't noticed her little burp.

Sauntering up to the pole acting sexy. I'd always be the one to catch her trip. I couldn't help but laugh, and she'd give me the finger from the stage—yes, in front of everyone—and laugh too.

In the lap dance room, she'd writhe and grind in men's laps. But when it was time to remove her G-string with the clips at her hips, she'd fumble. Tsk-tsking loudly, she'd stand up and muck around with those glittery clasps until she finally dropped the G-string the regular way to step out of the underwear. All the dancers wore G-strings that unclipped at the sides. It worked well with our lap dances, as we were rather talented at removing the tiny piece of material with one hand for our unsuspecting audience: ta-da! In one surprise movement the final piece of thread on our bodies was gone.

Except for Amy.

Amy stumbled on this move every single time.

Then one night a guy broke the most important rule in the club. Amy had her back turned to her client, and performed the move we all do once naked: reach for the floor. For a few seconds we placed our hands on the sticky carpet and admired our rhinestone manicures before standing back up with a dramatic hair flick. This particular time, while Amy had her butt in her client's face, he swept his hands right up her thigh and touched her between the legs.

'What the fuuuck?' Amy's scream topped the pounding dance music. She flew around to slap him and I've never seen a grown man run so fast. He leapt from his seat and before he could escape the lap-dance room, Amy took one of her nine-inch stripper heels and pegged it at his head. It missed, thankfully, otherwise I'm sure with the force of her throw and the point of her heel, I'd have seen him on the mortuary table the next day. It did whack him in the back though. Loudly. Amy, however, forgot she was still wearing one shoe and began to run after him, but the shoe-less foot had a long way to the ground compared to her stilettoed foot, and she face-planted in the middle of the lap-dance room with her bum in the air.

Yes, even when trying to be tough, Amy made me laugh.

Amy was always herself. She never lied to anyone. She couldn't if she tried. She hardly contained her goofy personality while attempting to remain in seductive character for an eight-hour shift.

* * *

By the time I met Amy, I'd experienced my fair share of partying. I'd secured myself an apartment in the middle of the city in my early twenties; my grocery store was next door to a nightclub and I zig-zagged through drunken queues just to buy bread and milk. When attempting a quiet night in, the rumbles of surrounding club music rattled the spoon in my ice-cream bowl. I'd try to resist, but I swapped ice-cream scoops for lipstick, joining the sweaty dance floors. Yes, I'd had enough cocktails and whiskeys (neat) to last a lifetime when I crossed paths with Amy.

But the pretty dancer, bless her soul, offered a level of partying I thought was reserved for Hollywood's Viper Room. Charlie Sheen and Lindsay Lohan, eat your heart out.

'Snoop Dogg is in town at the weekend!' Amy squealed one night in the dressing room, hugging me with such force I dropped the fake lashes I was trying to apply to my eyelid. 'I bought us tickets!'

That weekend, I arrived at Amy's apartment in my little black dress and Doc Martens. I'd clipped a pink hair extension to my hair for a flash of colour; I had glitter on my eyelids.

'*What* the fuck are you wearing?' said Amy when she answered the door. She wore a snapback cap backwards, an oversized tee and jeans torn at her knees. 'We're going to a hip-hop concert. Not a disco. Get in here, you idiot.'

It was like a scene from the nineties movie *Clueless*, where cool girl Alicia Silverstone transformed the geek played by Brittany Murphy. Half an hour later, I swept through the lobby of the apartment building hand in hand with Amy, dressed like Missy Elliot complete with a chunky gold chain and hoop earrings so heavy my ears ached for days afterwards.

A group of Amy's non-dancer friends waited for us at the stadium entry gates.

'Hey girl!' They fist pumped, hugs and kisses aplenty. 'Whaassup?'

'This is Madison,' she introduced me excitedly. They hugged me as if we'd been friends for years too, complimenting my hoops. During the performance, the air was heavy with weed haze from not only the audience but the superstar himself. Between songs he reached for the joint offered by stage crew, and he continued performing with his eyes tiny slits. Amy held me from behind most of the concert, dancing against me with her slim solarium-tanned arms slipped around my waist. I was totally in love with her, the moment, the music … actually maybe it was just the weed. No, I was definitely in love with her.

Afterwards we headed to an afterparty held in a city penthouse. A huge standalone spa overlooked the glittering city horizon, and one of Amy's friends had Snoop Dogg playing on the sound system to continue the hip-hop festivities.

'I can't believe we just saw fucking Snoop Dogg!' They danced around, retrieving bottles of gin and vodka, whiskey and schnapps from a cupboard. They'd checked into the room earlier in the day and prepared for the party that would go on well into the morning.

At some point, a few of us were seated around the table playing some card game, when Amy turned to me and uncurled one of her hands to reveal a cluster of what looked like dried potpourri. It looked just like the pouches of lavender we left behind on the pillow after transferring the dead from their beds.

'Mushies,' Amy giggled.

I had no idea what they were, but she looked excited, I felt safe, and what could be so wrong with these herb-looking things? They weren't pills made up of crazy dangerous substances. These had been harvested from a garden and dried, it seemed, so I threw them in my mouth the same time as Amy did. It was like crunching on a dry Weet-Bix, but I managed to swallow them and continued playing the game … whatever it was. Or maybe we weren't playing a card game at all. Because a short time later, I noticed the walls had begun to grow grass. *Wait. What?* The cream-coloured walls had a garden of grass crawling from the floor right up to the ceiling, with cartoonish flowers blossoming and showing off their psychedelic petals. I blinked hard, and gulped. Was that a butterfly? And … *a waterfall?*

Okay, I was tripping.

Literally.

Suddenly, Amy's friends' faces morphed into the hip-hop artists I had seen earlier at the concert and they began braiding my hair. But when I reached for my new braids to feel them, they were gone and I realised they had never braided my hair at all.

'I'm … going to bed …' Amy whispered to me at one point, and I wanted to ask her if she was okay and if I could go with her, but my jaw was locked and I was on my back suctioned to the ground, unable to look away from the rainforest blooming around me.

I'm not sure how long it was until I managed to crawl into the bedroom where Amy was huddled in bed, the blankets pulled up to her cheeks. I found her big blue eyes darting around the room at whatever it was that she could see.

'Amy, I'm here …' I think I said. It's what I wanted to say anyway. I crawled into the bed with her and pulled her in close.

'I'm so sorry,' she whimpered. 'I had no idea it'd be like this.'

'It's all good.' I think I chuckled and then I lay down next to her. Our heads touched, our cheeks flushed, we hugged and hugged and hugged watching birds, bees and butterflies flutter about us.

Thinking back now, even if we hadn't been tripping, I think it would have felt like a version of utopia to be hugging her all night anyhow.

CHAPTER 50

MADISON

I guess it seems hypocritical of me to defend the adult industry and the beautiful souls twirling within it, when I kept Madison secret the whole time.

Growing up, Mum and I weren't exactly close.

When I was in high school she told me she was my parent, not my friend, and this stuck with me like fake-eyelash glue. She wasn't the one to turn to when a boyfriend crossed my name out from the love heart on his textbooks. She was the one I turned to for tuckshop money and a signature on permission slips. We loved one another with our whole hearts, but let's just say, Mum wasn't going to be the first person introduced to Madison and told that I was a dancer now.

Which is why one day at the grocery checkout, I lied to her face over eggs and bread.

In the early days of my (exotic) dancing career, Mum was in town for a conference. We went grocery shopping together, something I don't think we'd done as a pair since I entered adulthood. This was before the awful mysterious phone call threatening to unveil my secret. I'd only been dancing a month.

'I'll pay,' I had insisted as our groceries crawled along the conveyor belt. I reached into my handbag for cash when the envelope from the club, with Madison written across the front, fell out by a loaf of bread. I hoped to fetch the envelope before her eyes caught glimpse of it, but it was too late. A mother is always on the lookout for juicy info.

'Who's Madison?' she asked, high-pitched.

'Oh, just a friend.'

I don't recall much more about this moment—whether I said more, or Mum's expression. Did she know I was lying? Or did she simply not feel the need to ask why I had a friend's envelope of cash in my bag? Writing this, I sent her a text and asked her about this day. She doesn't remember it at all, yet I remember it vividly as if the eggs in my fridge right now were the ones we bought that day.

* * *

I'm almost certain my brother figured it out during a stay with me following a break-up of his own.

'Ummm … what the heck is this?' Bro laughed, holding up a pearl G-string. He was hanging my washing on the line as I read close by in the sun. 'Are you a stripper now or something?'

I just laughed. And so did he.

He even had breakfast ready for me some mornings when I arrived home, makeup painted on my face like I had just stepped off a flight from Las Vegas. I told him I was working a side gig as a bartender, but I think he worked it out when he did the laundry.

As a dancer living a double life, you learnt who you could tell, and who you couldn't, about the glassy dancer's heels you wore on your feet after dark.

* * *

Time has passed since keeping my secret, so I can happily and proudly scream from my lungs, 'I am Madison! I love her!' but back then while keeping my two lives separate, it was simply easier to lie.

The reason I kept my second life hush-hush was to prevent heartache for others. I knew the adult industry was beautiful and misunderstood, but was aware not many saw it the same way. No parent wants to learn their daughter spends her evenings pirouetting on stage in a G-string when she should be at home eating dinner with clothes on. And the funeral directors, well. Ethically it clashed, surely. I wasn't keen to find out. I'm sure they'll find out soon enough now that I've written this book!

* * *

Emma Jane kept Madison a secret.

Madison kept Emma Jane an even bigger one.

I had entered beauty school with hopes of becoming a mortician; now I used my makeup skills to create Madison, the exotic dancer. Some days I'd drive straight to the L&L from the funeral home, with only an hour to spare before dancers draped themselves around poles. Those nights I never felt very glamorous. I could smell death seeping from my pores no matter how many layers of candy-scented spray tan I applied.

My favourite nights were those that didn't back onto a shift with death. I'd sleep most of the day, gathering energy for the night on stage. I'd wake in the afternoon, brew coffee, comb the eyelash extensions. I prepped my skin, curled my hair, I outlined my lips making them appear fuller. No one at the club would ever know how plain Emma Jane really was. Chubby cheeks would now benefit me, as I learnt many dancers plumped theirs with collagen. Blonde lashes were disguised, my love for pasta hidden beneath a corset.

Madison was prettier than Emma Jane.

I don't mean this egotistically.

I had known from a young age what a showgirl looks like, and these late-night dreams had prepped Emma Jane for these getting-ready marathons. I decorated my eyelids with gold glitter, making my brown eyes pop. Napoleon Perdis Aphrodite lipstick, the shade that helped me smash sales targets working at the beauty counter, suited my fake-tanned skin.

Hair extensions were huge for Madison. The frizzy-mopped kid on the farm would have been less traumatised by schoolyard bullying if she had known one day it could be hidden beneath fake hair and hairspray.

Almost symbolically, Madison's blonde locks were big, like my childhood dreams.

I'd finish my makeover with a spritz of perfume, and slip into a Juicy Couture tracksuit to further allow my tan to dry. Juicy Couture tracksuits were a dancer's staple outfit to arrive at the club in. A kiss on Cupcake's fluffy head, double-checking the locks, I'd skip out to thc car, costume jewellery jangling.

Emma Jane was left at home. I'd picture the funeral director as a ghost sitting on the couch eating nachos and watching Netflix while the physical body headed towards the twinkling city horizon and even brighter lights of the stage.

* * *

'Madison! The happy blonde dancer!'

'The one with the smile,' the men requested, approaching the booking counter. I know this because Beck told me how I was described. Wait? They didn't care I spent hours getting ready? It was the smile.

I was smiling because I was happy. Madison was happy. I was at home within the walls of the strip club decorated with framed photographs of *Penthouse* Pets, fringed lampshades and red velvet drapery.

My happiness became my signature look. Not the extensions. Not the makeup. The glee glowing from within. I was the performer I'd always dreamt of being.

* * *

Writing this chapter, I don't want to over-glamorise the moneymaking potential at the Lace and Lipstick, because some nights, you simply didn't make any. After working all day at the funeral home, I'd curse myself during these penniless nights at the club. I should have been home in bed, not strutting about in heels hustling for my rent. My envelope at the end of the night thin with less than a hundred, I'd spent more on getting ready.

Disheartened, I'd pack away my glitter hairspray, glitter pots pushed behind my funeral director 'natural makeup'.

I'd vow never to step foot in the place again.

Two nights later, I'd strut supermodel-like into the sunrise, headed for the breakfast buffet at the casino reserved for winners, the pay envelope unable to be sealed with the volume of money stuffed inside.

* * *

There was more to filling that envelope than pretty hair and flawless makeup.

It was a skill to make a client feel like he was the only man in the city, even if his face resembled a chicken. I took on board all advice offered, or overheard, including showing up to the monthly dancers' meetings.

One particular summer afternoon in the depths of daylight saving, dancers retreated to the cool of the club. The sun should have set by now, but with clocks forward an hour, the avenue outside was as bright as midday. I'd left the funeral home early to attend, and excitedly I nestled in between Sugar and Porsche who napped behind their Ray-Bans.

The lights usually on low were now bright and I noticed paint peeling from the corners of the ceiling and grime marks on the stage. The back wall, where dancers usually sat in the shadows in sequinned costumes, was now lined with girls in denim shirts, crop tops and flushed makeup-free faces.

A stool was placed in the middle of the stage and the star was Patrick. He took a seat. Patrick looked a little like Tommy Lee Jones. I anticipated the anthem 'Men In Black' to break out at any moment when he strode into the club in his suit and dark shades. 'Where's Will Smith?' I'd joke to myself. (It doesn't take much to amuse me.)

Patrick owned our club, and multiple others interstate and over the date line. He only showed up for these meetings. I enjoyed them, always learning something from the man who had owned strip clubs longer than my parents had been alive. I wondered what skin care he used; he looked amazing for his age. His gold-encrusted shades twinkled on his head as he gave us the lowdown on new rules and tips on how to increase earning potential.

'… and stop moaning to the patrons!' he said. 'The men come in here to escape their wives, not be reminded of them. If you've had a fight with your boyfriend, please leave the dispute at the door!' He pointed to the entrance, where Pauly, our security guard, prepared the venue for opening.

'And if the guy has a face that should be in horror films, for the club's sake, and your wage envelope, stop looking away in some sort of daydream. He's paying for your attention! Gaze right here …' and he pointed to the place between the eyebrows, the third eye for yoga enthusiasts. 'This tricks them into thinking you're looking into their eyes. Just do it, would ya? Or I'm getting rid of the dancers' bar tab.'

That afternoon, while I should have been cleaning hearses, I learnt never to whine about my love life and to pretend a taco was sitting between the eyebrows of an ugly guy.

* * *

Sophia and Amy had become dear friends of mine. But there was another dancer I had grown close to.

Madison.

I now had two best friends.

Madison and Death.

I pictured them playing together like patterns blending in a kaleidoscope.

Sad? Clip in the hair extensions and step on stage.

Missing hubby? Step into the mortuary and witness someone younger than me on the table who never got to experience marriage at all.

Lonely? Prep the face of an elderly lady, picturing her husband left behind. My loneliness didn't match that sort of grief.

Feeling ugly? Reach for sequins and lace, twirl around a stripper pole.

Yes, Death taught me to live my best life. I came to appreciate the smallest of things, like a fresh cup of coffee and the sound of wind at night. In any moment I could cease existing. And I was, and am, aware of this every waking moment. Death has enriched my life in the most beautiful way, and has strengthened my soul like I never thought possible. Some of the things I've seen as a funeral director … well, I've mentioned just a few in this book. There's so much more and it's made me courageous beyond belief.

But Madison, my good friend Madison, she's taught me I can be pretty. I can be powerful. *All women* are powerful, especially those willing to hang upside down on a pole in seven-inch stilettos. She's taught me how fit I can be and that my body looks damn fine with abs. Madison has taught me I don't need a spouse to help me in life if I choose singledom; I can pay my own way.

Wait, that was me. *I* taught myself these things. I *am* Madison. And I could not be fucking prouder.

CHAPTER 51

LOST CORPSE

'We can't find the body!'

'Well, there's funeral arrangements in place for him tomorrow and the paperwork says he is certainly here at your facility.'

'Well, he ain't in the fridge.' The morgue attendant sighed. I noticed her stare lingered on Byron, who had accompanied me on the transfer. 'I'll go get my manager.' And off she trotted, swaying her hips side to side dramatically.

'I think she likes you,' I said, nudging Byron. I could feel his rock-hard obliques under his suit. Was he constantly tensing just in case someone came along and happened to touch him?

Standing behind the black and yellow tape at the forensic science unit, we waited for the delivery of our corpse, if it could be found.

'How can a body disappear from the fridge?' asked Byron.

'Oh, it happens all the time.' I snapped on some gloves. 'Sometimes when rigor mortis sets in, the body can sit up all on its own and walk around.'

Byron's face turned white.

'I'm kidding, Byron!'

'Okay, let's see what we have going on here.' An important-looking man approached us, dressed in dark blue scrubs, different to all the assistants' light blue ones, and he wore a surgical mouth cover down on his chin. He smelt of blood, secret body gases and innards as he flicked through the loose paperwork in the manila folder in his hands.

Did he just walk out of an autopsy? I wondered, hopeful. *He literally had his hands in an open body cavity only moments ago!* Apart from wanting to be a showgirl, a funeral director, a mortician, a writer, an astronaut and an airplane mechanic, I had always wanted to become a forensic investigator. It was like the film set of a murder mystery. Black body bags, police officers wandering about, aroma of decomposition wafting through the air … heaven!

'You've lost Mr Johnson, have you?' said the man.

'Well, technically, *we* haven't lost him! We have the release paperwork which means he should be here. It looks as though *you* have lost him!' I said.

Nervous chuckles from all of us filled the air. 'Well, he couldn't have gone too far,' he replied, his spectacles fogging up. 'I'm sure we will get to the bottom of this in no time!'

Off he shuffled with his bubble-blowing assistant on his heels. (Or on the back of his blood-splashed gumboots.)

'So …' Byron turned to me, straightening his tie. His sandy hair was flicked back stylishly with gel. I felt like we were the trendy A-team at A Touch of Comfort. All those scandalous misconceptions about the death care workers: crooked smiles, mixing potions in test tubes in dark basement-like mortuaries … I liked to think we quashed this fallacy, Byron and I. Young, shiny and not a hunchback in sight. We listened to modern pop music and swam at the beach on weekends. We brought *cool* into funeral, and the *sexy*, in Byron's case.

'You never talk about yourself, Emma Jane.' He leant against the stretcher.

'I just don't have that much to say, I guess.'

I actually wanted to explain to him that BM (Before Marriage), I was a platinum-blonde bubble of fun. Since my separation, I had darkened the hair, quietened down a little. I was no longer the loudest one in the room. I was now a hermit who overindulged in Uber Eats and wine, unless of course I was on stage at the Lace and Lipstick. He needn't know about that.

'I think there is plenty to tell,' he said with a wink.

'Right! We found him!' The pathologist returned with a gleaming smile.

The assistant by his side blew a bubble that burst across her face. 'We couldn't locate Mr Johnson because he was not in the fridge at all. He was in the deep freeze!'

'The deep freeze?' Byron spluttered.

'Yes, sir. Mr Johnson arrived at our facility some years ago. No one had claimed him so he's been stored. All is well now, so won't be long!' And with that, he turned on his heels—sorry, his blood-splashed gumboots—and returned to the wonderful place of mystery I longed to witness … the autopsy room.

Destitute funerals (usually a direct cremation paid for by the government) are not uncommon. Sadly, some people simply don't have a single loved one.

A few minutes later, the bubble-gum enthusiast brought out our corpse in a frosty body bag covered in shards of ice. She retrieved an arm from inside, scanned the barcode and rolled the gurney over to us.

In my time in the funeral industry, I had touched bodies in all stages of death, but never one quite like this. Mr Johnson was completely frozen.

'I can't … secure … the … wrist tags,' I grunted, taking his heavy wrist in my hands. Not bending at the elbow, the frozen man's arm slipped from my grasp and he punched me right in the crotch.

Nothing quite like an arctic punch to the vag to cool down sexual tension, let me tell you!

After a few heaves and hos, we loaded the Ice Man into the back of our van and the roller door of the super-secretive morgue lifted, casting sunshine onto the bonnet of our body-collecting vehicle.

I was actually thankful for the icy punch. If it wasn't for that, I may have succumbed to the burning sensation between my thighs and totally ruined the professional relationship between Byron and me.

CHAPTER 52

OUTCALLS

For $480, a man could buy a dancer for the night. Well, for a few hours anyway. As well as dancing there was another way an exotic dancer at the Lace and Lipstick could earn big money.

Outcalls.

If a client thoroughly enjoyed his time with a dancer he had the opportunity to take her out on the town for a while. Some men actually preferred to spend time with a lady while she was wearing clothes. Very strict protocols were in place for outcalls; this is not leading to a dark story about how a client kidnapped a dancer and murdered her in the woods. They were to remain in the city, have a work phone on them and call the club on the hour, and if they could hear that you were not in a public place you could be done for soliciting sex from the venue. Outcalls could not be extended past three hours.

As they left, arm in arm, the entertainer continued to perform outside of the club. She doted on her client as he proudly bought her dinner and drinks. She was his girlfriend for just a while. The dancer was wined and dined and when the three hours came to an end, she pranced back into the club well-fed and continued with her night at the club.

To be honest, when I first learnt about outcalls, I was hesitant. I hardly liked socialising with my friends let alone a stranger.

My first outcall, thankfully, was a group booking. Three guys from a well-known reality TV series glided into the club and from the shadows, I recognised them immediately. A Red Bull in my hands, I made my way over to my favourite star of the show. Within ten minutes, they'd booked Amy, Sophia and me for the VIP lounge.

'Let's do an outcall!' Amy chanted, dancing around naked in the middle of the lap-dance room holding her champagne flute high in the air. 'The Presets are performing at the club across the street tonight! Let's paaartaay!'

Not needing much more encouragement than that, the men paid well over a thousand dollars and in a flash, my friends and I were among the sweaty partygoers at a nightclub dancing to one of Australia's biggest techno groups of the time.

I hardly remember talking to the guys that booked us. Draining my vodka Red Bulls, it could have been just the three of us for all I cared.

When the three hours drew to a close, we left our clients at the door and hobbled back into the club, returned to our costumes and resumed lap dancing while high on alcohol and life. Inevitably I woke the next afternoon with a headache but with green hundred-dollar notes splashed across my cosmetics vanity, I could afford a packet or two of Nurofen. I couldn't believe I'd spent my twenties hitting nightclubs for free. The new line at the end of my lap dances switched from, 'Would you like to extend your naked striptease for half an hour?' to 'Would you like to go on an outcall? We can hit the clubs! The casino! Are you hungry? Let's go to Santino's, the new Italian restaurant on Oxford!'

I was addicted to getting paid to eat pasta.

This addiction led me to Peter, a lovely middle-aged man who claimed to work at a fast-food restaurant. With his pocket bulging with the club's 'funny money' I suspected he had other sources of income, but I continued to smile and nod as he chatted about his day flipping burgers.

Every Friday night for two months, Peter showed up at the club in a suit and paid the $480 outcall fee. I knew not to eat on Fridays as my dinner would be generous at a restaurant I'd never been to before. One week it was Italian, the next French cuisine where I ate scallops and snails marinated in garlic butter. Then it was a Turkish feast where jewelled belly dancers rolled their sexy bodies around our candlelit table. For weeks, we 'dated' and my purse fattened. If wasn't for all the pole dancing, I would have fattened too.

* * *

During our final dinner together, my night job seemed to bleed into my funeral career.

The night started off like any other typical Friday outcall. Peter escorted me to a seafood restaurant where lobsters scraped at the walls of giant fish tanks, and the chef scooped his hands into the water to retrieve our meal. Can't get fresher than that!

We cracked lobster shells in flickering candlelight, sipped Moët and Johnny Blue, when Pete began to turn pale.

'Are you okay?' I gasped, dropping my fork.

He could not speak a word.

'Are you allergic? Pete! Pete! Someone help!'

The next thing I knew, I was in the back of an ambulance holding his clammy hands as a paramedic tested his blood pressure. The lighting bounced with the bumps in the road as I was tossed about in my sparkly heels.

Peter was admitted to a ward once we reached the hospital, and I rang the club to let them know I'd be late.

'I'll pay you,' he whimpered, falling in and out of sleep.

Watching the doctors connect my client to patches and tubes, my mind wandered to the funeral home. Many men had arrived in the mortuary still wearing their expensive trousers and fancy shoes. Before this night, I assumed the dead diner had been enjoying time with his family.

From then on I'd wonder: *had they died on an outcall?*

* * *

From that night, something in me had changed.

I found myself relating my clients to corpses, and vice versa. When I danced for a man who was high on drugs, I hugged him. What if he overdosed? Would I be the last woman to touch him?

When I prepped young men dead by overdose, I wondered if he dropped the drugs at a strip club.

My two worlds were colliding. Beating hearts, dead hearts, warm skin, cold skin, hard cocks, floppy ones in death, expensive lobster and body bags. I was no longer living a double life. The two worlds amalgamated, haunting me like a ghost.

CHAPTER 53

DREAMS

'Please get high with me, Maddy, it's my last night here!'

I peered down at the white powder Amy had cut into lines on the toilet seat.

'You have to, Maddy! I'm moving to the Gold Coast! Can you believe it? *Holy shit!* I need you to be on the same level as me!'

Fighting the sneeze that would send her precious powder flying, I tied my hair back with the scrunchie around my wrist. I could hear Warrant's 'Cherry Pie'; Sophia's final song, and then my turn on stage. I knew her performance playlist like clockwork by now.

'Okay, sure,' I said, kicking off my stilettos by the tampon disposal. Amy squealed and kissed my cheek.

'It's really good stuff, babe!'

Damp toilet paper gathered on my knees as I took a hundred-dollar bill from the neat bundle tucked in the lace around my thigh. I rolled the note into a tight tube, popped one end into my nostril and leaned down. With the dim lighting and given Amy's state, I knew she wouldn't notice that the line reserved for me remained.

'What did I say? Great, right? Okay, hold back my hair? I'm going to snort the rest. It's my last night in Sydney! I need to get wasted!'

* * *

The iconic Harbour Bridge looked as glamorous as Amy with the sunrise breaking through the clouds. Hand in hand, we walked along Circular Quay, the sails of the Opera House glowing against the backdrop of peach and pink sky.

'I'm really going to miss you,' I said as Amy leaned into me. I held onto her as we walked, and I realised it was the most romantic moment I had experienced since my wedding day. I loved this girl.

'I'm excited but scared,' the brunette beauty sighed as we took a seat on a bench to watch the morning take over the skies. 'The Gold Coast looks so … fancy. Maybe I'm not fancy enough?'

'Amy.' I turned to her, squeezing her small, cold hands. 'You must stop doubting yourself! You are one of the sweetest people I know! Can I ask you something?'

She nodded, licking her cracked lips.

'Think for a moment. I know you want to be a showgirl, but other than that, if you could be anything in the world, what would you be?'

She nibbled on her windburn in thought.

'A vet!' Her eyes shone.

'What's stopping you?'

'I'm not smart enough,' she said. Her eyes lowered and she fiddled with a ring on her finger. 'I always wanted to help animals, ya know? Like, when I was a kid, if I ever saw an injured animal on the side of the road I would take it home to nurse it back to health. I really would love to be a vet, Maddy. So much.'

There it was! Our souls *were* connected. As kids, we both collected animals that needed our help. She would try to save them, I would take care of them when they had died. I wasn't sure if I was about to make the right decision, but with her trembling hands in mine and remnants of white powder on her nose, I decided to tell Amy something I had feared saying for some time. But I felt I should. I'd now seen far too many drug overdoses in the mortuary, too many young adults leaving families behind. While I didn't think she would end up as a number in a mortuary fridge, if I could at least point her in the right direction she might thank me one day.

'Amy, I want to tell you something about me.' I gulped, loosening my grip on her cool hands, and turned to the harbour. The green and yellow ferries hooted their horns, steam bursting into the crisp air. Tourists with shiny cameras and glossy smiles embarked the boats excitedly.

'Tell me!' Amy moved in closer. 'You never talk about yourself. I would love to know!'

'I'm not a mobile makeup artist. I lied to you.'

'You lied to me?'

'I didn't want anyone to know about my profession, because if anyone found out that I was working at the L&L, I would probably lose my job. Please forgive me, but I was just being cautious.'

'Of course.' Amy grabbed my hands once again, hopeful. 'You can tell me. I understand. I have heaps of friends who've kept their professional lives separate to the club. It's only natural to protect yourself! What do you do? Are *you* a vet?'

'No,' I chuckled, gazing up into her glassy eyes. 'I'm actually a funeral director. A mortician. Amy, I work with the dead.'

Her face paled.

'Like, the TV show, *Six Feet Under*?' she gasped. 'Like, you touch dead bodies and do their makeup?'

'Yes.'

'That's the best fucking thing I've ever heard!' she screamed, people frowning at her as they passed by with coffee in their hands.

'Shhh! Amy!' I laughed. 'Be quiet! Nobody knows. Well, no one at the club anyway.'

'Maddy, that's the coolest fucking thing ever!'

'Amy, can you call me Emma Jane? Madison, the dancer, is my *second* job.'

'Okay, okay, I don't give a shit about formalities. Tell me some cool stuff. Want some more coke?' She started fishing into her purse for the powder.

'No, stop!' I grabbed her hand and she looked at me with furrowed brows.

'This is cause for celebration, bitch.' She pushed me jokingly. 'We need to celebrate! So much good shit is happening here. I am moving to the Goldy, and you put makeup on dead people! This is seriously cool!'

'Hon …' I took her diamante purse away from her. 'There is a point in telling you this.'

She faced me and pretended to put on a stern face, only to break out in laughter. She was higher than the seagulls that soared over the Harbour Bridge.

'Amy. You don't have to be like this.'

'Like what?' she snapped.

'Like *this*! I know you have had a lot of shitty things happen to you, but so have I! I was stuck in a difficult marriage, I am going through a divorce and at one point, I was sleeping in the back of my goddamn car! My morals are more important to me than shiny gadgets and an in-ground swimming pool. My point is, no matter how shit life may seem, you can always make it through. And to be honest, that's the most exciting part of it all! You can change your circumstance, right here, right now! You can totally reinvent yourself and create a brand-new life!'

'Can I have my coke back now?' Amy ignored my splendid speech.

'No!' I flew to my feet and held her purse hostage. 'I will throw it into the harbour if you don't listen to me!'

'So, what you're trying to say is, I'm a loser?' Amy's nose met with mine.

'No! That's the total opposite of what I am saying!'

'So, because you can apply a bit of blush to a dead guy's face, you're better than everyone, is that what you're trying to say?'

Crap. This wasn't going to plan.

And I don't put blush on men.

'Amy, this is not coming out right at all! What I mean is, I can't even cook scrambled eggs. I'm hopeless! But I always wanted to be a funeral director so I went for it. You want to be a veterinarian, you can be! I want to help you to achieve your dreams!'

'I've achieved my fucking dreams.' Amy snatched her studded clutch from my hands. 'My dad can't hurt me anymore and I'm making shitloads of money and moving to Queensland. Fuck you, Madison!'

My heart ached as I watched her storm off into the busy morning crowd.

PART THREE: LIFE

CHAPTER 54

TUG OF WAR

'You shaved off Mr Smythe's beard!' Mags screeched, steaming her spectacles. 'Apparently he spent over a decade growing that thing, Emma Jane. His family are not impressed!'

I'd made a few mistakes in my time assisting the mortuary, but none quite as big as this. I had applied red lipstick instead of pink, curled hair instead of straightening it, and tidied ear hairs when in fact, it was part of the deceased's character and his grandkids knew him as 'Mr Hairy Ears'.

'Did you not read the mortuary care form?' Mags's face scrunched with anger. 'You know what this means?' She moved in closer to the mortuary table. I continued clearing out the dead man's nasal cavities without taking my eyes from his snot.

'You must recreate a beard,' she demanded. 'I don't care how you do it, just ensure Mr Smythe is buried tomorrow with facial hair!'

'I will, Magda,' I promised, restraining my tears. Would I need to buy those plastic spectacles attached to a plastic moustache? Would I need to trim hair from his head and glue it to his lip? Yes, that's exactly what would have to be done.

'You're not yourself lately, Emma. When you're finished with this body, I want you to get out of the mortuary for the day and go out on a funeral. Get some fresh air. And then I want you to take a week off. There's obviously something going on with you, and I have been patient but your work is suffering.'

'Please, Mags. Don't make me take a week off!' With everything going on in my life and losing Amy to the glitzy Gold Coast, I *needed* to be at the funeral home. The place kept me balanced.

Mags rubbed her pudgy chin.

'Okay,' she finally said, taking off her specs and polishing them with her blouse. 'But you are not to work in the mortuary. You are on funerals only.' And with that, she left. The mortuary utensils rattled as she slammed the door behind her.

I spritzed some Brut on the old man's decaying body, flicked off my gloves and headed towards the locker room to slip into my suit.

'Heard you're on my service!' Macca's small eyes twinkled as he polished his hearse.

'Yeah.' I attempted to look enthusiastic. My two lives had intermingled and it was time to fix this dilemma before I dressed a dead man in a frock by accident.

* * *

The eulogy follows a common structure:

'Mum was born in 1941 and lived in Newcastle until she met my dad in 1960 ...'

'Dad grew up on a cattle station until he got a job promotion in Sydney and moved us to the big smoke … and along came our youngest sibling …'

'Mum worked as a nurse until she retired and spent her days camping and fishing with Dad …'

It's rare for a eulogy to shake us in our polished shoes. I wanted to know the *guts* of their lives …

What was their favourite food?

What were their greatest *passions* in life?

What gave them goosebumps?

What made them slip into bed each night fulfilled and happy to be alive?

I guess we don't hear of these details too often because the only person who knows these special stories is the person themselves, so how cool would it be if the deceased could pop up for a couple of minutes to tell us?

Well that's exactly what happened the day I was allocated funeral duties.

No, the coffin lid didn't spring open.

In charge of the media, I pressed play. Twelve months earlier, Robin, our deceased, had been sitting on the back porch talking with her daughter. Unbeknown to Robin, her daughter was recording the entire conversation and this recording was now playing. Robin told stories of her adolescence and she left out no juicy bits. The chapel was loud with laughter as Robin told jokes and spilled secrets. The daughter stood at the lectern, tears creeping down her flushed cheeks as her mother's voice echoed off the four walls.

The recording finished, I pressed stop, and Robin was gone forever.

As the pallbearers carried Robin down the aisle with heads lowered, I decided I would quit dancing at the Lace and

Lipstick. I'd made the money I needed and now my work at the funeral home was suffering. I was becoming withdrawn from the dead and shaving the beards off corpses when I wasn't meant to. I was wrapped up in the glamour, fast cash and excitement of it all, and the time had come to slow it down.

I was in the midst of a giant tug of war: a team of dancers in heels at one end of the rope, a group of funeral directors in suits and ties at the other, determined to pull Emma Jane back to them.

Mardi Gras was coming up, a busy time for Sydney nightlife. As I watched Robin get pushed into the flickering flames of the cremator I decided that after the parade of feather boas and rainbows I would hang up my stilettos and say farewell to the stage.

* * *

I spent a lot of time looking at myself in the mirror as a dancer. I spent an hour just on my hair. Ten minutes was reserved for buffing foundation into my skin to achieve a flawless look; the time it took to brew coffee was spent just on hairspray setting my hairstyle. I spent all of this time perfecting my appearance yet only five minutes on the body beneath the shimmer and fake tan.

A strong coffee, a piece of avocado toast if my body was lucky, then on to abuse it with espresso martinis to make it through the night and then the following day at the funeral home, I potentially poisoned it with caffeinated energy drinks.

One night close to the end of my time as an exotic dancer, reality hit me.

I was rolling my hips in a wealthy man's lap as he sipped on his scotch.

My tanned cleavage attracted his piercing blue eyes. His glossy skin had me asking about his skin care. My playful smile paid my rent.

While lying on the carpet performing floor work, I revisited the time I held onto the brain in the mortuary. Were the lungs of my client blackened with cigar smoke, his liver inflamed with too many after-work drinks and strip-club visits?

What did my heart look like after all the pain from my divorce? There is such a thing as dying from a broken heart, I was certain of that. Too many times I'd helped bury someone, then their spouse weeks later. Did my pulsating heart have a giant crack through the middle? My period pain had worsened lately. Were my bad eating and drinking habits causing havoc on parts of my body I'd forgotten about?

In the attempt to recover my bank account, I'd become obsessed with what I looked like on the outside, and shuddered at the thought of holding a mirror to my insides. I paused mid lap dance, my legs crisscrossed reaching for the crystal chandelier hanging above. I knew this gave my client a grand view of what he essentially came for, so I paused in this position, tilting my head back until my calvarium touched the floor.

I promised myself no McDonald's breakfast after work. Instead, I'd have a green smoothie and try to go for a run.

In hindsight, that was the most unrealistic goal I could have aimed for. It was obviously followed by an egg roll and bed, sneaking two hours of sleep in before the funeral home opened. But at least the roll was from an organic café, not a fast-food chain.

* * *

I self-medicated during my divorce with Mac and Cheese, and red wine binges, and I left out that many a time the red-wine glasses were spiked with brandy.

I nursed a broken heart, but were the microwave meals clogging the arteries of the physical organ? Was my brain slowing down because I'd replaced water with wine?

Wait. Was I poisoning my bloodstream with the bottles of fake tan? I could part with the macaroni, but not the tan.

The following afternoon, I glided into my kitchen like Madison on stage, and pulled open the pantry door. Cupcake watched in confusion as I filled garbage bags with toxic microwave meals and poured bottles of red down the drain.

No more phoney pasta! No more alcohol! I crawled into bed that night with a herbal tea next to my to-be-read pile, rather than the regular glass of cola for when I woke up through the night desperate for hydration.

The next morning I scolded myself for throwing out all the cereal and crunched on a carrot.

I starved myself that day, not because of an impending eating disorder but because I'd binned most groceries and was too busy assisting in the mortuary to visit the cafeteria down the street. By the end of the week, wine and fake pasta-free, I felt my organs were thanking me already. I'm pretty sure my suit seemed bigger too. I was determined to become so healthy that a mortician would have been impressed with my insides if they were to hold them in their gloved hands.

I'd no longer just care for my soul and appearance, but my organs too.

CHAPTER 55

HOLD ON, DAISY!

'Shelly said what?' I blasted, turning to Macca who was filling out paperwork in the passenger seat. It was my turn to drive and we were off on an hour-long trek to a hospital morgue out of town. The swanky vans used for body removal were out on the road when Macca and I were allocated the transfer, so we had no choice but to take the ancient Commodore station wagon with no barrier between the stretcher and our seats. It spluttered at the lights and you often had the poor old soul kicking you in the back of your seat around corners. Also, the air con was stuffed and the radio would only play one AM station. It would be a long trip.

'She said you love yourself.' He coughed behind his pen.

My knuckles reddened on the steering wheel. Shelly was my mentor and so-called friend, but I had overheard snickers myself in the locker room when I removed my blouse and the female funeral directors caught a glimpse of the fakies.

'I don't love myself!'

'Don't shoot the messenger.' Macca wiped his glasses on his tie.

I'd had a boob job long before I became a dancer. I was an athletic teenager, forming into an even lankier adult with a flat chest, unable to wear a dress comfortably. Despite the Wonderbras piled up at home, I'd never experienced cleavage. So at 18 years old I marched into the bank and applied for a personal loan. Back when I had my surgery, implants were far less expensive than they are today, so with a tick of approval on my loan application, I was in surgery within weeks. I didn't even tell my family or closest friends at the time that I had a boob job.

Aside from the boobs, it was becoming increasingly difficult separating my two identities. When I started getting the eyelashes done, one particular woman grew increasingly protective of her husband who also worked at A Touch of Comfort. I wanted to explain that the new lashes and tan wasn't Emma Jane the funeral director on the prowl. I did my best 'downing' my appearance during the day—no contour or mascara, hair slicked back, and I wore flattening sports bras. Still, Madison seeped through the tight bun and minimal makeup. She was screaming out loud and everyone was listening.

Have you ever noticed that women can stand as one, but in the same breath condemn one another for looking a certain way? Watch the next time you're in line at a store or café. I find it fascinating when a beautiful, contoured cashier is smiling and bubbly to every customer paying for their latte, but when they come face to face with someone who matches their beauty, they often carry out the transaction with much less enthusiasm. And you only have to scroll comments on social media, audiences condemning celebrities for choosing cosmetic surgery. Shouldn't we all love one another whether our hair is mousy brown or bleached blonde? Whether we have a small bust or an enhanced one? When faced with a pretty face contoured with better makeup skills than we ourselves possess, why not clap hands in an almighty high-five and say, 'Can you teach me?'

One morning following a shift at the L&L, I accidently fell asleep on the couch rather than removing my makeup. An hour later I jolted from sleep with 30 minutes to be at work. Smoky eyeshadow, plum blush and red lippy still on, I headed to the funeral home. Later, standing by the hearse in the buttery sunshine, a woman grunted at me as the coffin was slid into the back of the death car. I anticipated with dread a written complaint about the 'tart by the hearse'.

The look that earned money at night wasn't as welcome in the funeral home. My white blouses were stained yellow from fake tan and the blonde highlights that glowed in the lights on stage now had the women at the funeral home whispering 'bimbo' under their breath. And I'm sure it wasn't just the new hair. Perhaps I was becoming a little too big for my high heels since gaining all this extra attention at the club? Maybe it wasn't just the looks I had to downplay—was I mistaking caskets for tabletops? At the club, it was common knowledge *'the men know when you've just had sex!'* If a dancer had been bonking all afternoon, bare-faced and hair tousled from the romp between the sheets, she would make more money than the entertainers who'd spent hours in the makeup chair.

Were my sweaty nights on stage like the dancers' afternoons of sex? Was I bringing my new hot and heavy pheromones from the lap dances to the hearses?

I would have to be more aware of this, I thought to myself as Macca and I headed into the hills, butterflies slapping against the windscreen.

Today we were collecting an elderly lady named Daisy. What should have been a two-hour return trip turned into a four-hour expedition. There was an accident on the freeway and we were stuck in standstill traffic on the way back.

'Do *you* think I love myself?' I asked Macca, Daisy thudding into my back as I pressed the brake pedal in the traffic jam.

'No.'

Thud.

'Thank you.' I smiled weakly.

Thud.

Macca eventually fell asleep and with no good music I was stuck with his snoring and little old Daisy's secreting gases, the smell wafting through to the front.

Mags rang at 5 pm letting us know that everyone was heading home and to ensure we would lock up after we were done. Dusk had fallen and brake lights illuminated the freeway. Macca woke when we were only 50 metres from our street. We were starving and tired. Well, I was. Macca had had a lovely rest. Our street being visible only frustrated us more.

'Just overtake,' Macca said with a wink. 'You'll make it.'

'We will be on the wrong side of the road!'

'We will be here all bloody night if you don't!'

'Okay,' I gulped. I tucked a bleached blonde curl behind my ear, fiddled with the sports bra as if doing so would ensure our safety, and nodded. There was no oncoming traffic, but my heart was thumping and my hands sweaty on the steering wheel.

'Hold on Daisy!' I called out, and floored it. The station wagon grunted as we took off and I may have closed my eyes slightly, praying for the best. Gathering speed, we passed fists being shaken from car windows. I swerved into our street like I was competing in the Grand Prix, and sped into the operations facility. Daisy bounced about in the back and our laughs loosened our shoelaces. Screeching to a halt outside the mortuary, we slammed a high-five, our hearts racing in our suits.

'This bimbo can drive!' I laughed as we fell out of the car.

'You're no bimbo.' Macca wiped sweat from his forehead. 'You're bloody cool.'

Macca recorded Daisy in the mortuary register as I massaged barrier cream on her face and hands that were still quite warm. Rigor had only set in slightly and as I coated her fingers with lotion, she seemed to hold my hand. I wondered to myself as I gazed down at her sweet old face, *Why should my appearance matter when I'm brushing a deceased's hair for the final time or polishing their coffin?*

I zipped up Daisy's body bag and slid her in a shelf. Shelving that I will be lying in one day. Shelving *everyone* will be lying in eventually.

And then, looks won't matter at all.

CHAPTER 56

SMALL ROOMS AND FLOWER POTS

There's nothing quite like a nursing-home transfer to jolt you back to reality, reminding you that in the end material objects truly mean nothing at all. Before marriage, before I was working in a funeral home, I lived in a tiny city apartment with a sexy city view and Korean buffet within reach. I didn't own much—a few books, a queen-size bed and television, so when I visited my friends who had actual mortgages and four-bedroom homes brimming with dressing tables, desks and cupboards full of linen, I felt a twinge of jealousy. I felt they had their shit together by owning all this stuff. So when I finally wore a wedding ring and had my own overflowing linen closet, I'd thought I'd made it. We had so much shit that it took me a week just to launder our pillowcases. Owning expensive non-stick fry pans and an impressive TV in the cinema room somehow validated me. We had a home stuffed with belongings, we were successful.

Weren't we?

When my marriage ended, leaving almost all my possessions behind, I felt unsuccessful some days. Transferring rent to the real estate agency, I wished the funds were paying off my own mortgage.

While my lack of belongings got me down at times, on the good days I felt flighty and carefree. Deep down I knew material objects didn't define me, yet I felt a constant nagging that I needed to grow up and buy a leather couch with an expensive, matching floor rug.

Whenever I was overcome with this internal monologue, I'd be summoned on a nursing home transfer. Whether it was coincidence or the universe telling me to sit down and stop being so shallow I'm not sure, but the experience was always welcome and appreciated.

The nursing home transfer tells such a story of the deceased, their entire lives compressed into one room. They could have chosen anything from their homes so the possessions inside their small space show what was most precious to them during their time on earth. I always found myself scanning the walls of family photographs while snapping on my gloves, distracted by all the cherished items: ornaments, war medals, books and stuffed toys showing wear and tear, perhaps from their childhood, passed through generations. Never was there a flat-screen TV or DVD collection. Although I doubt either would fit into the small room. The objects always represented passions like gardening, reading and family.

One morning following a sleepless night, I was off to an aged care facility.

Puffy-eyed and feeling hungover without a drop of liquor in my system, I was into my suit and off into peak-hour traffic with my transfer partner offering to drive. Thank goodness. We would have ended up in a morgue ourselves if I was behind the wheel after my evening of singing along to depressing break-up love songs. We finally arrived on the other side of town where we would collect Frances, from her tiny nursing home bed surrounded with flower pots.

'She loved gardening,' the nurse sighed as we slid Frances into a body bag. 'She even helped with our gardens here.'

Frances's family lived overseas and would arrive on the day of the funeral. This lovely old botanist had lived her whole life creating memories with her family, building a home with material objects, no doubt, as I could see some of them in her small room, yet here she was, having died alone with her pot plants her only company. I zipped up the body bag and heaved Frances into the back of our body-collecting van and shed a little tear.

Every single time I seemed to lose my way, Death swept in to remind me that nothing really mattered. Not the divorce. Not my shiny Louboutins and garter full of cash at the club. No amount of money mattered in the end. I wondered for a moment as I closed the back of the van, why was everyone in such a hurry to get mortgage applications approved? To fill homes with nonsense belongings only to more than likely die in one tiny room without any of it?

I knew more than anyone, growing up in a tiny farmhouse sleeping in rickety bunk beds, that the less you have the happier you can be.

As I jumped up into the passenger seat with Frances's paperwork in my lap, I realised there was no one I needed to convince of this but myself.

CHAPTER 57

LIGHTNING STRIKES

'Are you the undertakers?' a squeaky voice blasted through the intercom.

'Yes, ma'am,' Byron replied into the speaker as I stood by his side, flicking off chipped nail varnish. 'It's Byron and Emma from A Touch of Comfort funeral home. We are here to take Mr Thompson into our care.'

'Won't be long!'

'So …' Byron twiddled his thumbs, leaning on the stretcher. 'How's life?'

I squirmed in my suit, peering into his sparkling eyes that reflected the storm brewing above us.

He is always so interested in my life.

'Everything is fine.' I blushed, nibbling on my thumbnail. Saving me from an awkward conversation, the nurse appeared at the door.

'Bad night to be out on the road, huh?' The small lady in scrubs passed us the paperwork as she peered up towards the stormy sky.

As we wheeled our stretcher behind the nurse, I could smell the remnants of dinner as we passed the closed rooms with name tags on the doors. The laminated signs were decorated with butterflies and flowers like the name tags above desks at a preschool. These elderly residents had once been children; now they were relying on others once again as they entered the final years of life. I could smell the familiar scent of death as we approached the room where Mr Thompson had died. We could hear eerie screaming echoing in the dark and Byron turned to me.

'So sad,' he whispered.

'Whoo hoo!' As we approached the room, the wailing, we suddenly realised, was not a heartbroken wailing at all. It was a cheer!

With the turn of the final corner, Byron and I giggled into the sleeves of our suits when we found an old lady wiggling her bare buttocks on the floor.

'Whooo hoooo …!' she sang. 'I'm out of bed again!'

'Yes, yes you are,' the nurse said, nodding as she opened the door that led to our deceased.

'I'm wiping the floor with my bum again!' the elderly resident announced.

'Right, he is in here,' said the nurse. 'There are three residents in this double room. We are running out of space. So be careful not to wake the others. I will meet you at reception when you're done.'

Careful *we* don't wake others? What about the one out there wiping her butt on the floor? I opened the sheer curtain that separated the elderly men sleeping in their beds. The first resident, mumbling in his sleep, was evidently not our man. Quietly, we swept open the next curtain to find our deceased in his bed with his mouth gaping. Byron prepared the stretcher and I reached forward to place wrist tags on the old soul, when the man's eyes snapped open, staring back at me with horror.

'Jesus Christ!' Byron toppled against the bedside, barley sugars rolling onto the linoleum floor. Almost instantly, the man fell back into his slumber.

'That was close.' Byron shivered. 'I watched a documentary the other night about a man who was accidently cremated while napping on a gurney! I've been frightened of mistaking a dead person all week, and it almost happened!'

'Shows that even the alive can appear dead,' I found myself saying as we finally approached our corpse.

* * *

By the time we got back to the funeral home, the storm was in full swing, hammering the body van with heavy rain.

'It's not opening.' Byron's teeth chattered as he repeatedly pressed the buttons on the remote that controlled the electronic front gates. '*It's not working!*'

Wow! This guy was losing it! Were storms his secret fear?

'Byron, honey, it's okay.' I placed my hand on his forearm, tense beneath his suit. 'I will go and open it manually.'

He looked as if I'd just asked him to drive off a cliff together. 'Don't go!'

'Byron, stop panicking, it's fine! I will use the side door and open up manually. I will only be a couple of minutes.

We have no choice. Mr Thompson is in the back and has earned his rest.'

'Okay.' He wiped his face, flicking sweat onto my trousers. Ignoring the splatter in my lap, I dived out into the rain, small hailstones bouncing off my head. I heaved myself up and over the front gate and raced to the side door of the operations facility. I fetched the key from my suit pocket, unlocked it and retreated to the safety of the garage area. The hearses parked side by side were hauntingly beautiful in the intermittent flashes of lightning. I pushed the button on the wall and the roller doors groaned open and, barely missing the door with the van, Byron sped inside. The smell of wood shavings and mortuary chemicals tickled my nostrils as I flicked on some lights and met Byron by the driver's side door. I was home.

'You okay, mate?'

'Yeah,' he nodded. 'I'm fine. Let's get Mr Thompson into the fridge.'

In this moment it occurred to me I had grown used to the dead, while Byron was certainly taking his time getting used to The Corpse. And I didn't blame him, I thought as I coated Mr Thompson's face with lotion. I gazed down at his pale face, his mouth in a silent scream.

'All done,' I chirped, pulling the coolroom door behind me. 'Let's go home.'

'Actually, I don't want to drive home right now, and I don't think you should either. It's not safe.'

A clap of thunder had us almost jumping into a hug.

'Okay,' I agreed. 'I'll close up and we can go upstairs and wait out the storm.'

'Thank you, Em.' Byron shook off his suit jacket, draping it over a casket close by.

I closed the front gate and garage doors and with Byron's breath on the back of my neck, we passed the lunch room and made our way upstairs where futons were available to sleep on after late-night calls like this one.

'I'm sure there's candles up here,' I said, ploughing through boxes of old suits and funeral information brochures. 'We have spares for church services.'

Byron continued to fidget and I was determined to find light, but it wasn't the storm I was afraid of. I didn't want Byron freaking himself into premature death and shelf allocation in the mortuary fridge. Personally, sleeping in a dark funeral home listening to a storm is peaceful to me. We lit the wicks of tealight candles and lay down on floor staring up the ceiling.

Byron finally broke the silence.

'So … I have some gin in my car.'

'You're not suggesting we drink while on shift?'

'We're not on shift anymore, Em. It's past 3 am! The phones have just switched over to Murray and Albert.'

'Well, we can't have alcohol on the premises at all,' I said, secretly applauding his suggestion.

'Just one shot won't hurt anyone.'

'You can, sure.'

'I'll be right back!' Byron leapt to his feet and disappeared, returning quickly with the light blue bottle.

'Want some?' he grinned.

'I don't think I like gin …' I had served it while bikini waitressing and it smelt awful.

'Did you know gin is the only alcohol that can't be smelt on the breath?' Byron swigged straight from the bottle.

No glasses? No juice?

He handed it to me. I hesitated.

'Do you drink on the job, Byron?'

'Never on the job.' He shook his head, wiping his lips on his sleeve. 'I only have it in the car so I can have a drink sometimes after work.'

'Right. Coz drink driving is *so* much safer.' I rolled my eyes.

I took the gin from him, pressed my lips against the bottle and the bitterness burnt my throat but warmed my gut. After a few more gulps, we lay down, piles of *Funerals Today* magazines as footrests.

'Emma. I want to apologise to you about tonight.'

'Apologise?'

'I panicked tonight, a few times. It was completely unprofessional. Tonight, you saw a side of me that no one has seen in a long time. I have a little PTSD, you know. From the military. This job still freaks me out a little.'

I sat up to face him.

'I thought I was getting better, ya know,' he pressed on. 'Please don't tell anyone, Emma. This job means everything to me.'

'Of course I won't,' I promised, and he leant in to cuddle me. I inhaled his hair gel.

'So, tell me why you're here.' I pushed him away playfully before I could kiss him. 'Why are you working at A Touch of Comfort funeral home? Do you think it's the right place to be right now if you're feeling like this?' At this point in my life, I knew very little about PTSD, but I suspected dealing with the dead couldn't have been helpful.

'Well, I've seen a lot of death. I am grateful to be here just to talk to you. I lost my best mate …' His eyes welled up again. 'I wanted to die right there with him, but something inside me made me get up and keep going. You see, when I was a kid, my dad died. Suicide. I was too young to understand death or why he went away. I remember, at his funeral everyone was crying when that bloody hearse pulled up. I couldn't understand why my father would choose to lie in a box when he could have played footy in the backyard with me. I spent years angry with my dad, Em. Not only did he leave *me*, but he also took away my mother. She never smiled after that day. My mother had died too. So, I became determined to face the villain. Death. I wanted to look the fucker straight in the eye. I still don't understand why Death is such a bastard and won't rest until I figure it out.'

A candle flame was sucked into darkness as if extinguished by a ghost.

'I'm sorry,' I whispered, my world muted.

How selfish I felt. My life consumed with glitter and wads of cash while this troubled soul slipped into his car each afternoon sipping on gin. His best friend and dad were dead.

'You know what I reckon?' Byron's tone brightened as he lay back down and faced the ceiling. 'Life should be backwards. You ever read that that thing online about living life in reverse?'

I shook my head as a flash of lightning lit up his chiselled face.

'It tells a story of life lived backwards. Born elderly, eyes opening for the first time in a nursing home. You get kicked out for being too healthy. Then you go to work until you're too young. You go to school, drink too much alcohol, experience sexual encounters and party hard. Then you become a child with no responsibilities before becoming a baby, floating in blissful unconsciousness.' His eyes twinkled. 'Then you die as an orgasm.' He laughed. 'Not a bad thought, huh?'

'Not a bad thought at all.' I felt my cheeks blush, and it sure as hell wasn't the gin.

* * *

'Jesus! Byron.' I shook him. 'Wake up!'

'Huh? What?' Byron squinted in the morning rays reaching in through the window.

'Byron! It's 8 am! We start work in ten minutes! Get up!'

'Shit!' he gasped, hurriedly fastening his top buttons. Pulling my eyes away from his morning bulge, I scrambled to my feet and began collecting the remnants of candles.

'Just act normal,' I begged. 'No one can know what happened here last night! No one!'

'No one must ever know *anything*!' Byron's eyes glazed over. 'I'm pretty sure I blurted my entire soul out to you ...'

'I don't remember a thing,' I lied. 'Let's just forget the whole night even happened and get to work.'

'Right!' Byron agreed, but as we looked into one another's flushed, startled faces, we both knew that nothing from the previous night could possibly be erased.

Whether we liked it or not, we were more than partners who collected the dead at night.

CHAPTER 58

THE DECOMP PLAN

My beautiful Madison, I regret the morning on the harbour. I'm sorry I stormed off on you. The Gold Coast is all I thought it would be, I have room service available at the touch of a button and I am so happy. The club here is amazing! I just wanted to let you know I am doing well and I'm making my dreams come true, just like you. I hope you are doing well and not missing me too much, haha! People you touch at the funeral home are blessed to have you work on them. Love you, Amy xo

I stared down at the text message, a huge grin on my face. My Amy was happy! I clicked my iPhone lock and slipped it back into the deep pockets of my scrubs, returning my attention to the decomp case lying on the mortuary table. The woman was unrecognisable but the beautiful mess in front of me was an elderly lady who had died in her kitchen and wasn't found for almost two weeks.

Looking down at the decomposed woman, I pictured Amy and myself, living side by side in a posh retirement village with lawn bowls and spas on site, spiking our tea with vodka and making fun of the old men who farted around us. Neither of us would ever be a decomp case. We'd never die alone, we'd promised one another that! Back when Amy and I were growing closer, we had developed the decomp plan. It came about because the ageing air-conditioning unit in my rented cottage rattled above my bed as I slept. One morning I stared up at the square hunk of metal thinking, *If that thing fell on my head and with my family interstate, I could easily become a decomp case.* I sent Amy a text, asking her to message me every day and to call the authorities if she didn't hear back from me, as it meant my head had been flattened. She agreed, and in response she confessed to taking an extra sleeping tablet outside of her prescribed amount, unable to wind down following a night performing on stage.

So I promised to check on her, too.

Amy and I had an anti-decomp plan—we'd be found long before our skin turned to sludge.

* * *

'I'm thinking of leaving the strip club,' I said to Sophia as she refilled my champagne glass.

'What do you mean? You're one of the best girls there!' She fell into the sun lounge next to me and together from the penthouse balcony, we absorbed the twinkling city skyline. It was one of the dancers' birthdays and although I didn't know Dyanna very well, Sophia had insisted I come along for a drink or two. Since it may have been my last week working at the Lace and Lipstick, I seized the opportunity to spend time with the crimson-haired beauty outside of work. I had come to admire the dancer who had taught me many lessons since my first shift at the club. It seemed so long ago now. Sophia had chosen my stage name. She taught me to lap dance. Taught me laser beams were better for my bikini line than razors and that it was perfectly okay to crush on a girl. I'd almost tripped in my stilettos the night we met, and now I'd be able to run down the stairs to level one of the luxury apartment with a pair on my feet, at speed. I sipped my champagne, smiling to myself, recalling how Sophia had peeled her clothes off over her head during our first meeting. I had been mortified, and now it was rare to see me with a thread on my own body when getting ready in the dressing room. I was a 'Baby Stripper' back then, and still was, really. Baby Stripper is the term used by dancers for a newbie; the young, fresh face with so much to learn. An amateur yet to discover there was far more to the hustle than glitter eyeshadow, winged liner and a cute costume.

'You can't leave the club, Maddie,' said Sophia, flicking a gathering of ringlets from her shoulder. 'You just can't. You're only just finding your feet. The customers love you. Beck loves you. I love you!'

'It's really distracting lately.' I turned to her, emptying my champagne flute. 'I'm losing concentration at my day job …'

'The stiffs?' She raised an eyebrow. Noticing the horror on my face, she gasped. 'Shit, sorry. Amy told me you're a mortician. It really is kinda cool. But are you really going to choose the funeral home over the club?'

I wanted to be upset at Amy for opening her (gorgeous) big mouth, but I never could be mad at her. She'd been so excited to learn I apply makeup to stiffs (her words) I should have expected she'd tell Sophia. Rather than saying anything, I reached forward and snatched the full champagne glass from Sophia's hands and gulped it down.

'Hey!' she laughed. 'Bitch.'

'Can I ask you a question?' I shimmied closer.

'Depends what it is. And if you're wondering, yes they're real.' She cupped her boobs. I knew they were real; I'd seen enough fake pairs to know the difference by now.

'What's your real name?'

'That, my dear—' she grinned, leaning in and kissing my cheek, '—you'll never know.'

'Fine,' I chuckled, resting my head back on the lounge chair. The girls inside the apartment were squealing and dancing to deep house, rattling my sternum through the floor.

'I'm heading inside.' Sophia stood up and looked down at me. 'Coming?'

She held her hand out to the Baby Stripper. I took her chilly hand and followed her inside to find some guys had arrived now, and the lounge room had become a mirror image of the lap-dance room. Girls slithered naked on laps, on the floor and even on the kitchen bench, skolling champagne and having the time of their lives. I even caught glimpses of Ebony, Heaven and Pleasure snorting cocaine from a plate in the kitchen.

I'd miss these characters, the seductive lap dancing, the sultry lips, the tanned athletic bodies draped with lace, and even the thirsty men gawking with eyeballs springing from their sockets. However, despite my love for the sexy chaos, it occurred to me that the only place I wanted to be in that moment was the cemetery. I yearned for a stroll among the headstones, to be with the souls passed over. I missed the mortuary, the coolroom hum, my funeral family.

The adult industry had become like an older sister to me, one I never had, holding my hand and teaching me life lessons the way only a sister could, but it was time to head back out in the world without her.

'I'll pay you extra …' I caught the tail-end of a discussion as Candy led a man to one of the bedrooms, and more than ever, I missed my dog. I remembered I had freshly laundered socks in the dryer and couldn't wait to slip my feet into them.

Without saying goodbye, I slipped out the door and into the plush-carpeted corridor, and realised I was smiling to myself all the way to my car, to my home. To my pet Maltese, my bed.

I was smiling all the darn way until I reached my fluffy odd socks.

CHAPTER 59

A FINAL BOW

Taking to the stage for the last time felt like I was saying goodbye to a dear friend. The final bow, stepping down out of the spotlights and hanging up my stilettos was similar to lowering a body into the ground. I had grown to love Madison. I looked forward to creating her; curling the platinum-blonde hair extensions, buffing thick foundation into my skin, painting my lips with bright lipstick. Slipping my shellac pedicure into heels, I was someone else for the night. When I was Madison, nothing else mattered. Everyday life was a distant thought as I played, flirted, twirled beneath bright lights.

Madison would be truly missed. I was afraid of laying her to rest; I'd grieve her just like a real death.

* * *

My left ankle twisted and pain shot up my leg as I stepped down into the shadows. I was out of view now, in the darkness by the stage. I had just taken my final bow.

All this time dancing at the Lace and Lipstick on those damn stilettos and I had never missed a step. Hobbling from the spotlight, I wondered if it was a sign that it wasn't time for me to leave. I pushed open the change-room door and the chanting from the audience faded as it swung shut behind me.

'Madison! Madison! Madison!'

Alone in the change room, I stared at my reflection in the body-length mirror. My defined calf muscles bulged from my legs and my newly gained six-pack glittered. Not only had dancing on stage been fun, it was a bloody good workout and it showed. Flabby Emma Jane, no more. I flopped my shapely arms by my side and my posture slumped. Tonight would be the last time I wore those twinkling sequins. Never again would I take to the stage at the L&L; the stage floor beneath my seven-inch heels would now exist only in my dreams. Tears had loosened the glue holding the fake lashes to my already artificially-extended ones, and I peeled them off. Each morning I got home from the club, it took a good 30 minutes to undress each layer of Madison: the eyebrows Sophia had taught me to pencil into an arch higher than the Sydney Harbour Bridge; the blush; the bronzer. I usually peeled the layers through yawns and tired eyes, but right now I didn't want to reach for a makeup wipe at all. If the hair extensions weren't so heavy, encouraging premature hair loss, I would have kept them in for days, hanging on to every last part of Madison.

I heard the crowd being ushered out of the club and yellow light streamed in under the dressing-room door as the main floor lights were turned on.

I wasn't ready to leave the club yet, so I frantically gathered my things, shoving my lingerie, bikinis and rainbows of cash into my bag. I ran over to the door that led to the storage room. Inside it was dark but I had been inside the room many times before and knew exactly where to tread. I tiptoed carefully in the dim light to where I knew I could hide until all the dancers had collected their earnings and carried on dancing into the dawn light.

I needed some time alone, to be with the costumes, the wigs, the items that brought the show to life. I needed to avoid the goodbyes, the final hugs with my new friends. If I could just hide here then reappear just as Pauly locked up, I could avoid all human interaction and tears. The dust on the wooden floorboards gathered on the soles of my feet and by the time I reached the back of the room, I felt like I was wearing socks.

'Madison?' Beck's voice called out from the change room.

I scurried to the chest I planned to crouch behind until the coast was clear. With footsteps approaching, my heart flattened against my spine and I ducked behind the chest just in time. The darkness was disturbed by light as the door blasted open.

'She must have already left. Now, I think it's time for breakfast, what do you say?' I recognised Sophia's voice.

The door closed and their voices ebbed into the chatter of dancers as they piled into the dressing room to retire for the night.

I scrambled to my grubby feet and wiped the dirt off my naked buttocks and headed to the centre of the room. In slow motion I circled the room, running my hands along glittery garments. Oh, how I was going to miss the stage, my clients, bills paid on time. I would even miss Pauly, the friendly security guard.

I had learnt to love myself again, danced for celebrities, built a strong body and equally strong friendships. I had already lived out my dream and my thirties had only just begun. The adult industry, just like death care, had saved me.

But the Lace and Lipstick was not quite done with me just yet. If I had known what was to come, I would have hid behind that chest of costumes and pearls in the dusty room forever.

CHAPTER 60

AN UNEXPECTED GOODBYE

My mobile phone vibrated in my pocket as I ordered my skinny latte. I stepped to the side to wait for my caffeine fix and reached into my suit pocket. I missed the call.

The voice message was converted to text: *Hi, Maddie. It's me, Sophia. Call me back when you can please. It's urgent.*

My heart dropped and I stared blankly at the screen. Sophia and I hadn't really spoken since I'd left the club and my intuition told me something was very wrong.

Once I'd received my coffee, I found cover from the weeping skies in a graffiti-covered side alley.

'Sophia, what's wrong?'

'It's Amy.'

'What about her?'

'Madison, I'm so sorry, but we've lost Amy. I don't know anything other than that at this time. It's not clear whether the overdose was intentional or not. We have no answers just yet.'

I collapsed against the brick wall and screamed. Trying to regulate my breath, I rang work to let them know I would not be in, hailed a cab to the airport and boarded the next flight to Brisbane.

* * *

I arrived in Queensland still in my funeral director attire, and blasted into the hospital. Leaning on the reception desk gasping for breath, I demanded to speak with the mortuary manager. The eyes of the triage nurse darted to the company badge pinned on my blouse and she nodded. Any close family member or friend can spend time with their loved one once they have died. It's just that not many people know that they can. It helped that I was in my funeral director's uniform. I knew what to say. The staff at the hospital where Amy was kept were wonderfully accommodating. I felt embarrassed at my manners, or lack thereof, when the mortuary manager approached me with a clipboard in his hands. I knew Amy's real name was on that paperwork, her surname first, then given names.

'I am a funeral director …' I blurted, panicky. 'I go to mortuaries every day and I need to go to yours. I'm her family. Take me!'

The balding man's small eyes were too close together, as if his nose was planted on his face after the rest of his facial features. He blinked them at speed. It annoyed me. Everything was annoying me. The bright artificial lights. The babies crying, representing life. The conversations all around. *How could they go on? Amy is dead!* 'Take a seat, ma'am, I shall organise the viewing for you.'

My body trembled and I could not stop my hands from shaking. Was this shock? Anger? I felt unusually cold and rubbed my arms swiftly with my chilly hands. To stop from passing out, I took a seat by the water cooler and hung my head in my hands.

* * *

Every single day, *I* am the one organising viewings, visiting mortuaries to conduct transfers, pallbearing loved ones down church aisles and lowering bodies into the ground! This wasn't supposed to happen to me! I'm the funeral director!

I thought my experience in the industry and the workshops on grief would assist when sudden death touched my own life.

My gained knowledge, in fact, made it far worse.

I knew exactly what was happening to Amy's body. I knew what her body bag looked like. I knew what a mortuary viewing entailed: folding the body bag down, the body hidden within sheets and the lights dimmed strategically to soften her stiff face. I knew she was placed in the mortuary fridge with a barcode. I knew shortly the funeral home staff would arrive and transfer her delicate body into their care while they chatted about their favourite TV shows or the latest workplace gossip.

Amy was now a number and all 29 years of her life would soon be compressed into a 30-minute funeral service.

The mortuary manager returned and led me to a small room at the end of many brightly lit corridors. He opened a door and instructed me to take a seat. *It was so cold.* I knew we were seated right next to the body coolroom. I could hear the droning hum, the sound that usually comforted me at the funeral home.

Hum … huumm … huuummm …

'Your friend is on the other side of that curtain.'

I nodded.

'Now, ma'am, your friend doesn't look the same as when she was alive …'

I knew all the lines.

'It's fine,' I snapped.

'You know you can wait until the funeral home …'

'No,' I sniffled. I imagined her mouth suture, the makeup, the plugging with cotton wool …

'I want to see her before all of that.'

'Okay …' His voice trailed off for a moment, before adding, 'you may smell an odour. You may see slight discolouration of the skin …'

I know! I know!

'As you can appreciate, working in the industry yourself—' he pressed on, nodding towards my name badge, '—she will need to be relocated to the forensic science unit for further investigation.' A moment's silence. 'I will give you some time,' he said finally, leaving me alone to enter the viewing room.

'Oh, Amy.' I reached deep within the frosty body bag so I could hold her entire body. Green spots were already forming, the early stages of decay. The diamond tattoo on her thigh would soon disfigure, the decomposition taking over her trim thighs that once carried her across the stage.

* * *

The sun stung my face as I leant against the hire car in the car park. In the heat of Queensland summer, I wailed so hard I brought on a migraine.

I suddenly missed my ex-husband.

No! I shook my head as if to clear it of polluting thoughts. *You're just lonely. Upset. Don't even think about it!*

I found myself dialling a phone number, holding the phone shakily to my ear.

'Hello?' Byron answered.

'Byron,' I stammered. 'When your best friend died …'

'Yes …' His voice trailed off.

'I now know how you feel.'

* * *

Since I was in the state, I thought I'd best visit my parents. We hadn't spoken since they'd discovered I'd become an exotic dancer. Although the tension lingered, I found comfort in their presence and in the sprawling backyard showcasing all of Dad's hard work. The fruit trees and fishponds took me back to the farm before all of this had happened. Before I'd grown up. Before I experienced the gruelling pain that accompanies adulthood. I wanted to cry and cry and cry. Hold on to Dad. Ride my pony he bought for me when I was seven. Rewind to the nineties. I wanted to be a child again and never get married. Never fall in love. Never have met Amy so this wouldn't hurt so much. I revisited the funeral of Adam, the young man who died by suicide, when I'd questioned why a young man would kill himself. Had Amy ended her life? *Could I?* I shook my head and scolded myself … *Low point! Low Point!*

My parents' backyard smelt of Queensland: barbequed sausages, bananas and burnt-off sugar cane from nearby fields. Humidity itching my scalp, I slipped into an outside dining chair as Dad cracked open two beers. Mum remained inside tossing a caesar salad. After discussing the weather, the garden gnomes he had bought from Bunnings and the price of fuel, Dad cracked open his third beer and flicked froth from his moustache. The small talk was done.

'Do you know when the funeral will be?' he asked, fiddling with the can in his suntanned hands.

'No,' I stuttered, wiping dampened curls from my forehead. I held the icy beer can to my throbbing temples. 'I really don't want to think about it right now.'

'Her poor parents, they must be a wreck.' Dad peered up towards the kitchen where Mum paused a beat, and then resumed tossing lettuce leaves. 'I can't even imagine the pain. We've been scared too, about *things*. The club.'

'Not now, Dad!' I emptied my Fourex. 'It's all over now anyhow. Just so you know,' I said with another pang in my heart. 'Do you mind if I have another beer?'

Dad fetched a beer and with a cicada chorus our backdrop, we got drunk beneath the sunset and thankfully, avoided the subject of the Lace and Lipstick.

* * *

With very little family, Amy's service was small, held at a quaint chapel on the outskirts of the Gold Coast. Beck and Sophia held onto one another, sobbing in the front row, and one of Amy's favourite dance tracks played at soft volume. 'Just Dance'. Lady Gaga. Amy had the coffin she deserved. A Swan. Pure white with gold handles; twinkling fairy lights were strung through the flower display. My tears felt like lava as they fell. The photo montage showed Amy as a curly-headed child with braces. She wore gumboots in the rain. She hugged a man I assumed was her dad. I could take no more. I stepped outside to cry and curse the sunshine. How could the sun glow right now? *Fuck off, happy sky.* I was weak at the knees and took a seat on the front steps of the chapel, watching the funeral directors prepare the hearse for Amy's departure.

When it was time, I ducked behind a rose bush out of sight from the other dancers, and watched the funeral staff slide my friend into the back of the shiny death car. The coffin locked in and secure, the hearse turned out onto the main road and off towards the crematory as dandelion fluff floated on the wind.

And just like that, my Amy was gone forever.

CHAPTER 61

TIME OUT

The stages of grief—denial, anger, bargaining, depression and acceptance—were modelled by psychiatrist Elisabeth Kübler-Ross in the 1960s.

As a funeral director it's important to understand the grieving process to serve the families experiencing it. It was common to hear the identified framework for grief bouncing off the walls at the funeral home.

'Oh, yes, Joan is at the depression stage. That is why it was hard to communicate with her during the arrangement this morning…'

'Jim has reached the stage of anger … did you see his blood boil when I asked him about the music for the service'

Assuming the stages evolved sequentially, I'd observe the family when working on funerals to establish the stage of grief they were at: experiencing denial then anger and so forth until reaching the finish line with *ACCEPTANCE!*

printed on a shiny banner. *Yes! We did it! It's all over! Where's the confetti?* However, when Amy died, I discovered I'd been rather naive. I learnt there's no concrete framework for grief at all. I also discovered how lonely the grieving process can be. It's hard to stomach when everyone is continuing with life as if nothing has happened at all.

'Mourn for a little while, but not too long. They wouldn't want that. Don't mope. Remember him/her and keep on living. It's what they'd want for you …' A particular celebrant weaved this message into his final words of comfort at the lectern almost every service. It's a lovely sentiment and I can appreciate what he was saying, but what is wrong with falling to pieces if someone you love has died? Acknowledging the ache in places you never knew existed? Why the rush to get on with things? Why try and outrun the terror of grief?

Well, I was no expert, but I wasn't about to mourn just for a day, then get back on with it. A quiver ran through me whenever I saw lace. I staggered at the glimpse of a sequin and recoiled at red lipstick where I once wore it every day. It felt like that scene near the end of the movie *Titanic* where terrified passengers gripped the priest's hands as the ship sank. I didn't lock away my glassy stilettos; I placed them by the front door next to my sandals, so I could remember the neon spotlights playing tag across her skin every time I used the door. I was indeed crying while wearing makeup.

* * *

I'd only known Amy a short time. Did I even have the right to grieve her?

The short time I'd spent getting to know the dancer, I felt I'd learnt things about her that you wouldn't discover with your closest friend in a year.

Losing Amy to death wounded me deeply. I would have to convince myself it was okay to cry over the lady I'd known as briefly as a kiss on the cheek.

* * *

Years earlier when Poppy, my grandfather, passed away, my mum busied herself with her career and cooking perfect roasts while her brother appeared deeply troubled and cried often. If I'd been my uncle, I'd have compared myself and felt inadequate and weak. *'Wow, look at her, I wish I was as strong as her!'* But you see, Mum did cry—in private. She channelled her pain into art as the director of a childcare centre. (I still find it ironic that Mum assists little ones starting out in life while her daughter takes care of them at the end.)

Every person mourns differently; it's an individual journey, so when we lose someone we love we must not compare our progress with others. We have to stop being so hard on ourselves. It's hard to believe, but there are people out there who haven't experienced deep grief. They're not close to their family and it's common that they discover family deaths years later. I missed someone because I was blessed to have that person in my life. My life was affected by her absence and pausing to reflect a moment, it truly is a beautiful thought.

My heart was in shards because I once gave it full and beating to someone else.

Many aren't so lucky.

CHAPTER 62

GRIEF FUN?

Following Amy's death, I took a month's leave without pay from the funeral home. My days consisted of stirring whiskey into morning oats, eating corn chips as dinner and sleeping with an eye mask on throughout the day. And oh, I moved out of the cottage. I couldn't stand to stare up at that air-conditioning unit reminding me of the anti-decomp plan I'd shared with Amy. 'I'll only take it if the air conditioning is ducted,' I mumbled when inspecting potential homes.

On the final weekend of leave, I met a character dealing with grief the best way I'd seen in some time.

Around midday I hid my tired eyes behind dark shades and headed off to visit my lover, a.k.a. my barista. Cradling my takeaway coffee lovingly in my hands, I almost ran into a skeleton. A life-size cardboard cut-out tied onto a pole with tinsel. Glued to its ribcage was an address hosting a garage sale. It was time I bought a second-hand book anyhow. So, off I went. Sparkles, skeletons and coffee—had to cheer me up, right? I followed the arrows tied to street signs to a large house on the hill with a giant plastic skull on the letterbox. I checked the date on my mobile phone—was it Halloween already? The host was a vibrant middle-aged man dressed in a skeleton onesie. His face beamed with a smile and he offered his customers a sausage sizzle and soft drinks. Looking at the price tags attached to items, I imagined it would have cost him more to set all of this up than what he'd make in sales.

'Check it out!' he trilled, holding up a plastic skull to an elderly lady who winced and backed away. My out-loud laugh captured his attention, and our eyes locked over tables of pre-loved DVDs and crockpots. It didn't take long before we were chatting about books, movies and death.

'So, are you moving?' I asked, sipping my complimentary Coke.

'Well actually, my partner died.' He pointed towards the skeletons and skulls. 'It's the reason for the theme. He was a funny bastard. It's mostly his stuff. He'd laugh. Oh, some of it is my dad's too. He died a few years ago. Hey, do you like plants? There's heaps for sale around the corner!'

'No, I always kill them.'

'Me too!' he belly-laughed.

And right there, I made friends with a stranger in the depths of grief, using his experience to give to others. The bookshelves were bulging with classics—I bought an entire collection of Charles Dickens novels, *The Andy Warhol Diaries* and a first edition of *Watership Down*. As a lover of literature, I knew this garage sale was worth a fortune.

I bought as much as I could afford. This guy deserved every dollar.

'Thank you.' He pulled me in for a hug, one I was unable to reciprocate with the box piled with old books and movies in my hands.

During my divorce, a friend said to me: 'Time doesn't heal all wounds, it's what you do with your time that heals you.' I wondered if the man in the skeleton onesie had heard the same thing. As I drove away, I watched the twinkling tinsel disappear into the distance in the rear-view mirror.

It was time to get back to work.

CHAPTER 63

CRYSTAL GARDEN

'Can you come over and help me massage the blood out of this guy?' the embalmer asked in a squeaky voice caused by her PPE mask pressing down on her nose.

'Sure, just let me finish what I'm doing here. One moment …'

I was holding a 90-year-old man's ankle in the air, washing poop from his bottom. Gently placing down his leg and patting him dry with a towel, I moved to the table where the embalming was taking place. A stocky Italian man was slowly turning pink and lifelike as the preserving fluid flowed through his veins. Together, the embalmer and I massaged his legs and thick arms to help the formaldehyde flow rapidly and evenly through the body.

'So, how are you holding up?' she asked, not taking her eyes from the rivers of blood streaming down the sides of the table.

'I'm okay.'

On this rainy afternoon, as I pushed and pulled the flesh of the Italian man, I was summoned to the office.

'When you're finished there!' Mags demanded, poking her head through the door.

Tossing my bloodied gloves into the chemical waste bins and removing my soiled disposable apron, I flicked off my gumboots, anticipating the worst. I made my way to the office, taking a seat across from Mags.

'One moment!' she said as she typed furiously. She finally turned to me, taking off her spectacles, and folding them carefully she placed them next to a pile of 'The Grieving Process' brochures.

Unable to look her in the eye, I was petrified of what my manager was about to announce. I was afraid it would be the death of me, no pun intended. What on earth would I do without my job? Just the thought of not seeing the dead each day, polishing the hearses, preparing the coffins, even that repetitive paperwork!

'Emma Jane,' she began, strumming her desk with her fingers. I could feel that she was staring at me, but I continued to peer down at my feet wiggling nervously in my socks.

'How do you enjoy being out on funeral services?'

'Very much.'

'Well, I'm glad.' Mags leant in closer, her chubby arms leaning on her desk. I pulled my eyes from the floor to hers. 'The office has received quite a few emails from families praising your work. Emma Jane, they love you.'

What?

'Emma, we'd like to offer you a new position.' Mags sat back in her swivel chair, resting her arms across her bosom proudly. 'We would like you to be a conductor.'

Me? A conductor?

'Excuse me,' I coughed. 'You want me to be a conductor?'

'Yes,' Mags beamed. 'We need another female conductor. We only have one other and when we have baby services or young women, families feel comforted seeing another woman holding the show together. It's not just a job to you and we can see that and so can our families. They need you.'

I thanked Mags for her time, accepted the offer and casually walked to the locker room. Once inside the change room, I squealed hysterically using a suit to muffle the volume. Little old me? A conductor? It was time to press my suits full-time and take the lead!

Like I had done so many times before, I rang Amy's number knowing her voicemail was still active, so I could hear her beautiful voice.

'I know you can hear me,' I whispered down the phone line. 'I miss you and I'm going to make you proud.'

* * *

Before I could take the lead, I had to undergo two weeks of intense training with a fellow funeral conductor. As with most positions in the funeral home, there was no printed manual to study in bed at night, it was all on-the-job training. I did, however, study many scribbled notes I had written for myself. On my bedside accompanying *Pet Sematary* by Stephen King and two memoirs written by famous escort Samantha X (it's all about variety) were scrambled sticky notes cluttered with my reminders.

- ***Always remember to ask the family if they would like to take the flower arrangement home. You don't want to lower them into the grave if they wanted to keep them!***

- *On church services, always fold the pall at the end of the service slowly. Don't rush, you'll look nervous to everyone watching!*
- *Explain instructions to the pallbearers clearly. They are grieving and won't understand long sentences and fast directions. This may be the first time they've ever carried a coffin!*

For two whole weeks, I followed on the conductor's heel. I was the assistant at the back of the chapel no more! I would be on show, and given I was known to trip over my own two feet while stationary, this could be a challenge, but I was more than ready. Surely dancing on stage had prepared me for the task.

And apart from knowing everything about the big day, there was one thing as important to the conductor as a shortcut to the church. The plush leather folder that never left their side, filled with cheques, notes and other mystery forms I was to learn about.

I followed my superior as she asked the organist to sign her cheque. I was on her heel as she wandered beyond the church altar asking Father to sign his. Yes, priests are paid to deliver a homily. The conductor taught me when and where to bow within the church when carrying out these formalities, when to walk down the aisle and invite the pallbearers to come forward. She taught me east from west in a minefield of headstones, as most Christians are buried with their feet facing the east in case resurrection is indeed a possibility. I considered buying a pocket compass.

As I watched the conductor speak to pallbearers, the musicians, the priests and cemetery staff, I doubted myself.

I put milk in the pantry most mornings and always misplaced my keys. Was I cut out to conduct one of the most important events in life? Unlike a wedding, there's no second chance at a perfect funeral.

* * *

The morning of my first solo shift as funeral conductor, the feared CEO had driven to the operations facility. Working from the swanky head office in the city, it was rare she visited. While others hid upon her arrival, I used her occasional attendance to thank her for the day she hired me. Every single time. The CEO of A Touch of Comfort funeral home had worked in death care for as long as I'd been alive, and despite the responsibilities upon her, she hadn't a single frown line. I found her to be a very inspiring woman. So on this very exciting morning when she arrived, I was happy to see her. Maybe I could ask her for an extra pen with all the paperwork I'd now be in charge of.

'Emma, can I speak with you?' she asked, once I exited the change room in my suit. Did I have deodorant marks at the armpits? Were my shoes not shiny enough? I followed her from the morning chaos to a quiet space by a hearse. I checked my lipstick in the shiny paintwork, as she said my name again. Sternly.

Shit.

'I have something for you.' She pulled out of her handbag the leather folder with *Conductor* embroidered on the front. The folder I had seen the conductor carry around at funeral services for almost two years. I held that damn folder in my hand the way I'd cradled my newborn niece all those years ago. As well as the conductor folder, the CEO handed me a shiny gold pen with A Touch of Comfort carved on it. 'You are the first one to receive one of our new pens.' She smiled.

'Congratulations Emma Jane.' She pulled me in for a hug, then looked into my eyes proudly. 'You'll be amazing.'

As well as handing me the folder and new pen, she tucked a small box in my hands and told me to read the instructions once I got home that afternoon.

Once home, I retrieved the gift box: she'd gifted me a 'Crystal Garden'. The directions on the box instructed to water the small crystals and they would grow, just like flowers. *'These crystals will grow just like you. You're becoming a wonderful funeral director,'* the note inside read.

It had been a long time since I actually felt proud of myself. Since my separation, it was milestone after milestone to get back on my feet, but I hadn't actually taken the time to reflect upon these achievements. I thought back to the days I slept in my car wondering what this crazy life had in store for me. The day I admitted myself to hospital. I even thought back to the nights during my childhood where death anxiety kept me awake. I had not only overcome this fear; Death had become my friend. My best mate!

Death needed me as much I needed Death. I would help the dead and in return, they would help me grow again, just like my crystal garden.

I nursed a broken heart, but my soul was on the way to being as strong as ever. Strong as fucking crystal.

CHAPTER 64

STANDING OVATION

In suit and tie I stood by the hearse with my assistant by my side. I had gone from Funeral Director's Assistant to *having* an assistant. The family of the deceased were gathering at the entrance of the chapel wearing large dark sunglasses, looking much better than I did in their suits. My head was buzzing with the intricate details:

The son of late Mr Peterson is named Roger …
Must wait until one minute and 14 seconds of the opening song before walking down the aisle of the chapel …
Must remember to place framed photographs on top of the casket at the end of the first song …
Oh dear, I still have to get the bagpiper to sign his cheque and where on earth is Father Stevens? He was meant to be here by now.

Thankful for my stage makeup battling my anxious sweat, I continued to pep-talk myself.

I can do this.

'I'll go get the slideshow ready,' the FDA whispered.

During training, having an experienced conductor by my side to swoop in and save the day allowed me to sleep at night. Now I was on my own.

Nothing could go wrong today. Mags and my CEO believed in me, I had a crystal garden growing at home just like I was, supposedly. And I was allocated the largest service of the day. I had to do this. Perfectly.

Finally, Father Stevens arrived, flustered and adjusting his robe that I knew he had thrown on over his casualwear in the car.

'Traffic,' he puffed as he dashed past me towards the sacristy.

It was time to gather the pallbearers and, disguising my panic, I explained how to remove their dad from the back of the hearse: 'As I release the coffin, please each take a handle. The head is the heaviest end so the strongest men come forward please.' Nervously, I continued. 'We will wait at the entrance of the chapel until halfway through the song, then we will head down to the front and place Dad on the bier.'

'Thank you,' the men in dark suits and matching shades nodded and followed my lead.

Showtime.

And no stilettos or hair extensions needed.

We stood at the back of the chapel, waiting for the nod from the FDA by the media controls indicating it was time, then I led the pallbearers down the red-carpeted aisle.

Throughout the service, while Father Stevens read Bible passages and relatives shared stories of Mr Peterson's life, I tended to the weak with water and filled out the conductor's paperwork.

When it was time to close the service, I was required to walk down the aisle once more, acknowledge the coffin with a bow, then ask the pallbearers to come forward once again to return dad to the back of the hearse.

'Pallbearers come forward, please,' I called over the hymn, 'Amazing Grace'. They reappeared from the crowd of black suits, and just as we began our procession, something incredible happened. A man in the front row began to clap. Then another, and another until every person in the church was on their feet in applause. The pallbearers and I proceeded down the aisle, my skin raised in goosebumps, and as we passed the media controls I looked to my assistant who smiled and winked at me.

The clapping turned to cheers when we reached the hearse, with whistles and a *'Well done, mate! Well done!'*

This wasn't directed at me of course, they were cheers of farewell for Mr Peterson, but how perfectly timed, this wonderful applause? My first funeral as a conductor and it ended with an ovation.

When the conductor closes the back door of the hearse, they are required to bow in acknowledgement and respect to the deceased.

So, I locked the coffin securely into place and just like so many times on stage, to the sound of applause, I took a bow.

EPILOGUE

We are sitting at the traffic lights, my boyfriend and I, with Miss Hogan secured in the back on the stretcher.

'I love you.' Byron winks.

'I love you too.' I blush.

'Happy six-month anniversary.'

Byron squeezes my knee from the driver's side and flashes his striking white teeth in a huge smile.

I smile back, then return my gaze to the walks of life at the intersection: an elderly lady in fluorescent pink tights waiting to cross the road with her fluffy Maltese in tow; she has no idea she is standing only metres away from a dead body. A young man in a dusty white ute meets us at the red lights. He fiddles with his radio and gulps down an enormous can of energy drink, oblivious to the fact that he has just pulled up next to a lady who'd died earlier in the day.

We aren't always in our shiny hearses. Death shares the roads 24 hours a day, seven days a week. We are right here pulled up in traffic with 'life extinct' forms in our laps.

The world rotates, lattes guzzled, traffic banks up. And while all of this carries on, Death is watching, waiting and can strike at any time.

Smell flowers. Go on, try the extra spicy satay! *Feel* those bubbles in the bath. Dance as if it is indeed your last.

Be safe, love plenty and *always* be grateful.

ACKNOWLEDGEMENTS

Thank you to my agent, Tara. I'll never forget the day I entered the literary agency and saw my first draft printed and sprawled across your desk. The moment was a dream come true, let alone what was to come. I owe this publication to you! Samantha X, the reason I met Tara in the first place. Your ongoing strength and advocacy for the adult industry is truly special. I am humbled to have you in my life. You've taught me so much along this journey; forever thankful.

Jo Mackay, Nicola Robinson, Annabel Blay, Alex Craig, Natika Palka, everyone at Harlequin and HarperCollins publishers. The team that have worked tirelessly for an unknown author are the unsung heroes. Thank you with all my heart.

To Joy, my writer's coach. You've had no idea until now, that I'm the 18-year-old who sent you that terribly inexperienced work of fiction. Thirteen years later I sought you out and emailed you this book at its earliest stages. The cards you posted, the ongoing Skype appointments, the continuous words of inspiration; thank you for the encouragement and believing in me.

To Jake, for the meals you cooked for me, the cups of tea you delivered to my study when I was in a zone writing for days; the post-it notes I discovered on my computer screen after taking a nap. I love you, baby brother. To Dad, you're my hero. Mum, Jessie, Lucas, Haylee, I love you. My niece and best friend Aaleah. You keep me going.

Vanessa McCausland, you gem. I'm so grateful to have met you at the Author Day in Sydney. Your writing inspires me and I'm proud to call you a friend. Kelly Arrowsmith aka Queen of the Desert. Writing can be a solitary journey, but with you I felt less alone.

Michelle, who has no idea that I wrote these acknowledgements in her reading space by the bay window. To Dave, for everything but there is not enough paper in the world to list it all. Matt Black (not his real name, but he knows who he is!).

To my beautiful dancer friends. Love you all. Glitter and sequins for life.

To the dead, each and every one I have dressed, held hands with, beautified, closed the coffin lid upon. You have changed my life. To all of the funeral directors I have worked with, you have enriched my mortal journey in poignant ways. I have the most special (and hilarious) memories with every single one of you.

Duncan Ball, Anne M. Martin and R.L. Stine. You probs don't like being mentioned in the acknowledgments section of a memoir with 'G-Strings' in the title, but your books are the reason I wanted to become an author when I grew up.

Lastly, to the farm my dad bought when I was three. Where my childhood dreams of becoming a writer manifested. It's not a place, She's a soul: the animals, water, air, paddocks, birds, lady beetles, jasmine flowers; you're within me forever.

talk about it

Let's talk about books.

Join the conversation:

@harlequinaustralia

@hqanz

@harlequinaus

harpercollins.com.au/hq

If you love reading and want to know about our authors and titles, then let's talk about it.